English in Action
Teacher's Guide

Barbara H. Foley

Elizabeth R. Neblett

John Chapman

HEINLE
CENGAGE Learning

Australia • Brazil • Japan • Korea • Mexico • Singapore • Spain • United Kingdom • United States

W9-AJN-290

HEINLE
CENGAGE Learning

English in Action 2, Teacher's Guide
Barbara H. Foley, Elizabeth R. Neblett, and
John Chapman

Publisher, Adult and Academic ESL: James W. Brown

Senior Acquisitions Editor: Sherrise Roehr

Developmental Editor: Sarah Barnicle

Editorial Assistant: Audra Longert

Marketing Manager: Eric Bredenberg

Director, Global ESL Training & Development:
   Evelyn Nelson

Senior Production Editor: Maryellen Killeen

Senior Frontlist Buyer: Mary Beth Hennebury

Project Manager: Tünde A. Dewey

Compositor: Pre-Press Co., Inc.

Text Designer: Sue Gerould

Cover Designer: Gina Petti/Rotunda
   Design House

Photo Researcher: Claudine Corey

Unit Opener Art: Zita Asbaghi

Illustrators: Scott MacNeill; Ray Medici;
   Glen Giron, Roger Acaya, Ibarra
   Cristostomo, Leo Cultura of Raketshop
   Design Studio, Philippines

Cover Art: Zita Asbaghi

For product information and technology assistance, contact us at
Cengage Learning Customer & Sales Support, 1-800-354-9706
For permission to use material from this text or product,
submit all requests online at **www.cengage.com/permissions**
Further permissions questions can be emailed to
permissionrequest@cengage.com

ISBN-13: 978-0-8384-5193-9

ISBN-10: 0-8384-5193-4

Heinle
20 Channel Center Street,
Boston, MA 02210
USA

Cengage Learning is a leading provider of customized learning solutions with office locations around the globe, including Singapore, the United Kingdom, Australia, Mexico, Brazil, and Japan. Locate your local office at **international.cengage.com/region**

Cengage Learning products are represented in Canada by Nelson Education, Ltd.

Visit Heinle online at **elt.heinle.com**
Visit our corporate website at **www.cengage.com**

Printed in the United States of America
4 5 6 7 11 10 09

Acknowledgments

We would like to acknowledge the many individuals who helped, encouraged, and supported us during the writing and production of this series. In keeping with an open-ended format, we would like to offer a matching exercise. Please be advised, there is more than one correct "match" for each person. Thank you all!

Jim Brown	• for your creative eye for art and design.
Eric Bredenberg	• for your enthusiasm and support.
Sherrise Roehr	• for your support, patience, and humor while guiding this project.
Sarah Barnicle	• for your faith in the authors.
Maryellen Killeen	• for your smiles and your stories.
Audra Longert	• for your encouragement, comments, and suggestions.
Tünde A. Dewey	• for putting up with us!
All the Heinle sales reps	• for your understanding of the needs of teachers and programs.
The students at Union County College	• for your keeping us all on schedule.
The faculty and staff at UCC	• for your help with research.
Our families	

The authors and publisher would like to thank the following reviewers and consultants:

Linda Boice
Elk Grove Unified School District, Sacramento, CA

Rocio Castiblanco
Seminole Community College, Sanford, FL

Jared Erfle
Antelope Valley High School, Lancaster, CA

Rob Kustusch
Triton Community College, River Grove, IL

Patricia Long
Old Marshall Adult School, Sacramento, CA

Kathleen Newton
New York City Board of Education, Bronx, NY

Alberto Panizo
Miami-Dade Community College, Miami, FL

Eric Rosenbaum
Bronx Community College, Bronx, NY

Michaela Safadi
South Gate Community, South Gate, CA

Armando Valdez
Huantes Learning and Leadership Development Center, San Antonio, TX

Contents

Contents

Many years ago, I attended an ESL workshop in which the presenter asked a full audience, "How many of you read the **To the Teacher** at the front of the text?" Two participants raised their hands. Since that time, I have begged my publishers to release me from this responsibility, but have always been overruled.

As a teacher, you can form a clear first impression of this book. Flip through the pages. Will the format appeal to your students? Look carefully through the table of contents. Are most of the structures and contexts that your program has established included in the text? Thumb carefully through a few units. Will the activities and exercises, the support, the pace be appropriate for your students? If you wish, you can even read the rest of **To the Teacher** below.

English in Action is a four-level core language series for ESL/EFL students. It is a comprehensive revision and expansion of *The New Grammar in Action*. The popularity of the original edition delighted us, but we heard the same requests over and over: "Please include more readings and pronunciation," and "Could you add a workbook?" In planning the revision, our publisher threw budgetary concerns to the wind and decided to produce a four color, redesigned version. The revision also allowed us, the authors, an opportunity to refine the text. We are writers, but we are also teachers. We wrote a unit, then immediately tried it out in the classroom. Activities, tasks, and exercises were added, deleted, and changed in an on-going process. Students provided daily and honest feedback.

This second book is designed for students who have had some exposure to English, such as students who have taken a basic course, false beginners, and adults who have lived in the United States for a few years.

The units in Book 2 branch from introductions to school, home, and neighborhood; to work; and to past activities and future plans. The contexts are everyday places and situations. The units build gradually, giving students the vocabulary, the grammar, and the expressions to talk about the situations and themselves. Students see, hear, and practice the language of everyday life in a great variety of exercises and activities. Because this is the second book and students are somewhat unsure of themselves, there is ever-present support in the form of grammar notes, examples, vocabulary boxes, and so on. By the end of Book 2, students should feel comfortable talking, reading, and writing about their lives using basic English phrases and sentences.

Each unit will take between five and seven hours of classroom time. If you have less time, you may need to choose the exercises you feel are the most appropriate for your students. You can assign some of the activities for homework. For example, after previewing **Writing Our Stories,** students can write their own stories at home, instead of in class. The short descriptions that follow give you an idea of the sections in each unit.

Finally, the book comes with an audio component. You need the audio program! The listening activities in the units are motivating and interesting. They provide other voices than that of the teacher. We have encouraged our adult students to buy the book/audio package. They tell us that they listen to the audio at home and in the car.

Dictionary

Each unit opens with a one- or two-page illustrated **Dictionary.** Students are asked to listen and repeat each item. All teachers realize that one repetition of vocabulary words does not produce mastery. Ask students to sit in groups and study the words together. Stage spelling bees. Play word bingo. Look for the same items in the classroom or school environment. Students must also study the words at home.

Active Grammar

Three to six pages of structured exercises present and practice the grammar of the unit. This first book integrates the new vocabulary and the grammar throughout all the activities in the unit. Students can be expected to learn the basic structures of English and to feel more comfortable using the language. As students progress through this section, they will find a variety of supportive features. Artwork and photos illustrate the context clearly. Answer boxes show the verbs or nouns to use in the answers. For many of the exercises, the entire class will be working together with your direction and explanations. Other exercises have a pairwork icon 👥 — students can try these with a partner. You can walk around the classroom, listening to students and answering their questions.

Pronunciation

Within the **Active Grammar** section is an exercise that focuses on pronunciation. These are specific pronunciation points that complement the grammar or vocabulary of the lesson, such as plural *s*, contractions, numbers, and syllables.

Working Together

For these one to two pages, students work in pairs or groups, trying out their new language with cooperative tasks, such as interviewing partners, writing conversations, or arranging a person's daily schedule. The Student to Student exercises are information gap activities in which the students look at different pages and share information about maps, jobs, menus, prices, and other contexts. Be prepared—students will make lots of mistakes during the practice. This exploration of the language is an important step in gaining comfort and fluency in English. If your students represent several different languages, group students with classmates who speak a language other than their own.

The Big Picture

This is our favorite section. It integrates listening, vocabulary, and structure. A large, lively picture shows a particular setting, such as a street scene, a job interview, or vacation plans. Students listen to a short story or conversation, and then answer questions about the story, fill in exercises, review structures, or write conversations.

Reading

A short reading expands the context of the lesson. We did not manipulate a selection so that every sentence fits into the structure presented in the unit! There are new vocabulary words and structures. Teachers can help ESL readers learn that understanding the main idea is primary. They can then go back over the material to find the details that are interesting or relevant. If students can find the information they need, it is not necessary to master or look up every word.

Writing Our Stories

In this writing section, students first read a paragraph written by an ESL student or teacher. By using checklists or fill-in sentences, students are directed to brainstorm about their own schools, families, jobs, etc. Students then have an opportunity to write about themselves. Several teachers have told us about the creative ways they share student writing, including publishing student magazines, designing a class Web page, and displaying stories and photos taken by their students.

Practicing on Your Own

This is simple: It's a homework section. Some teachers ask students to do the exercises in class. Another suggestion for homework is the audio component. Ask students to listen to it three or four more times, reviewing the vocabulary and the exercises they did in class. Our students tell us that they often write the story from **The Big Picture** as a dictation activity.

Looking at . . .

This is a convenient place for forms, math problems, or interesting information we located about the topic as we were writing the units.

Grammar Summary

Some teachers wanted this summary at the beginning of the unit; others were pleased to see it at the end. Use this section if and when you wish. Some students like to see the grammar up front, having a clear map of the developing grammar. We have found, though, that many of our students at this beginning level are confused with a clump of grammar explanations at the beginning of a unit. There are small grammar charts as needed throughout the unit. The ending summary brings them together.

Teacher's Guide

We have developed the *English in Action 2 Teacher's Guide* to be a support to teachers of all levels of experience. New teachers will benefit from the clear, step-by-step instructions on using the Student Book, while more experienced teachers will find creative and fun ideas for expanding on the Student Book material. Each **Teacher's Guide** page includes a reduced Student Book page, along with guidelines for effectively teaching and expanding on the activities on that page. At the bottom of many of the **Teacher's Guide** pages are audio scripts for the listening activities on that page. These audio scripts are for listening activities that do not already appear on the Student Book page. The audio scripts are also included at the end of the Student Book. The audio scripts allow teachers who do not have access to the audio to read aloud to their students the audio portion of the listening activities.

The **Teacher's Guide** also features a helpful grammar section in the appendices. This section, the **Grammar Summary Expansion,** is designed to give teachers more information about the grammatical structures and points taught in each Student Book unit.

I am sure we will be revising the text again in three or four years. We will be gathering your input during that time. You can always e-mail us at **www.heinle.com** with your comments, complaints, and suggestions.

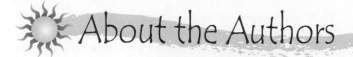

Liz and I both work at Union County College in Elizabeth, New Jersey. We teach at the Institute for Intensive English, a large English as a Second Language program. Students from over 70 different countries study in our classes. Between us, Liz and I have been teaching at the college for over 40 years! When Liz isn't writing, she spends her time traveling, taking pictures, and watching her favorite baseball team, the New York Mets. Liz took many of the pictures in the texts, for which our students eagerly posed. In the warm weather, I can't start my day without a 15- or 20-mile bicycle ride. My idea of a good time always involves the outdoors: hiking, kayaking, or simply working in my garden.

Barbara H. Foley
Elizabeth R. Neblett

Photo Credits

This page constitutes an extension of the copyright page. We have made every effort to trace the ownership of all copyrighted material and to secure permission from copyright holders. In the event of any question arising as to the use of any material, we will be pleased to make the necessary corrections in future printings. Thanks are due to the following authors, publishers, and agents for permission to use the material indicated.

All photos courtesy of Elizabeth R. Neblett with the following exceptions:

p. 4, top left: Jeff Greenberg/Photo Edit

p. 4, center left: Harry Sieplinga.HMS Images/The Image Bank

p. 4, bottom left: Bruce Ayres/Stone

p. 10, center left: AP Photo/Stuart Ramson

p. 10, bottom right: AP Photo/Lenny Ignelzi

p. 10, bottom left: AP Photo/Terry Ashe

p. 42: Michael S. Yamashita/CORBIS

p. 48: Bob Jacobson/Index Stock Imagery

p. 56, center right: Myrleen Cate/Index Stock Imagery

p. 56, bottom right: Michelle D. Bridwell/Photo Edit

p. 72: Reuters NewMedia Inc./CORBIS

p. 88: Steve Dunwell/Index Stock Imagery

p. 94: Stephen Frisch/Stock Boston Inc/PictureQuest

p. 95: Jeff Greenberg/Photo Edit

p. 104: Scott Barrow, Inc./SuperStock

p. 134: Sean Murphy/Stone

p. 148, top right: Robert Santos/Index Stock Imagery

p. 148, bottom right: FoodPix/Getty Images

p. 188, top left: REUTERS/Gary Hershorn/TimePix

p. 188, top right: Hulton Archive/Getty Images

p. 188, center left: AP Photo/Butch Belair

p. 188, center right: AFP/CORBIS

p. 191 and 192: Jeffry W. Myers/Stock Boston/PictureQuest

p. 196: Reuters NewMedia Inc./CORBIS

p. 207, center left: AFP/CORBIS

p. 207, center: REUTERS/Mike Blake/Time Pix

p. 207, center right: Reuters NewMedia Inc./CORBIS

p. 207, bottom left: AP Photo/Ric Francis

p. 207, bottom center: Damian Strohmeyer/IPN/AURORA

p. 207, bottom right: Reuters NewMedia Inc./CORBIS

p. 210: Duomo/CORBIS

p. 211: David Young-Wolff/Photo Edit

Unit 1
Nice to Meet You

Discuss the person next to the unit number. Ask:

• *Who is next to the number?* (A man)

• *What is he doing?* (He is tipping his hat, bowing, and holding out his hand.)

☀ Dictionary:
People and Places

📶 A. Listen and repeat.
   (CD1, Track 1)

• Ask students to talk about the picture. Ask:

> *Who are the two people?*
> *Where are they?*
> *What are they doing?*

• Have students listen as you play the audio. The second time through, have them repeat the words.

• Repeat the second activity until students feel comfortable saying the sentences.

Suggestion

Have students practice the dialogue in pairs. Then, ask them to stay with the same partner and practice the conversation using their own names. Move around the room as the pairs work, modeling pronunciation and intonation as needed.

Teacher Note

Point out that Esperanza and Carlos are smiling and shaking hands. Explain that when meeting someone for the first time, Americans sometimes shake hands. Ask:

> *Do people shake hands in your country?*
> *Do both men and women shake hands?*
> *In what situations do people shake hands?*
> *Do they use other greetings such as bowing?*
> *Do you shake hands with people in the United States? In what situations?*

1 ☀ Nice to Meet You

☀ Dictionary: People and Places

📶 **A. Listen and repeat.**

> **A:** Hello. My name is Carlos.
>
> **B:** Hi, Carlos. I'm Esperanza. Nice to meet you.
>
> **A:** Nice to meet you, too.

B. Listen and repeat.

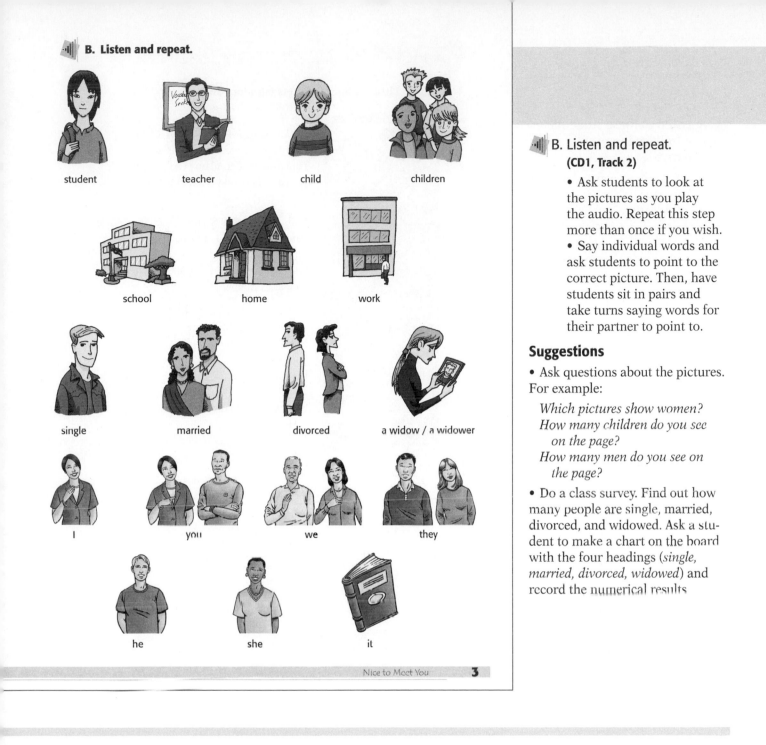

student

teacher

child

children

school

home

work

single

married

divorced

a widow / a widower

I

you

we

they

he

she

it

B. Listen and repeat.
(CD1, Track 2)

• Ask students to look at the pictures as you play the audio. Repeat this step more than once if you wish.
• Say individual words and ask students to point to the correct picture. Then, have students sit in pairs and take turns saying words for their partner to point to.

Suggestions

• Ask questions about the pictures. For example:

Which pictures show women?
How many children do you see on the page?
How many men do you see on the page?

• Do a class survey. Find out how many people are single, married, divorced, and widowed. Ask a student to make a chart on the board with the four headings (*single, married, divorced, widowed*) and record the numerical results

☀ Active Grammar:
Present Tense–Be

🔊 A. Listen to these students introduce themselves.
(CD1, Track 3)

• Before you play the audio, have students cover the introductions on the right as they look at the pictures on the left. Ask questions about each person. For example:

How old is he/she?
Where is he/she now?
Where is he/she from?

• Point to the person in each picture and have students listen as you play the audio. Present the introductions this way two or three times.
• After students have heard the introductions several times, invite them to ask questions about anything they don't understand.

Suggestion

Invite volunteers to read aloud one of the introductions.

B. Introduce yourself to the class.

Suggest that students fill in the blanks and practice their introductions several times before introducing themselves to the class.

Suggestion

If students are comfortable with the activity, tape record their introductions. These recordings will serve as evidence of the progress they have made when you play them back at the end of the course.

Suggestion

Have a world map posted on the wall in case students are unfamiliar with the location of each other's countries.

☀ Active Grammar: *Present Tense—Be*

🔊 A. Listen to these students introduce themselves.

Hi. My name is Pablo. I am from Mexico.
I am 17 years old. I live in Texas.
I am a student at Adams High School.
I am at school now. I am in Room 9.

Hello. My name is So Jung. I am from Korea.
I am 24 years old. I am single.
I live in California.
I am a student at Edison Adult School.
I am at work now.

Good morning. My name is Diego.
I am from Honduras.
I am 37 years old. I am married.
I live in Virginia.
This is my wife, Ana.
We have two children. Junior is 8 years old, and
    Melissa is 9.
I am a student at Lake Community College.
I am at home now.

B. Introduce yourself to the class. (Answers will vary.)

My name is _____. I am from _____.

I am _____ years old.

I live in _____.

I am married. *or* I am single. *or* I am divorced.
    or I am a widow / widower.

I have _____ children. *or* I don't have any children.

> When you meet someone for the first time, say *Nice to meet you.*

C. Pronouns. Say each sentence again, using *he, she, it,* or *they.*

Pablo is at school. →	**He** is at school.
So Jung is at work. →	**She** is at work.
This school is large. →	**It** is large.
Adam and Anna are at home. →	**They** are at home.

1. Pablo is from Mexico.
2. So Jung is from Korea.
3. Adam and Anna are married.
4. Pablo is single.
5. So Jung is at work.
6. Adam and Anna are at home.
7. This school is large.
8. The students are at school.
9. The teacher is in the classroom.
10. The book is on the desk.
11. The books are on the table.
12. The students are from India.
13. The door is open.
14. The teacher is at work.

D. Pronunciation: Contractions. Listen and repeat.

I am a student. →	I'm a student.
You are at school. →	You're at school.
He is single. →	He's single.
She is at home. →	She's at home.
It is the capital. →	It's the capital.
We are married. →	We're married.
They are at work. →	They're at work.
He is not from Cuba. →	He isn't from Cuba.
They are not here. →	They aren't here.

Say these sentences, using a contraction. Practice with a partner.

1. We are at school.
2. You are in the classroom.
3. They are in Room 5.
4. I am married.
5. He is at work.
6. She is a student.
7. I am in the classroom.
8. He is here.
9. She is from Mexico.
10. It is the capital of Texas.
11. She is not here today.
12. He is not at home.
13. They are not married.
14. They are not from China.

C. Pronouns. Say each sentence again, using *he, she, it,* or *they.*

Ask students to say the sentences using contractions in place of long forms.

Suggestion

Provide additional oral practice by pointing to a row of students and giving the cue *at school.* Elicit the answer from the class–*They are at school.* Then, point to a man and give the cue *married.* Elicit the answer–*He is married.* Continue in this manner.

D. Pronunciation: Contractions. (CD1, Track 4)

Play the audio for the first part of the exercise as students follow along in their books. Repeat several times. Then ask students to repeat each pair of sentences aloud.

Say these sentences, using a contraction.

As students practice saying the sentences in pairs, move around the room offering pronunciation support as needed.

Suggestion

Before asking students to work in pairs, play "Same or Different." Read pairs of similar sentences aloud. When you read identical sentences (*She's at home. She's at home.*), students call out *Same!* When you read different sentences (*She's at home. She is at home.*), students call out *Different!*

A. Circle the correct answer.

Ask students to point out Keren and Kimberly in the picture. Then, have them complete the activity individually and check their answers with a partner.

B. Answer.

• Point out the short answers in the box. Say each answer aloud and ask students to repeat. Then, invite different students to read aloud one pair of answers.

• Ask students to read the questions and practice saying their answers to a partner. Then, call on individuals to answer the questions.

C. Put the words in the questions in the correct order.

Have students write the questions on their own. Then, have them ask and answer the questions in pairs. Ask them to change roles so each student has a chance to practice both questions and answers.

☀ *Yes/No Questions*

Keren and Kimberly are 18 years old. They're from Haiti.

A. Circle the correct answer.

1. Is Keren 18 years old?   (Yes, she is.)   No, she isn't.
2. Is Kimberly from Peru?   Yes, she is.   (No, she isn't.)
3. Are Keren and Kimberly twins?   (Yes, they are.)   No, they aren't.
4. Are they happy?   (Yes, they are.)   No, they aren't.
5. Are you 18 years old?   Yes, I am.   No, I'm not.
6. Are you a twin?   Yes, I am.   No, I'm not.

B. Answer. (Answers will vary.)

1. Are you a student?
2. Are you at school now?
3. Are you married?
4. Is your teacher from the United States?
5. Is your teacher married?
6. Are the students from the United States?
7. Is your school large?
8. Is today Monday?

Short answers	
Yes, I am.	No, I'm not.
Yes, you are.	No, you aren't.
Yes, he is.	No, he isn't.
Yes, she is.	No, she isn't.
Yes, it is.	No, it isn't.
Yes, we are.	No, we aren't.
Yes, they are.	No, they aren't.

C. Put the words in the questions in the correct order. Ask your partner the questions.

1. you / married / are / ? Are you married?
2. from / are / Japan / you / ? Are you from Japan?
3. school / this / in / Texas / is / ? Is this school in Texas?
4. from / the teacher / is / California / ? Is the teacher from California?
5. all the students / today / are / in class / ? Are all the students in class today?

6   UNIT 1

☀ Completing a Registration Form

◀)) A. The alphabet. Listen and repeat.

Aa	Bb	Cc	Dd	Ee	Ff	Gg
Hh	Ii	Jj	Kk	Ll	Mm	Nn
Oo	Pp	Qq	Rr	Ss	Tt	Uu
Vv	Ww	Xx	Yy	Zz		

◀)) B. Numbers. Listen and repeat.

1	2	3	4	5	6	7	8	9	10
11	12	13	14	15	16	17	18	19	20
10	20	30	40	50	60	70	80	90	100

◀)) C. Listen and complete the registration form.   Please spell that.

SCHOOL REGISTRATION

Boris Galkin
NAME
514 North Avenue
ADDRESS
Richmond   Virginia   23223
CITY   STATE   ZIP CODE
555-7833
TELEPHONE NUMBER
Russia
COUNTRY

☀ Completing a Registration Form

◀)) A. The alphabet. (CD1, Track 5)

Play the audio several times and have students repeat the names of the letters.

Suggestions

• Write on the board any letters students are having difficulty pronouncing and practice them intensively. If you know the student's native language, you might contrast the pronunciation of the letter in the two languages.

• Students may confuse certain English letters. For example, Spanish speakers sometimes have difficulty distinguishing between *b* and *v*, and *e* and *i*. Write such pairs on the board and have students repeat the two different sounds as you point to the letters.

◀)) B. Numbers. (CD1, Track 6)

Introduce and practice the numbers as you did the letters in Exercise A. Practice the difference in pronunciation between -*teen* and -*ty* using pairs such as *14* and *40,* and *15* and *50.*

◀)) C. Listen and complete the registration form. (CD1, Track 7)

Ask students to complete the activity on their own. You can ask pairs of students to check each other's work.

Audio Script

C. Listen and complete the registration form. (CD1, Track 7)

A: I need some information for the registration form. What's your first name?

B: Boris.

A: And your last name?

B: Galkin.

A: Please spell that.

B: Galkin–G-A-L-K-I-N.

A: What's your address?

B: 514 North Avenue.

A: And the city?

B: Richmond.

A: What's your zip code?

B: 23223.

A: And what's your telephone number?

B: 555-7833.

A: 555-7833?

B: Yes.

A: And what country are you from, Boris?

B: I'm from Russia.

D. Match the question and the answer.

Ask students to complete the activity on their own. Students can then practice asking and answering the questions in pairs.

E. Complete with information about yourself.

Ask students to fill in the form as if they were registering for the school they are in right now.

F. Sit with a partner.

Students use the questions in Exercise D to find out the necessary information about their partners. When they finish filling out the form, have them check it against the completed Exercise E in their partner's book.

D. Match the question and the answer.

1. What's your name? (d.)   a. It's 23223.
2. What's your address? (f.)   b. It's 555-7833.
3. And the city? (e.)   c. I'm from Russia.
4. What's your zip code? (a.)   d. My name is Boris Galkin.
5. What's your phone number? (b.)   e. Richmond.
6. What country are you from? (c.) f. 514 North Avenue.

E. Complete with information about yourself.

```
                SCHOOL REGISTRATION
                 (Answers will vary.)
  NAME
  _____
  ADDRESS
  _____
  CITY              STATE              ZIP CODE
  _____
  TELEPHONE NUMBER
  _____
  COUNTRY
```

F. Sit with a partner. Ask the questions in Exercise D. Complete the form with information about your partner.

```
                SCHOOL REGISTRATION
                 (Answers will vary.)
  NAME
  _____
  ADDRESS
  _____
  CITY              STATE              ZIP CODE
  _____
  TELEPHONE NUMBER
  _____
  COUNTRY
```

☀ Working Together: Student to Student

A. STUDENT A: Look below.
STUDENT B: Turn to page 10.

PART 1: Read these sentences to Student B.

1. She is married.
2. He isn't at work.
3. We are at school.
4. Boston is a city.
5. It isn't in Mexico.
6. She isn't from China.
7. I'm not a teacher.
8. He is 20 years old.
9. We are at school.
10. You are in class.

PART 2: Listen to Student B. (Circle) the verb form you hear.

11. He (is) / isn't a student.
12. She is / (isn't) at school.
13. We are / (aren't) from Russia
14. I'm / (I'm not) married.
15. You (are) / aren't in Room 2.
16. They are / (aren't) at work.
17. She (is) / isn't single.
18. (I'm) / I'm not a student.
19. It is / (isn't) Monday.
20. They (are) / aren't from Japan.

☀ Working Together: Student to Student

A. Student A.

• Point to the two people in the picture. Ask:

Who are these two people?
What are they doing?

• Remind students not to look at the other student's page. The goal of the exercise is to practice speaking clearly and understanding spoken English.

• The pairs take turns speaking and listening. When they finish circling their answers, have them check their own work using the other student's page.

Suggestion

Poll students and list the numbers of any questions in Part 1 or Part 2 that several students got wrong. Then, have different students read these statements aloud. Discuss why the listener may not have heard them correctly. Point out specific pronunciation errors that may have caused problems. For example:

T: *Part 1. Sentence 5.*
   Listen carefully.
   1. *It is in Mexico.*
   2. *It isn't in Mexico.*

Ask students to repeat each form several times.

B. Student B.

See instructions for page 9.

C. People in the news.

• Have students bring to class newspaper or magazine pictures of famous people. You can also bring several pictures to ensure that people from a variety of different walks of life are represented–politicians, singers, etc.

• If possible, display the pictures in the classroom before class begins and encourage students to identify each person.

• Point to each picture in the book and read the related sentences with the class. Then, have students form small groups. Suggest that they discuss the pictures they brought in and practice saying their sentences aloud to each other before they begin writing. They can use the sentences in Exercises A, B, and C as models.

• Invite different students to hold up a picture and read the sentences they wrote.

Suggestion

Display pictures and sentences in the classroom.

B. STUDENT B

PART 1: Listen to Student A. Circle the verb form you hear.

1. She **is** / isn't married.
2. He is / **isn't** at work.
3. We **are** / aren't at school.
4. Boston **is** / isn't a city.
5. It is / **isn't** in Mexico.

6. She is / **isn't** from China.
7. I'm / **I'm not** a teacher.
8. He **is** / isn't 20 years old.
9. We **are** / aren't at school.
10. You **are** / aren't in class.

PART 2: Read these sentences to Student A.

11. He is a student.
12. She isn't at school.
13. We aren't from Russia.
14. I'm not married.
15. You are in Room 2.

16. They aren't at work.
17. She is single.
18. I'm a student.
19. It isn't Monday.
20. They are from Japan.

C. People in the news. Bring in pictures of people in the news: athletes, politicians, actors and actresses, singers, etc. In a group, talk about each person. Write three or four sentences about each person.

This is Gloria Estefan. She is a singer. She is married. She has two children. She is from Cuba.

This is Ichiro Suzuki. He is a baseball player. He's from Japan. He's on the Seattle Mariners team.

This is Hillary Clinton. She is a U.S. senator from New York. She is married. She has a daughter. Her name is Chelsea.

10   UNIT 1

D. Class list. Introduce yourself to the class. Write your name on the chalkboard. Show your class the location of your native country on a world map.

Hello.
My name is Soji.
I'm from India.

Make a list of all the students in your class. Write their native countries.

Name	Country
(Answers will vary.)	

D. Class list.
Display a world map and have students point out their native countries as they introduce themselves.

Suggestion
If the lettering on the map is small, you may wish to have students write their countries of origin on the board along with their names.

A. Listen and complete the form. (CD1, Track 8)

- Discuss the picture with the class. Ask:
  Who are the two people in the picture?
  Where are they?
  What is the woman on the left doing?
  What is the woman on the right doing?
  What is the paper on the counter?

- Have students just listen as you play the audio the first time. Then, present the dialogue again at least two more times. During one presentation, you may wish to pause after you play or read each question-and-answer exchange to give students time to fill in the lines on the form.
- Discuss vocabulary items such as *first name, last name, zip code,* and *birth date.* Write the four terms on the board and ask students to give specific examples of each. For example: *John, Chen, 07632,* and *October 10, 1980.*

Suggestion

Ask groups of students to write more questions about the picture. Then, have them read their questions aloud and call on other students to answer.

A. Listen and complete the form.

SCHOOL REGISTRATION		
Akiko Tanaka		
NAME		
337 Bay Avenue		
ADDRESS		
Kendall	Florida	33156
CITY	STATE	ZIP CODE
March 4, 1980		
DATE OF BIRTH		
555-4739		
TELEPHONE NUMBER		

Audio Script

A. Listen and complete the form. (CD1, Track 8)

Akiko is a new student at Miami Adult School. She's in the office now. She's registering for class.

A: What is your first name?
B: My first name is Akiko.
A: A-K-I-K-O?
B: Yes.
A: And your last name?
B: Tanaka.
A: Please spell that.
B: T-A-N-A-K-A.
A: What's your address?
B: 337 Bay Avenue.

A: And the city?
B: Kendall.
A: What's your zip code?
B: 33156.
A: What's your telephone number?
B: 555-4739.
A: 555-4739?
B: Yes.
A: What's your birth date?
(Continued on page 13.)

B. Put the words in the questions in the correct order. Then, write short answers.

Yes, she is.
No, she isn't.

1. at / is / work / Akiko / ?

   Is Akiko at work?   No, she isn't.

2. Akiko / school / is / at / ?

   Is Akiko at school?   Yes, she is.

3. she / the office / is / in / ?

   Is she in the office?   Yes, she is.

4. in / she / is / her classroom / ?

   Is she in her classroom?   No, she isn't.

5. student / a / new / is / Akiko / ?

   Is Akiko a new student?   Yes, she is.

6. Vietnam / she / is / from / ?

   Is she from Vietnam?   No, she isn't.

C. Listen and write the questions.

1. What's your name?   My name is Akiko Tanaka.
2. What's your address?   337 Bayard Avenue.
3. What's your telephone number?   555-4739.
4. What's your birth date?   March 4, 1980.
5. What country are you from?   Japan.

D. Conversation. Practice this conversation with a partner. Write a new conversation with *your* names.

A: Are you a new student?

B: Yes, I am. My name is Akiko.

A: Hi, Akiko. My name is Marie.

B: Hi, Marie. Nice to meet you.

A: Nice to meet you, too. Welcome to our class.

B. Put the words in each question in the correct order.

• Remind students that Akiko is the young woman who is registering for class in the picture on page 12. Review the first item and have students complete the rest of the questions and fill in the answers on their own. They can check their answers with a partner.

• Have them practice asking and answering the questions in random order.

C. Listen and write the questions. (CD1, Track 9)

Students listen and fill in the questions. You may wish to play the audio more than once.

D. Conversation.

• Ask students to read the conversation to themselves. Answer any questions and have pairs practice the conversation together.

• Have partners write a similar conversation using their own names. Have them practice their conversation several times. Invite volunteers to read their conversations to the class.

(Continued from page 12, Exercise A.)

B: Birth date?

A: Yes, your birth date.

B: I don't understand *birth date*.

A: Your date of birth, the day you were born, maybe 1979 or 1980.

B: Oh! I understand. March 4, 1980.

A: And what country are you from?

B: I'm from Japan.

A: Thank you, Akiko. You are in Miss Bayard's class. That's room 217.

B: Excuse me?

A: You are in room 217. That's two-one-seven, 217. It's upstairs. Go up those stairs to Room 217. Give this paper to Miss Bayard.

B: OK. Thank you.

C. Listen and write the questions. (CD1, Track 9)

1. What's your name?
2. What's your address?
3. What's your telephone number?
4. What's your birth date?
5. What country are you from?

A. Before You Read.

• Ask students to answer the two questions above the passage. Then, talk about the picture. Ask:

Where is this woman?
What is her job?

• Ask students to read the passage on their own. Explain that they won't understand everything. Suggest that as they read they just try to understand the main ideas. Then, read the story aloud to the students.

Suggestion

You can help students understand the story by following these steps:

• Read the story to the class.
• Ask, *Do you understand the story? Read me a sentence you understand.*
• Have several students tell the class facts they know about the ESL program and the teacher, Lynn Meng. For example: *The program has 1,800 students. Lynn Meng is an ESL teacher. She is married. She has two children.*
• Read the story again.

B. Complete this chart about Union County College and about your own school.

Have students reread the story and complete the information about Union County College. Then, discuss statistics and information about your own school and have students complete the "My School" column together.

A. Before You Read.

1. What is the name of your school?
2. What does ESL mean?

My name is Lynn Meng. I am a teacher at the Institute for Intensive English at Union County College. Union County College is in Elizabeth, New Jersey. Elizabeth is a big city. People from all over the world live in this city. We have a large English as a Second Language (ESL) program. More than 1,800 students are studying ESL. Our students are from 72 different countries and they speak 80 different languages. We have 70 teachers. I teach Level 3 and Level 5. The students are friendly and talkative. They study hard. I love my job!

My students like to ask me questions. Where are you from? Are you married? How old are you? I am from the United States. I live in New Jersey. I'm married and I have two daughters. One is in high school, and one is in college. My husband is from China. He is a librarian. Don't ask my age! I always say that I'm 25.

B. Complete this chart about Union County College and about your own school.

	Union County College	My School
Name of school	Union County College	(Answers will vary.)
Number of students in the ESL program	more than 1,800	
Number of countries	72	
Number of teachers	70	

Writing Our Stories: An Introduction

A. Read.

My name is Bibiana. I am from Slovakia. I am 27 years old. I am single. I am studying English at Union County College. I am in Level 5. I study three days a week, Monday, Wednesday, and Friday. On Monday and Wednesday, my class is from 8:00 to 10:30. My class is in room 403. My teacher is Lynn Meng.

B. Write about yourself. (Answers will vary.)

My name is _____. I am from _____,
_____. I am _____ years old. I am _____.
     country   married / single / divorced
I live in _____. I am studying English at _____.
        state   school
I am in _____. I study _____ days a week:
        class
_____. My class is in Room _____.
     days
My teacher is _____.

Writing Note
The days of the week begin with capital letters: Sunday, Monday, Tuesday, Wednesday, Thursday, Friday, Saturday.

Writing Our Stories: An Introduction

A. Read.
Read the story aloud to the students. Ask them to point out any sentences they don't understand. Explain what they mean.

B. Write about yourself.
• Students can use Exercise A as a model as they complete this activity.
• Invite some students to read their stories aloud to the class.

Suggestion
Circle errors on students' papers and have students work in pairs to make the corrections.

Practicing on Your Own

A. Pronouns.

Review the sample answer with the class. Then, have them complete the exercise on their own.

B. Contractions.

Have students complete the activity orally with partners before writing the answers in their books. One student reads the sentence with the full form and the other says the sentence using a contraction.

C. *Be.*

Students complete the activity on their own. Tell them to check the chart in Exercise D on page 5 if they need help with any answers.

Practicing on Your Own

A. Pronouns. Rewrite these sentences, using *he, she, it,* or *they.*

1. Mary is a student. — She is a student.
2. Tom is at school. — He is at school.
3. Peter and John are students. — They are students.
4. The teacher is here. — He/she is here.
5. School is open. — It is open.
6. Ana is single. — She is single.
7. Lisa and Kate are at school. — They are at school.

B. Contractions. Rewrite these sentences, using a contraction.

1. I am a student. — I'm a student.
2. She is married. — She's married.
3. It is Friday. — It's Friday.
4. He is not at work. — He's not at work.
5. It is hot today. — It's hot today.
6. They are absent. — They're absent.
7. I am not a teacher. — I'm not a teacher.
8. She is not at school today. — She's not at school today.

C. *Be.* Complete these sentences, using *is, am,* or *are.*

1. He __is__ at school.
2. They __are__ at home.
3. I __am__ in class.
4. She __is__ on the bus.
5. We __are__ students.
6. Jack __is__ a student.
7. They __are__ not from India.
8. They __are__ married.
9. Marie __is__ single.
10. Tom __is__ friendly.
11. I __am__ not from New York.
12. It __is__ on the desk.
13. I __am__ 20 years old.
14. It __is__ Sunday.

16 UNIT 1

Grammar Summary

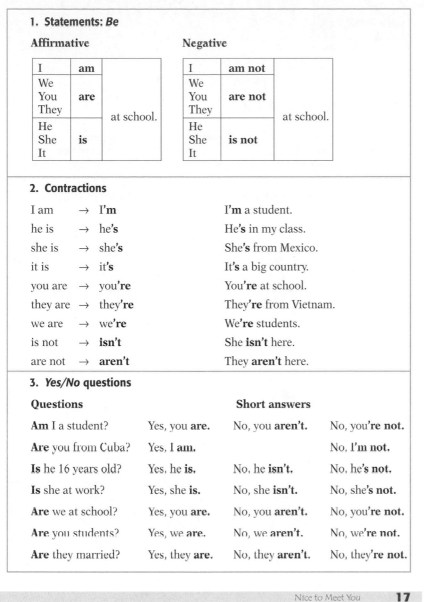

1. Statements: *Be*

Affirmative

I	am	
We You They	are	at school.
He She It	is	

Negative

I	am not	
We You They	are not	at school.
He She It	is not	

2. Contractions

I am	→	I'm	I'm a student.
he is	→	he's	He's in my class.
she is	→	she's	She's from Mexico.
it is	→	it's	It's a big country.
you are	→	you're	You're at school.
they are	→	they're	They're from Vietnam.
we are	→	we're	We're students.
is not	→	isn't	She isn't here.
are not	→	aren't	They aren't here.

3. *Yes/No* questions

Questions / **Short answers**

Am I a student?	Yes, you **are.**	No, you **aren't.**	No, you**'re not.**
Are you from Cuba?	Yes, I **am.**		No, I**'m not.**
Is he 16 years old?	Yes, he **is.**	No, he **isn't.**	No, he**'s not.**
Is she at work?	Yes, she **is.**	No, she **isn't.**	No, she**'s not.**
Are we at school?	Yes, you **are.**	No, you **aren't.**	No, you**'re not.**
Are you students?	Yes, we **are.**	No, we **aren't.**	No, we**'re not.**
Are they married?	Yes, they **are.**	No, they **aren't.**	No, they**'re not.**

Grammar Summary

• Review the summary with the class. Invite students to make up alternate sentences for each example in the chart. For example, in place of *I am at school,* a student might say *I am a student.* In place of *He is not at school,* a student might say *He is not married.*

• See the Grammar Summary Expansion on page 230 for a more complete explanation of these grammar points.

Unit 2
My Classmates

Discuss the people next to the unit number. Ask:

• *Who are the people next to the number?* (Two women or girls)
• *What are they doing?* (They are holding books and putting their arms around each other's shoulders.)

Dictionary:
Adjectives

A. Listen and repeat.
(CD1, Track 10)

• For now, focus only on the adjectives on page 18. Ask students to look at the words in the box and the pictures. Answer any questions they may have using simple English sentences. For example:

S: *What does* tired *mean?*
T: Tired *means you want to sleep. You feel* tired *after you work hard all day.*

• Play the audio and have students listen and repeat.

B. Describe each picture.

• Invite students to talk about whatever pictures they want to. Restate their comments in simple English. For example:

S: *This girl is shy.*
T: *That's right. She doesn't want to talk. She's shy.*

• Go through all the pictures one by one, asking different students to apply the correct adjective to each person. For each picture, have the class repeat a correct sentence containing an adjective from Exercise A.

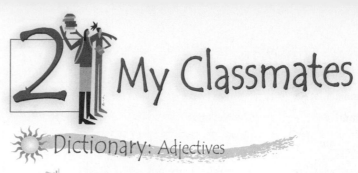

My Classmates

Dictionary: Adjectives

A. Listen and repeat.

messy	neat	thirsty	hungry
beautiful	handsome	hardworking	lazy
talkative	quiet / shy	intelligent	tired

B. Describe each picture. Use an adjective from Exercise A.

 1. ___thirsty___
 2. ___hungry___
 3. ___talkative___
 4. ___tired___

 5. ___handsome___
 6. ___messy___
 7. ___beautiful___
 8. ___hardworking___

 9. ___neat___
 10. ___lazy___
 11. ___quiet/shy___
 12. ___intelligent___

C. Opposites. Write the opposite of each adjective. Use the words on the right.

1. clean   _dirty_
2. happy   _sad_
3. hot   _cold_
4. safe   _dangerous_
5. friendly   _unfriendly_
6. nervous   _relaxed_
7. young   _old_
8. noisy   _quiet_
9. tall   _short_
10. expensive   _cheap_
11. easy   _difficult_
12. heavy   _thin_

old
dangerous
quiet
cold
sad
unfriendly
✓dirty
cheap
thin
relaxed
difficult
short

D. Describe. Use an adjective to describe these people, places, and things.
(Answers will vary.)

1. The United States is _____.
2. My car is _____.
3. The students in this class are _____.
4. This classroom is _____.
5. The teacher is _____.
6. Canada is _____.
7. The street outside this building is _____.
8. English is _____.

E. Describe yourself. Choose four adjectives that describe *you!* (Answers will vary.)

I'm _____, _____,

_____, and _____!

C. Opposites.

Do this activity with the whole class. Discuss each numbered adjective and help students find matches. For words they aren't familiar with, give several synonyms and sample sentences. For example:

S1: *What does* nervous *mean?*

T: *It means* worried *or* afraid. *I get nervous when I have to drive in a big city. Some people get nervous when they go to the dentist. Do you get nervous before you take a test?*

S1: *Oh,* nervous *means scared or* worried.

T: *That's right.*

D. Describe.

Ask students to complete the activity on their own and check their answers with a partner. Point out that there are several correct answers to each question.

E. Describe yourself.

Have students complete this exercise individually and share their sentences with a partner. Invite volunteers to read their sentences to the class.

Suggestion

If appropriate, have students write their sentences on small slips of paper. Collect the slips. Read each one aloud and ask the class to guess who is being described.

Active Grammar:
Present Tense Questions–Be

A. Complete the sentences using adjectives.

- Ask questions about the pictures. For example:

  What is the man at the top doing?
  What is the woman below doing?
  Where are Carmen and Juan?
  What are they doing?

- Ask pairs of students to take turns completing the sentences orally. Remind them that they can look back at the lists of adjectives on pages 18 and 19 if they wish. Then, have them fill in the blanks on their own. Review the exercise with the whole class.

B. *Who* questions.

- Model the question and the two answers in the box. Both the question and the answers end with falling intonation. Ask students to repeat the question and answers.
- Do the activity with the whole class. Then, ask:

  When one person is mentioned in the answer, what verb do you use? (is).
  When more than one person is mentioned in the answer, what verb do you use? (are)

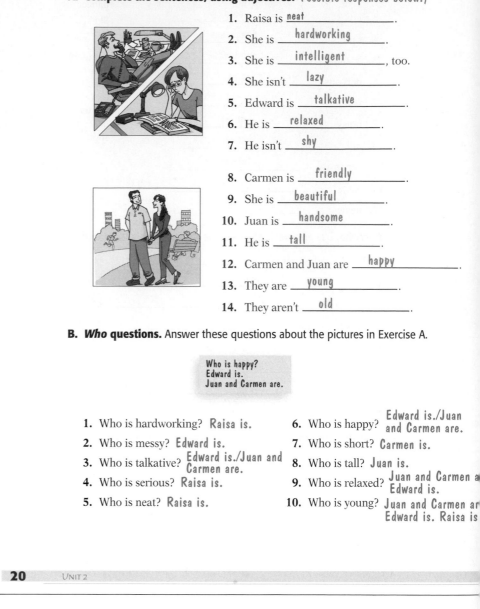

A. Complete the sentences, using adjectives. (Answers may vary. Possible responses below.)

1. Raisa is __neat__.
2. She is __hardworking__.
3. She is __intelligent__, too.
4. She isn't __lazy__.
5. Edward is __talkative__.
6. He is __relaxed__.
7. He isn't __shy__.

8. Carmen is __friendly__.
9. She is __beautiful__.
10. Juan is __handsome__.
11. He is __tall__.
12. Carmen and Juan are __happy__.
13. They are __young__.
14. They aren't __old__.

B. *Who* questions. Answer these questions about the pictures in Exercise A.

> Who is happy?
> Edward is.
> Juan and Carmen are.

1. Who is hardworking? **Raisa is.**
2. Who is messy? **Edward is.**
3. Who is talkative? **Edward is./Juan and Carmen are.**
4. Who is serious? **Raisa is.**
5. Who is neat? **Raisa is.**

6. Who is happy? **Edward is./Juan and Carmen are.**
7. Who is short? **Carmen is.**
8. Who is tall? **Juan is.**
9. Who is relaxed? **Juan and Carmen are./Edward is.**
10. Who is young? **Juan and Carmen are./Edward is. Raisa is.**

C. Answer these questions about your class. (Answers will vary.)

Yes, I am.	Yes, s/he is.	Yes, they are.	Yes, it is.
No, I'm not.	No, s/he isn't.	No, they aren't.	No, it isn't.

1. Is your classroom hot?
2. Is your classroom cold?
3. Is your classroom large?
4. Is your book on your desk?
5. Is English difficult?
6. Are the students hardworking?
7. Are the students friendly?
8. Are the students relaxed?
9. Are the students intelligent?
10. Is your teacher tall?
11. Is your teacher tired?
12. Are you thirsty?
13. Are you friendly?
14. Are you talkative?

D. Write. Look at the pictures on page 20. Answer these questions.

1. Is Raisa at home?   Yes, she is.
2. Is she messy?   No, she isn't.
3. Is Edward talkative?   Yes, he is.
4. Is he messy?   Yes, he is.
5. Are Juan and Carmen in the park?   Yes, they are.
6. Are they happy?   Yes, they are.
7. Are they nervous?   No, they're not.

E. Pronunciation: *Or* questions. Listen and repeat.

1. Is Raisa neat or messy?
2. Is Raisa lazy or hardworking?
3. Is Raisa at home or at work?
4. Is Edward relaxed or nervous?
5. Are Carmen and Juan at home or in the park?
6. Are they happy or sad?
7. Are they young or old?

> **Or questions**
>
> Is Raisa neat or messy?
> She's neat.

Ask and answer the questions above with your partner.

C. Answer these questions about your class.

• Begin by reviewing the short answers in the boxes. For each answer, ask students to suggest one or more correct questions. For example:

T: *Let's make some questions to go with the answer* No, they aren't.

S1: *Are Linda and Ari in class today?*

T: *No, they aren't. They're absent. Good work!* Model one question for students if they find this task difficult.

• Do the activity with the whole class. Allow for the possibility of different correct answers for some questions. For example, with item 5 some students may think English is difficult and others may think it's not.

D. Write.

Have students complete the activity on their own. Then, have different students write one answer each on the board. Review the answers with the class and answer any questions they may have.

E. Pronunciation: *Or* questions. (CD1, Track 11)

• Model the rising and falling intonation used with the *or* question in the box. Point out that the voice rises and falls almost like it does when you sing a song. Then, model the sentence again and ask students to repeat.

• Play the audio and have students just listen the first time through. The second time through, pause to allow time for students to repeat each question. Do the repetition step as many times as you wish.

Ask and answer the questions above with a partner.

Have pairs of students practice together. Observe.

☀ Countries and Cities

Suggestion

Bring to class a world atlas or almanac that shows all the countries
of the world, their populations, and
so on, so that you can refer to it,
if necessary, while completing
the following pages.

A. Continents.

• Point to the names of the
continents on the map and
model the pronunciation of
each. Ask students to repeat.
• Point to the names of the
countries in the box and ask
students to repeat. Ask students
what countries they are from,
write the countries on the board,
and ask the class to repeat.
• Read the sample dialogue and
ask students to repeat. Then, call
on pairs to ask and answer the
question about each country in
the box (and on the board).

B. Capitals.

Point out and explain the sample
answer. Then, invite students
to study the list and raise their
hands when they think they have
another answer. Call on students
one by one. Have them write
the unscrambled name on the
board. Ask the rest of the class
to copy each correct answer in
the appropriate space.

Suggestion

Explain that Americans often give
foreign place names an English
pronunciation instead of using
the native language pronunciation.
Practice the usual American
pronunciation for each capital.

☀ Countries and Cities

A. Continents. Where are these countries?

A: Where is <u>Korea</u> ?

B: It's in <u>Asia</u> .

Korea	Peru	Poland
Kenya	Egypt	Canada
Brazil	Vietnam	Turkey

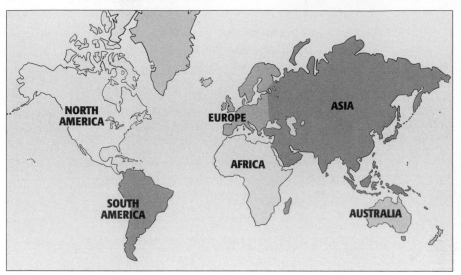

B. Capitals. What is the capital of each country? Unscramble the letters.

1.	Spain	D M A D R I	Madrid
2.	Russia	S M C O O W	Moscow
3.	Portugal	B I L N S O	Lisbon
4.	Canada	T T A A W O	Ottawa
5.	Chile	A O I N G S A T	Santiago
6.	France	S P R I A	Paris
7.	Japan	O O Y T K	Tokyo
8.	India	W E N L H I E D	New Delhi
9.	Thailand	G A K B O K N	Bangkok
10.	Ecuador	O T I U Q	Quito

C. Match the questions to the correct answers.

1. What country are you from?   It's about 66 million.
2. Where is your country?   It's Cairo.
3. Is your country large or small?   It's in Africa.
4. What is the population?   I'm from Egypt.
5. What is the capital of your country?   It's large.

D. Sit with a partner. Write a conversation about your country. Practice the conversation. **(Answers will vary.)**

A: What country are you from?   B: I'm from _____.

A: Where is your country?   B: It's in _____.

A: Is your country large or small?   B: It's _____.

A: What is the population?   B: It's about _____.

A: What is the capital?   B: The capital is _____.

E. This city. Answer these questions about the city that your school is in. What do you like about this city? What don't you like? **(Answers will vary.)**

1. What's the name of this city?
2. Is it large?
3. What's the population?
4. What state or province is this city in?
5. Is it the capital?
6. Is this city clean?
7. Is it safe in the daytime?
8. Is it safe at night?
9. Is this city busy?
10. Is this city quiet?
11. Is it hot today?
12. Are the people in this city friendly?

I like this city because _____.

I don't like this city because _____.

C. Match the questions to the correct answers.

Ask students to complete the activity on their own. Go over the answers with the whole class by having one person ask the question and another give the correct answer.

D. Sit with a partner.

Give the pairs several minutes to complete their conversations. Then, call on several different pairs to read their conversations to the class.

E. This city.

Do this activity with the whole class. As new pieces of information are mentioned (such as the population or the state or the province), write them on the board. Repeat the activity, asking different students to answer each question.

Suggestion

Have students close their books. Then ask the questions in random order and invite volunteers to answer.

Working Together

A. My classmates.

Suggest that the pairs or groups discuss each adjective and which student or students it might apply to. Then, have them write the sentences together. Call on groups to read three or four of their sentences to the class.

Teacher Note

Remind students to be sensitive to the feelings of the individuals in the class. For example, one student might enjoy being labeled *talkative*, but another might feel bad about receiving this label.

B. Student to student.

First, one student asks all six questions and circles his or her partner's answers; then, the other student takes his or her turn.

Working Together

A. My classmates. Sit with a partner or in a small group. Use the adjectives here, and write about students in your class. Then, read a few of your sentences to the class.

> Phoung is handsome.
> Yelena and Diana are intelligent.

intelligent   talkative   tall

thin   tired

busy   young   hardworking

friendly   happy

B. Student to student. Sit with another student. Ask your partner questions using these adjectives. Circle your partner's answer.

> happy   sad
>
> A: Are you happy or sad?
> B: I'm happy.
>
> happy   sad

1. happy   sad
2. relaxed   nervous
3. lazy   hardworking
4. shy   talkative
5. tall   short   medium height
6. old   young   middle aged

C. My country. Draw a simple map of your native country. Include the capital and the city or town you are from. Complete or circle the correct information. (Answers will vary.)

```
┌─────────────────────────────────────────────────┐
│                                                   │
│                                                   │
│                                                   │
│                                                   │
│                                                   │
│                                                   │
│                                                   │
│                                                   │
│                                                   │
│                                                   │
│                                                   │
│                                                   │
│                                                   │
└─────────────────────────────────────────────────┘
```

I'm from _____. It's a **large / small** country.

The capital of my country is _____.

It's here, in the **north / south / east / west / center** of the country.

The capital of my country is **big / small.** It's **noisy / quiet.**

The population of my country is about _____.

I'm from _____. (name of town)

My country is **hot / cold / hot and cold.**

The people in my country are **friendly / unfriendly.**

Tell your group or your class about your native country. They can ask questions for more information.

Suggestion

Many students will not be sure of the population of their native country. Bring in an atlas and help students find this information.

C. My country.

• Read the instructions aloud and invite students to ask about anything they don't understand. Review the statements below the map. Teach or review the directions *north, south, east,* and *west,* if necessary. Then, have students complete the maps and sentences on their own or with another student from his or her country. Move around the room helping as needed.

• If you have a large class, divide it into groups with a maximum of four people in each group. Encourage students in the groups to ask each other questions after each presentation.

Suggestion

If some students lack confidence when speaking in front of a group, pair them with a more fluent partner for a practice session. The two can rehearse in another part of the room (or outside the room) while the first few presentations are made. When they return, they can also listen to several presentations before doing their own.

A. Write three adjectives to describe Adam.

- Ask students to describe the two college students in the picture. You might use questions like these to get started:

  Who is this?
  Where are the boys?
  What are they doing?
  What is Ben buying?

- Ask students to write three adjectives to describe each student. Then, go over the answers with the whole class.

B. Listen to the conversation. Then, listen to the questions and circle the correct answers.

(CD1, Track 12 and Track 13)

Play the audio and have students just listen the first time. Then, play Track 12 along with Track 13 again and have students circle the correct answers. Play both Tracks 12 and 13 one more time so they can check their answers. Write the correct answers on the board and discuss any that students missed.

☀ The Big Picture: A New Student

A. Write three adjectives to describe Adam. Write three adjectives to describe Ben. (Answers may vary. Possible responses are:)

Adam	Ben
friendly	short
tall	happy
intelligent	young

Ben   Adam

B. Listen to the conversation between Adam and Ben. Then, listen to the questions and circle the correct answers.

1. **a.** in class   **b.** (in the bookstore)   **c.** in the cafeteria
2. **a.** (a dictionary)   **b.** an English book   **c.** a sandwich
3. **a.** Ben is.   **b.** Adam is.   **c.** (Mr. Baxter is.)
4. **a.** (in room 312)   **b.** at 9 o'clock   **c.** Mr. Baxter is.
5. **a.** Yes, he is.   **b.** (No, he isn't.)   **c.** Yes, they are.
6. **a.** Yes, he is.   **b.** (He's from Poland.)   **c.** He's from India.
7. **a.** to class   **b.** (to the cafeteria)   **c.** to the bookstore.

26   UNIT 2

Audio Script

B. Listen to the conversation between Adam and Ben. Then, listen to the questions and circle the correct answers. (CD1, Track 12)

Two students are standing in line in the college bookstore.

Adam: Are you buying a dictionary?
Ben: Yes, I am.
Adam: You know, I think you're in my class, English 2?
Ben: With Mr. Baxter?
Adam: Yes. At 9:00. In Room 312.
Ben: Yeah. We are in the same class.
Adam: My name is Adam.

Ben: Hi, Adam. My name is Ben.
Adam: Hi, Ben. Are you a new student?
Ben: Yes. This is my first week at school.
Adam: This is my second year here. What country are you from?
Ben: I'm from India. How about you?
Adam: I'm from Poland. What classes are you taking?
Ben: English, and Writing, and Math. How about you?
Adam: The same. And I have a computer class. I'm going to the cafeteria for a sandwich. Want to come?
Ben: Sure. I'd like a soda.

Listen and circle. (CD1, Track 13)

1. Where are Adam and Ben?
2. What is Ben buying?
3. Who is their teacher?
4. Where is their class?
5. Is Adam a new student?
6. Is Adam from Poland or from India?
7. Where are they going?

C. Write the answer.

Yes, he is.
No, he isn't.

1. Is Adam young?   Yes, he is.
2. Is Adam tall?   Yes, he is.
3. Is Adam talkative?   Yes, he is.
4. Is Adam hungry?   Yes, he is.
5. Is Ben heavy?   No, he isn't.
6. Is Ben friendly?   Yes, he is.
7. Is Ben a new student?   Yes, he is.
8. Is Ben happy?   Yes, he is.

D. Complete with *Who, Where, What,* or *What time.*

1. ___What___ country is Adam from?   He's from Poland.
2. ___Where___ are Adam and Ben?   They're in the bookstore.
3. ___What time___ is their class?   It's at nine o'clock.
4. ___Who___ is from India?   Ben is.
5. ___Who___ is their teacher?   Mr. Baxter is.
6. ___Where___ are they going?   They're going to the cafeteria.
7. ___What___ is Ben buying?   He's buying a dictionary.
8. ___Who___ is in the bookstore?   Ben and Adam are.
9. ___Who___ is buying a dictionary?   Ben is.
10. ___Where___ is their class?   It's in room 312.

E. Write a conversation. Sit with another student. Write a conversation between two students who are meeting for the first time.

C. Write the answer.

Ask students to answer the questions on their own. As you review the answers, replay the audio of Exercise B, if necessary, to confirm the correct answers.

D. Complete with *Who, Where, What,* or *What time.*

• Ask students to make up one or two sample questions using each question word. Then ask them to complete the following sentences.

Who *asks about . . .* (people)
Where *asks about . . .* (places)
What *asks about . . .* (objects, things)
What time *asks about . . .* (time)

• Ask students to complete the activity on their own. Go over the answers with the class. Correct any errors using one of the four statements above to explain the corrections.

E. Write a conversation.

Have students write the conversation with a partner. Encourage them to include things not mentioned on the audio, if they wish. Invite volunteer pairs to present their conversations to the class.

Suggestion

To provide a model, you can play the audio from Exercise B again and ask the students to listen for some of the questions in the conversation. As students tell you the questions, write them on the board. Ask "What other questions can you ask when you meet someone?"

A. Put an X on your home state on the map.

• Point out the states listed in the box and ask students to repeat each name. Then, have them point to the location of each state on the map.

• Write the words *north, south, east,* and *west* on the board. Ask students to tell where each of the states on the list is located. (California is in the West.)

• Have students point out their home state on the map and tell where it is located.

• Ask students to read the passage on their own. Then, read the story to the students. Explain that they won't understand everything and ask them to hold any questions until after they have done Exercise B.

Suggestion

Display a wall map of the United States and again point out the locations of the seven states in the box. Ask students if they have any relatives or friends in these states or in other states. Invite students to point to and make comments about any other states they wish.

B. Circle *Yes* or *No.*

Check the answers by reading the questions and calling on different students to answer.

C. Discuss.

Have a whole-class discussion. Restate any incomplete sentences or sentences with grammatical errors in simple English. For example: *You live in Nevada because there are a lot of jobs there.*

A. Put an X on your home state on the map.

Where are these states?

California	New York
Texas	New Jersey
Arizona	Illinois
Florida	

The United States is a country of immigrants. The population of the United States is 280,000,000. Ten percent of the population was born in another country. That means that more than 28,000,000 people came to the United States as children or as adults. Most immigrants live in seven states: California, Arizona, Texas, Florida, New York, New Jersey, and Illinois. Why are these states so popular? First, many immigrants live in these states. New immigrants often come and stay with their families. Next, three of the states, California, Arizona, and Texas border on Mexico. Almost half of the immigrants to the United States are from Mexico and these states are near Mexico. Finally, these seven states have many large cities. There are many jobs for the new immigrants.

B. Circle *Yes* or *No.*

1. Many immigrants come to the United States. (Yes) No
2. There are 280,000,000 immigrants in the U.S. Yes (No)
3. Almost half of all immigrants are children. Yes (No)
4. Many immigrants have family here. (Yes) No
5. Most immigrants want jobs. (Yes) No
6. Large cities have many jobs. (Yes) No
7. Florida borders on Mexico. Yes (No)
8. Most immigrants are from Mexico. Yes (No)

C. Discuss. What state do you live in? Why did you choose to live in this state?

A. Read.

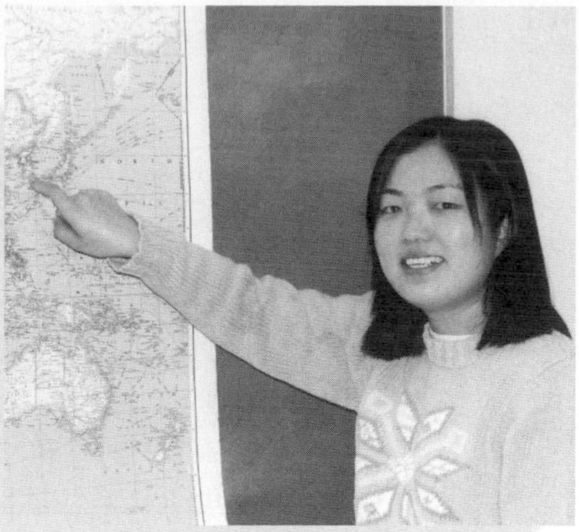

I am from South Korea. Korea is a small country in Asia. There are many people in Korea. The population is about 46,000,000. I am from Seoul. Seoul is the capital. It is in the north, on the Han River. Seoul is a big, busy city. Korea is hot in the summer and cold in the winter. The people in my country are busy, happy, and friendly.

B. Write. (Answers will vary.)

I am from _____. _____ is a _____.
$\qquad$ large/small

country in _____. The population is about _____.
$\qquad$ continent

I am from _____. _____

_____

_____

_____

_____

_____

Writing Note

The names of cities, states, and countries begin with capital letters: **Los Angeles, New York, Egypt.**

Writing Our Stories: My Country

A. Read.

- Point to the woman in the picture and ask:

  Where is this woman?
  What is she doing?

- Read the passage aloud to the class. Then ask questions such as:

  What is her name?
  What country is she from?
  How big is Korea?
  What city is she from?
  What is her city like?
  What are the people like?

B. Write.

- Students can use Exercise A as a model as they complete this activity.
- Invite some students to read their stories aloud to the class.

Suggestion

Students can draw large maps of their countries. Display the maps and student stories around the classroom.

A. Write the opposite of each adjective.

Students do the activity individually and check their answers with a partner.

B. My class.

Have students write the questions on their own. Then, have them ask and answer the questions in pairs. Ask them to change roles so both students have a chance to practice both questions and answers.

Practicing on Your Own

A. Write the opposite of each adjective.

1. dry _____wet_____
2. neat _____messy_____
3. small _____big, large_____
4. sad _____happy_____
5. new _____old_____
6. hardworking _____lazy_____
7. relaxed _____nervous_____
8. old _____young/new_____
9. friendly _____unfriendly_____
10. expensive _____cheap_____

B. My class. Put the words in each question in the correct order. Then, answer the questions.

1. you / are / tired / ?
   Are you tired?   (Answers will vary.)

2. teacher / your / is / busy / ?
   Is your teacher busy?

3. is / class / large / your / ?
   Is your class large?

4. friendly / are / students / the / ?
   Are the students friendly?

5. your / teacher / relaxed / is / ?
   Is your teacher relaxed?

6. hungry / you / are / ?
   Are you hungry?

7. students / are / the / talkative / ?
   Are the students talkative?

8. school / is / your / noisy / ?
   Is your school noisy?

9. classroom / small / is / your / ?
   Is your classroom small?

10. at / you / are / school / now / ?
    Are you at school now?

Looking at Numbers: Population Figures

A. What is the population of each country?

3,000,000	three million
37,000,000	thirty-seven million
356,000,000	three hundred fifty-six million

Kenya	30,000,000	Egypt	66,000,000
Ukraine	51,000,000	The Philippines	73,000,000
Canada	31,000,000	Russia	148,000,000
Turkey	65,000,000	Brazil	166,000,000
Kazakhstan	17,000,000	Nigeria	107,000,000

Grammar Summary

▶ **1. Adjectives**

   a. Adjectives describe a noun (a person, place, or thing).
      She's **tall.**

   b. Adjectives are the same for both singular and plural words.
      She's **young.**   They're **young.**

   c. Adjectives also come **before** a noun (a person, place, or thing).
      He's a **busy** <u>student</u>.

▶ **2. *Who* questions**

Who is intelligent?	I am.
Who is talkative?	Hector is.
Who is at school?	The students are.

▶ **3. *Or* questions**

Are you talkative **or** quiet?	I'm talkative.
Is Canada large **or** small?	It's large.
Are the windows clean **or** dirty?	They're clean.

Looking at Numbers: Population Figures

A. What is the population of each country?

- Model the pronunciation of the three numbers in the box and ask students to repeat. Point out that in English the word *and* is not used in these numbers.
- Call on individuals to say each of the numbers. Correct any errors and confirm each correct response by repeating the number.
- On the board, add the country names and populations for any other countries represented in the class. Continue to practice these larger numbers. (Refer to a current atlas for these statistics.)

Grammar Summary

- Review the summary with the class. Invite students to make up alternate sentences for each example in the chart. For example, in place of *Are you talkative* or *quiet*, a student might say *Are you neat* or *messy?*
- See the Grammar Summary Expansion on page 231 for a more complete explanation of these grammar points.

Unit 3
At School

Discuss the people next to the number. Ask:
- *Who is the person next to the unit number?* (A man or a boy)
- *What is he doing?* (He is reading. He's hanging upside down.)

Dictionary:
The Classroom

A. Listen and repeat.
(CD 1, Track 14)

- Read or play the audio several times and have students repeat the words.
- Ask students which words they don't understand. Write the words on the board. Ask students to point out these objects in the classroom. Ask students to repeat each word as you point to the object.

Suggestion

Ask students to study the list of words at home. During the next class, have them give each other spelling tests on these words. Ask them to work in pairs, taking turns giving each other the test. Students exchange papers to check their work.

B. Label the people and the classroom objects.

- Point out the five different category labels on page 32 and page 33. Check that students understand the meaning of each label.
- Have students label the pictures of classroom objects individually. Then ask them to compare answers with a partner.

3 At School

Dictionary: The Classroom

A. Listen and repeat.

backpack	computer	map	pencil	tape recorder
bookcase	desk	man	pencil sharpener	window
chair	dictionary	men	printer	woman
chalkboard	eraser	notebook	student	women
clock	examination	pen	table	

B. Label the people and the classroom objects.

People

student   woman   women   man   men

On the wall

map   clock   chalkboard

Furniture

desk   table   bookcase

32   Unit 3

Around the room

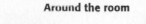

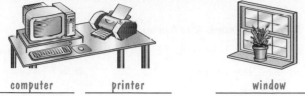

computer   printer   window

On the desk

pen   dictionary   tape recorder

eraser

notebook

pencil   backpack

C. Look around your classroom. Write 10 more classroom objects. Your teacher may help you with the vocabulary and spelling.

1. (Answers will vary.)   6. _____
2. _____   7. _____
3. _____   8. _____
4. _____   9. _____
5. _____   10. _____

At School   **33**

C. Look around your classroom.

- As you point to various objects in the classroom, ask:

  Is this a computer or a printer?
  Is this a backpack?
  What is this?

- Ask students to write the names of the objects on the lines provided.

Suggestions

- Invite students to point out other objects in the classroom whose names they would like to learn. Write the name of each object on the board and have students repeat it several times.
- Make labels for 10–15 of the new classroom objects students pointed out. Display the labels one at a time and have different students tape a label on the corresponding object.

Active Grammar: Singular and Plural Nouns

Suggestions

• Call students' attention to the box containing the rules for *a* and *an*. Ask students to study it for several minutes. Then, ask different students to explain the rules in their own words and give examples to illustrate each rule.

• Point out that when the *u* at the beginning of a word sounds like "you" (as it does in the word *university*), we use *a* before the word. When the *u* sounds like "uh" (as it does in *umbrella*), we us *an* before the word. Write some other examples on the board and ask students to choose *a* or *an*. For example: (a) unit to study, (a) used car, (an) upstairs bedroom, (an) uncle in Spain.

A. Singular nouns.

Ask students to complete the activity on their own. Review the answers with the class.

B. Plural nouns.

• Review the rules for forming plurals in the box at the top of the exercise. Point out the exceptions listed in the box below the exercise. Also mention that one-syllable words that end in *-y* do not use the *-ies* ending: *day/days* not *day/daies).*

• Have students fill in the answers on their own and check them with a partner.

Suggestion

Make up a set of 20 cards with singular words ending in *-s, -ch, -sh,* or *-y* on each one. Hold up a cards and ask a volunteer to spell the plural form. Call on another student to say whether the answer given was right or wrong. Recycle any words that students get wrong. After reviewing all the words, give a quick 10-word test and have students correct each others' papers.

Possible words: *boss, bus, guess, catch, match, lunch, dish, fish, push, baby, story, country.*

A. Singular nouns. Write *a* or *an*.

1. __a__ large bookcase
2. __an__ eraser
3. __an__ expensive pen
4. __a__ thin notebook
5. __an__ excellent student
6. __a__ U.S. map
7. __a__ handsome man
8. __an__ American teacher
9. __an__ electronic dictionary
10. __a__ young woman
11. __a__ pink eraser

12. __an__ English class
13. __a__ big desk
14. __a__ world map
15. __a__ sharp pencil
16. __a__ digital clock
17. __an__ Asian student

> Use *a* before a **consonant sound.**
> **b c f j k l m n p y**
> Use *an* before a **vowel sound.**
> **a e i o u**
>
> * Be careful with nouns that begin with **u.**
> **a university   an umbrella**

B. Plural nouns. Write the plural of the nouns.

> 1. Add *s* to make a plural noun: erasers, pens, students
> 2. Add *es* to words that end in -s, -ch, -sh: watches
> 3. Change *y* to *i* and add *es:* cities
> 4. Do *not* add an *s* to adjectives: young students

1. a bookcase — bookcases
2. a printer — printers
3. a computer — computers
4. a dictionary — dictionaries
5. a teacher — teachers
6. a desk — desks

7. a class — classes
8. a man — men
9. a map — maps
10. an exam — exams
11. a woman — women
12. a notebook — notebooks

> man—men   woman—women   child—children

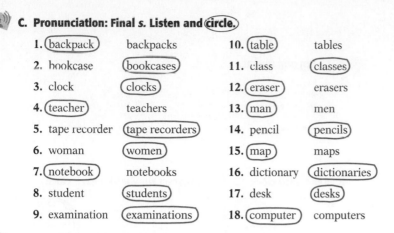

C. Pronunciation: Final s. Listen and circle.

1. (backpack)	backpacks		10. (table)	tables
2. bookcase	(bookcases)		11. class	(classes)
3. clock	(clocks)		12. (eraser)	erasers
4. (teacher)	teachers		13. (man)	men
5. tape recorder	(tape recorders)		14. pencil	(pencils)
6. woman	(women)		15. (map)	maps
7. (notebook)	notebooks		16. dictionary	(dictionaries)
8. student	(students)		17. desk	(desks)
9. examination	(examinations)		18. (computer)	computers

Practice reading the words with a partner.

D. Review. Look around your classroom. Write seven singular nouns and seven plural nouns. Add *a* or *an* to the singular nouns. Add *s* or *es* to the plural nouns.

Singular Nouns	Plural Nouns
a clock	windows
(Answers will vary.)	
_____	_____
_____	_____
_____	_____
_____	_____
_____	_____
_____	_____

C. Pronunciation: Final s.
(CD1, Track 15)

• Read the pairs of words aloud. Point out that the final *s* can have three different pronunciations. It sounds like /s/ on words like *maps,* /z/ on words like *pens,* and /iz/ on words like *classes.*

• Play the audio and have students circle the words they hear. Repeat the presentation of the words so students can check their work. Go over the correct answers with the class.

Practice reading the words with a partner.

Students take turns reading the pairs of words to a partner. Move around the room correcting pronunciation as needed.

D. Review.

• Have students complete their lists individually. Then, call on different students to read examples from each of their lists to the class. Ask students to raise their hands if they hear a word they don't understand. Write these words on the board and discuss their meaning.

Audio Script

C. Pronunciation: Final s. Listen and circle.
(CD 1, Track 15)

1. backpack
2. bookcases
3. clocks
4. teacher
5. tape recorders
6. women
7. notebook
8. students
9. examinations
10. table
11. classes
12. eraser
13. man
14. pencils
15. map
16. dictionaries
17. desks
18. computer

☀ Telling Time

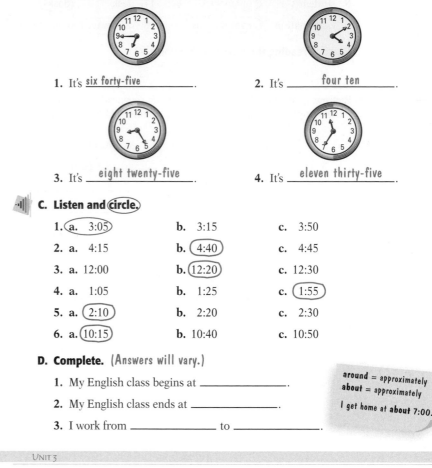

◁‖ A. Listen and repeat.

(CD 1, Track 16)

Read or play the audio once or twice all the way through. Then, play it again, pausing to have students repeat each clock time.

B. Read each clock.

Call on different students to read aloud the clock times shown. Then, have students write the time in words under each clock. Review the correct answers by having four students write the times on the board.

◁‖ C. Listen and circle.

(CD 1, Track 17)

Call on different students to read each set of three clock times aloud. Then, play the audio and have students circle the correct answer.

Suggestion

For additional practice, call out different clock times. Ask students to write the times in their notebooks. (Examples: *7:15, 2:10, 5:30*)

D. Complete.

Students complete the sentences and share their answers with a partner.

Suggestion

Discuss the definitions of *around* and *about* in the box. Invite students to make up original sentences using each.

☀ Telling Time

◁‖ A. Listen and repeat.

3:00	three o'clock	3:05	three-oh five	3:30	three thirty
6:00	six o'clock	3:10	three ten	3:45	three forty-five
9:00	nine o'clock	3:15	three fifteen	3:50	three fifty
12:00	twelve o'clock	12:00 P.M. — noon		12:00 A.M. — midnight	

B. Read each clock. Write the correct time under each clock.

1. It's <u>six forty-five</u>.

2. It's <u>four ten</u>.

3. It's <u>eight twenty-five</u>.

4. It's <u>eleven thirty-five</u>.

◁‖ C. Listen and circle.

1. a. (3:05)   b. 3:15   c. 3:50
2. a. 4:15   b. (4:40)   c. 4:45
3. a. 12:00   b. (12:20)   c. 12:30
4. a. 1:05   b. 1:25   c. (1:55)
5. a. (2:10)   b. 2:20   c. 2:30
6. a. (10:15)   b. 10:40   c. 10:50

D. Complete. (Answers will vary.)

1. My English class begins at _____.

2. My English class ends at _____.

3. I work from _____ to _____.

> around = approximately
> about = approximately
> I get home at about 7:00.

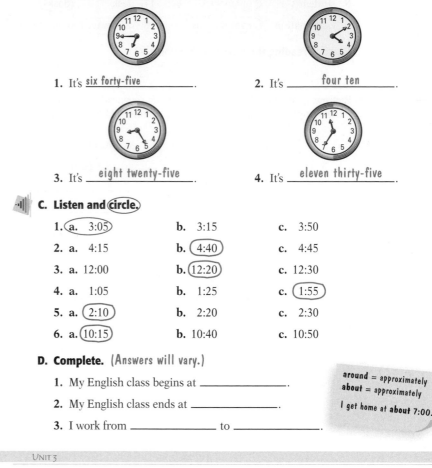

36 UNIT 3

Audio Script

C. Listen and circle. (CD 1, Track 17)

1. A: What time is it?
   B: It's three oh five.
2. A: What time is it?
   B: It's four forty.
3. A: What time is it?
   B: It's twelve twenty.

4. A: What time is it?
   B: It's one fifty-five.
5. A: What time is it?
   B: It's two ten.
6. A: What time is it?
   B: It's ten fifteen.

Dictionary: Inside the School Building

A. Listen and repeat.

the auditorium	the director's office	the principal's office	the ground floor
the bookstore	the elevator	the restrooms	the first floor
the cafeteria	the gymnasium / the gym	the stairs	the second floor
the computer center	the library	the theater	the third floor
the counselor's office	the nurse's office	the tutoring center	the fourth floor

B. Label the places in the school.

1. the gymnasium/the gym

2. the restrooms

3. the cafeteria

4. the bookstore

5. the stairs

6. the principal's office

7. the library

8. the nurse's office

9. the computer center

10. the theater

11. the counselor's office

12. the first floor or the ground floor

Dictionary: Inside the School Building

A. Listen and repeat.
(CD 1, Track 18)

After students have repeated the names of places in a school building, go back over the list to be sure they understand the meaning of each one. Ask questions about each place and call on individuals to answer. For example:

T: *Where is the auditorium in our school?*
S: *On the first floor.*
T: *That's right. The auditorium is on the first floor.*

Teacher Note

Some students may be confused by the numbering of floors. In the United States the floor that is on ground level is often called the first floor. The next floor up is called the second floor. However, in Europe and many other parts of the world, the floor that is on ground level is called something like "the ground floor" and the next floor up is called the first floor.

B. Label the places in the school.

Ask students to label the pictures on their own. Point out that all the words they need are listed in Exercise A.

Suggestion

If possible, tour the school with the class. Have them check off each item in Exercise A as they see it. You can also have them add the names of other places to the list in their books. For example, your school might have a security checkpoint or a swimming pool.

C. Read and circle about your school.

Ask students to complete this exercise on their own and check their answers with a partner.

Suggestion

After students complete the activity, have them close their books. Then, ask them to work in pairs. One person says the name of a singular or plural location and the other person makes a statement about it using *There is . . .* or *There are . . . .* For example:

S1: *Four floors*
S2: *There are four floors in our school.*
S3: *A big gym*
S2: *There is a big gym in our school.*

D. Pair practice.

• Point to the pictures and ask different students to identify each location.
• Review the use of *Yes/No* questions and answers with *Is there* and *Are there* as outlined in the box. Then, have pairs of students read aloud the sample dialogues. Answer any questions students may have.
• Ask pairs of students to practice the questions and answers using the picture cues. When they finish, call on different pairs to present each of the dialogues to the class.

C. Read and (circle) about your school. (Answers will vary.)

1. My classroom is on the third floor.   Yes   No
2. There is an elevator in my school.   Yes   No
3. There is a gymnasium in my school.   Yes   No
4. There is a library in my school.   Yes   No
5. There are restrooms on the first floor.   Yes   No
6. There is a nurse's office in my school.   Yes   No
7. There are three floors in this building.   Yes   No
8. There is a bookstore on this floor.   Yes   No

D. Pair practice. Ask and answer these questions with a partner.

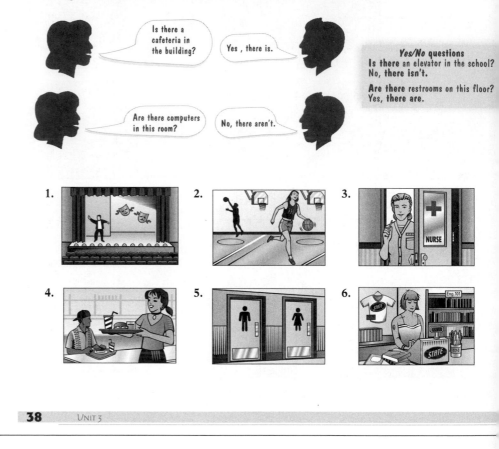

Yes/No questions
Is there an elevator in the school?
No, there isn't.

Are there restrooms on this floor?
Yes, there are.

Working Together

A. Look at the picture. With a group of students, write sentences about the picture. Use *There is / There are.* (Answers will vary. Possible responses below.)

1. There are two computers.
2. There is one bookcase.
3. There are ten students.
4. There is one window.
5. There is one printer.
6. There are eleven chairs.
7. There are three backpacks.
8. There are three maps.

B. The ideal classroom. With a group of students, design a classroom. What is in your classroom? On a sheet of paper, draw a picture of the classroom. Then, tell your classmates about your ideal classroom.

Working Together

A. Look at the picture.

• Divide the class into groups of no more than six students. Ask them to just talk about the picture together for a few minutes. Then ask:

What kind of room is this? Who are the people in the room? What are they doing?

• Have students work in groups to write sentences about the picture in their books. Then, ask different students to write one of their group's sentences on the board. Check what each one is going to write so that you don't have duplicate sentences. As you review the sentences, correct any errors.

B. The ideal classroom.

• Divide the class into small groups and give each group a large piece of paper and markers. Before they begin drawing, have them discuss what should go in the classroom and make a list of what they plan to draw.
• Ask each group to share their picture with the rest of the class. One person can do the basic description and other group members can add their comments. Encourage members of other groups to ask questions.

☀The Big Picture: My New Classroom

A. Vocabulary.

• Discuss the pictures with the class. Encourage them to make comments about the items in each room and the condition of the two rooms. Ask:

Is this room new or old?
Are there a lot of desks or only a few?
Is there a window?
Does the room have a computer?

• Have students write their vocabulary lists individually and then compare lists with several other students. Invite them to add missing items to their own lists.

• Complete the exercise by having students create two master lists on the board–one for the old classroom and one for the new classroom. Have them take turns adding items to the lists on the board until they run out of items.

Suggestion

During the discussion at the beginning of Exercise A, invite students to look back at the adjectives introduced in Unit 2, and include some of these words in their descriptions of the two rooms.

📶 B. Listen and look at the pictures. (CD 1, Track 19)

Ask students to listen and look at each classroom as the audio describes it.

☀ The Big Picture: My New Classroom

A. Vocabulary. Make a vocabulary list of the items in the classrooms below.
(Answers will vary. Possible responses below.)

Old Classroom

chairs
chalkboard
backpack
books
clock
table

New Classroom

computer
printer
chalkboard
tables
bookcase
window
maps
chairs
desk

📶 **B. Listen and look at the pictures.**

Audio Script

B. Listen and look at the pictures. (CD 1, Track 19)

I'm a teacher in an adult school. I teach math at night. My class meets every Tuesday and Thursday from 7:00 to 9:00. There are 15 students in my class. This is a picture of my classroom in September, 2000. Look at it. It's depressing, isn't it? There are no windows. There's no desk for me–only a very small table. I put my backpack on the floor. The room is ugly. The paint on the walls is old. There's a clock, but the clock's broken. There are many chairs in this small room, so the students are not comfortable. It's difficult for them to study in this room.

Now, look at this picture. This is a picture of my new room. It's great. The room is clean and bright. Now I have a big window. There are two maps on the wall: one of the United States and one of the world. There's one big bookcase, and there's a large chalkboard to write on. There are no desks for the students because now we have three long tables. Five students can sit at each table. And there's a computer and a printer. I really like my new classroom.

C. Listen and circle.

1. old classroom **(new classroom)**   5. old classroom **(new classroom)**
2. old classroom **(new classroom)**   6. **(old classroom)** new classroom
3. **(old classroom)** new classroom   7. old classroom **(new classroom)**
4. **(old classroom)** new classroom   8. old classroom **(new classroom)**

D. Complete.

> **There is** old paint on the walls.   **There is no** teacher in the old room.
> **There are** two bookcases.   **There are no** students in the old room.

1. _There is_ old paint on the walls in the old classroom.
2. _There are no_ desks in the old classroom.
3. _There is_ a clock over the door in the old classroom.
4. _There are no_ bookcases in the old classroom.
5. _There is_ a big bookcase in the new classroom.
6. _There are_ three tables in the new classroom.
7. _There is_ a world map in the new classroom.
8. _There is no_ digital clock in the new classroom.
9. _There is_ a big window in the new classroom.
10. _There are no_ windows in the old classroom.

E. Answer the questions about the new classroom.

1. Is there a window in the classroom?   _Yes, there is._
2. Are there three maps on the wall?   _No, there aren't._
3. Is there a bookcase in the classroom?   _Yes, there is._
4. Are there desks for the students?   _No, there aren't._
5. Is there a telephone in the classroom?   _No, there isn't._

At School **41**

C. Listen and circle.
(CD 1, Track 20)

• Play the audio and have students circle *old classroom* or *new classroom* to show which picture each statement applies to. For example, *1. There's one bookcase* applies to the picture of the new classroom. Play the audio as many times as you wish.

• Review the answers by reading each statement from the script and calling on individuals to give the correct answer and point to the part of the picture that illustrates the statement.

D. Complete.

• Review the statements in the box, which use *There is* and *There are*. Point out the use of *There is no* and *There are no* to make negative statements.

• Ask students to complete the sentences individually. Review the answers with the whole class.

E. Answer the questions about the new classroom.

• Have students complete this exercise in pairs. Encourage them to continue the exercise with questions of their own about both of the pictures.

C. Listen and circle. (CD 1, Track 20)

1. There's one bookcase.
2. There are two maps.
3. There is a small table for the teacher.
4. There are no windows.
5. There's a computer.
6. There's a small chalkboard.
7. There's a big desk for the teacher.
8. There are no desks.

☀Reading: A One-Room Schoolhouse

A. Before You Read.

• Help students locate Minnesota on the map on page 28 of Unit 2 or on the map on page 246. Ask them what they know about the state or nearby states. Then, discuss the two questions.

• Point out the one-room school in the picture. Ask students to guess what it is. Ask:

Does this look like your school?
What is different about it?
How many students could attend this school?

• Ask students to read the first sentence in each paragraph. Then, go back and read these three sentences aloud. Ask students what they think the story will be about. (It's about a one-room school in Minnesota.)

• Ask student to read the passage on their own. Explain that they won't understand everything. Suggest that as they read they try to understand the main ideas.

B. Read and circle.

After the students have read the article to get the main idea, introduce the idea of *scanning*. Have them scan the article to find the answers to the questions. Review the correct answers with the class.

Suggestions

• Explain that *scanning* means looking over the paragraphs very quickly for a certain word or group of words. It means you don't read every single word.

• Explain that we use scanning when we are looking for one certain piece of information. For this purpose, scanning saves a lot of time.

• Read questions 1 and 2 and ask them what words they will look for. (Example: *one-room schoolhouse.*) Then, have them scan the passage and find the sentences with *one-room schoolhouse* in them. This will give the answers to questions 1 and 2.

☀ Reading: A One-Room Schoolhouse

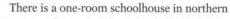

A. Before You Read.

1. Where is Minnesota?

2. How many rooms and classes are in your school?

Sometimes, there are only a small number of children in a community. For example, maybe there is only one child in the first grade, five children in the third grade, and three children in the sixth grade. Maybe there are no children in the fifth grade. In this situation, a regular-sized school is too big. In some small communities, there is a one-room schoolhouse, but this is very unusual.

There is a one-room schoolhouse in northern Minnesota, the Angle Inlet School. This school is near the border of Canada. In this school, there are students from kindergarten to sixth grade. In Spring 2000, there were fifteen students, seven girls, and eight boys. Some of the children live on islands. Some of the children live on the mainland of Minnesota, but there are no good roads for cars and buses. The students go to school by boat or by snowmobile in the wintertime.

Everything that the students need is in one big classroom. There is one teacher. There are only fifteen students. There are desks and chairs for the students. There is a big desk for the teacher. There is a U.S. map on the wall. For music lessons, there is a piano. There are three computers, so the students and the teacher can use the Internet. They can communicate with students in other schools. There is even a small library with five or six bookcases. This school is a small school, but the students are happy there.

B. Read and ⟨circle.⟩

1. There are one-room schoolhouses in big cities.   Yes   (No)
2. The one-room schoolhouse is in Minnesota.   (Yes)   No
3. There are three teachers for the class.   Yes   (No)
4. There are many rooms in the school.   Yes   (No)
5. The students go to school by bus.   Yes   (No)
6. There are music lessons for the students.   (Yes)   No
7. There are many computers in the classroom.   (Yes)   No

Writing Our Stories: My Classroom

A. Read.

This is our classroom. We're in Room 202. There are three men and twelve women in my class. Our classroom is small, but it is comfortable. Our teacher is Mrs. Mahoney. There is one computer for the teacher, and there is one computer lab on the third floor. There's a U.S. map on the wall. There are no bookcases, but there are desks for all the students.

There are two floors in our building. The building is small. There's a small library. There is no elevator, but we are comfortable here.

B. Check (✓) the objects in your classroom and building. (Answers will vary.)

_____ a man	_____ men	_____ a window _____ windows
_____ a woman	_____ women	_____ a cafeteria
_____ a teacher	_____ teachers	_____ restrooms
_____ a bookcase	_____ bookcases	_____ a computer center
_____ a clock	_____ clocks	_____ a theater / an auditorium
_____ a U.S. map	_____ a world map	_____ a library
_____ a computer	_____ computers	_____ an elevator

C. In your notebook, write about your classroom and school building.

> **W**riting Note
>
> Edit your story. Check all the plural nouns. Remember that most plural nouns use **s** at the end. Check all **irregular** plural nouns such as **men** and **women**.

Writing Our Stories: My Classroom

A. Read.

- Invite students to comment on the picture. Ask:

    How many students are there?
    How old are they?
    Are they in a classroom?

- Ask students to read the story all the way through without stopping. Then, read the story to the students. Ask: *Do you have any questions about the story?*

B. Check the objects in your classroom and building.

Students complete this exercise on their own.

C. In your notebook, write about your classroom and school building.

- Students should use the information from Exercise B as they complete this activity.
- The story at the top of the page can serve as a model for their writing. Show how they can adapt sentences to fit their own needs. For example: *There are three men and twelve women in my class* can become *There are two Japanese students and six Colombian students in my class.*
- Point out the Writing Note and remind students to check all the plural endings in their stories.

Suggestion

Choose several correct, useful sentences from different students' papers and write them on the board. Ask the class to repeat them. Then invite them to copy the sentences into their notebooks.

Practicing on Your Own

A. Write *a* or *an*.

Students do the activity individually and check their answers with a partner.

B. Change each sentence from singular to plural.

Point out that students will have to make two changes in each sentence–the number change and the change from singular noun form to plural noun form. Have students complete the activity on their own.

Suggestion

Ask students to work in pairs. Have them read sentences in B. again, but ask students to correct the sentences about their school or classroom that are not true. Share the corrected sentences with the class.

C. Complete with *There is a, There are, There is no,* or *There are no.*

Ask students to do the activity individually and check their answers with a partner.

Suggestion

Write the phrases *There is, There are, There is no,* and *There are no* on the board. Have students practice making original sentences about the class. Examples: *There are no French students in our class. There is a coffee machine in the classroom.*

Practicing on Your Own

A. Write *a* or *an.*

1. __an__ old computer
2. __an__ Applied computer
3. __a__ Bell computer
4. __an__ English teacher
5. __a__ large desk
6. __a__ small table
7. __a__ difficult exam
8. __a__ U.S. map
9. __a__ hardworking student
10. __an__ auditorium

B. Change each sentence from singular to plural. Use the number in parentheses ( ).

1. There is a woman in the class (six)
   There are six women in the class.

2. There is a computer in the computer lab. (twelve)
   There are twelve computers in the computer lab.

3. There is a dictionary in my backpack. (two)
   There are two dictionaries in my backpack.

4. There is an elevator in the school. (three)
   There are three elevators in the school.

5. There is a student in Room 421. (twenty-two)
   There are twenty-two students in Room 421.

C. Complete with *There is a, There are, There is no,* or *There are no.*

1. __There is a/There is no__ teacher in my classroom.
2. __There are/There are no__ students from China in my class.
3. __There are/There are no__ students from Central America in my class.
4. __There is a/There is no__ computer in our classroom.
5. __There is a/There is no__ map on the wall.
6. __There are/There are no__ men in our class.
7. __There are/There are no__ restrooms on this floor.

Looking at Numbers: The Internet

A. Look at the information in the chart.

Percent (%) of schools with access to the Internet

School	1994	1997	2000
Elementary	30%	75%	97%
Secondary	49%	89%	100%

B. Read and discuss.

1. Does your school have computer labs?
2. Does your classroom have computers? How many does it have?
3. What do you use your computer for?

Grammar Summary

1. Singular nouns

a. Use **a** before a **consonant sound:**   b c d f g h j k l m n p q r s t v w x y z
   a computer   **a d**esk

b. Use **an** before a **vowel sound:**   a e i o u   **an e**levator   **an u**gly room

c. Be careful with nouns that begin with *u.*   **a u**niversity   **an u**mbrella

2. Plural nouns

a. Add *s* to make a plural noun.   eraser**s**   pen**s**   student**s**

b. Add *es* to words that end in *-s, -ch, -sh.*   watch**es**

c. Change *y* to *i* and add *es.*   dictionar**ies**

d. Do <u>not</u> add an *s* to adjectives.   young student**s**

3. *There is / There are / There is no / There are no*

There is a chalkboard in the classroom.

There are many students in the classroom.

There is no desk for the teacher.

There are no computers for the students in the classroom.

Looking at Numbers: The Internet

A. Look at the information in the chart.

Discuss the chart with students. If necessary, explain what *access to the Internet* means. Ask whether Internet use in schools has grown quickly or slowly.

B. Read and discuss.

Ask individuals to answer questions 1 and 2. As you discuss question 3, make a list of possible uses for computers on the board. Invite students to copy useful vocabulary words into their notebooks.

Grammar Summary

• Review the summary with the class. Invite students to write on the board alternate examples for each item. For example, in place of *an elevator,* a student might write *an English class* or *an immigrant;* in place of *dictionaries,* a student might write *cities.*

• See the Grammar Summary Expansion on page 232 for a more complete explanation of these grammar points.

Unit 4
The Family

Discuss the unit title art. Ask:
• *What is this?* (It's a drawing of a family photograph in a frame.)

☀Dictionary: Family Members, Occupations

▪ A. Listen and repeat.
(CD1, Track 21)

• Discuss the picture with the class. Ask:

Where is the mother?
How many children are there?
How old is the boy (girl)?

• Play the audio several times and have students repeat the names for the members of a family.
• Talk about the relationships in the family. For example: *Susan is a mother. She has two children. Rich and Susan are married. Rich is Susan's husband.*

Suggestions

• Write four headings on the board: *old, young, boy/man,* and *girl/woman.* Ask students to take turns going to the board and writing names for various family members in the correct columns. You can have each person write only one name in one column or write one name in as many columns as possible. For example, *son* could go in two columns: *young* and *boy/man.*

• Invite students to describe the people in the pictures using words from previous units. For example: *She's young. He's old. He's handsome.* Then have students label each person in the picture.

▪ B. Listen and repeat.
(CD 1, Track 22)

• Point out the people who have been added to the picture. Ask:

---

4 The Family

☀ Dictionary: Family Members, Occupations

▪ A. Listen and repeat. Then, talk about the relationships.

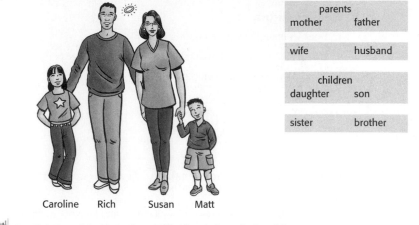

Caroline   Rich   Susan   Matt

parents	
mother	father

wife	husband

children	
daughter	son

sister	brother

▪ B. Listen and repeat. Then, talk about the relationships.

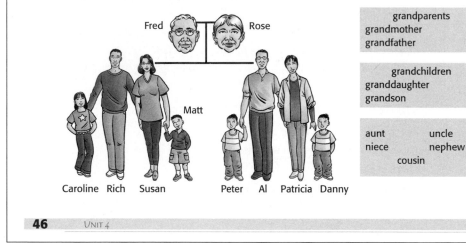

Fred   Rose

Matt

Caroline   Rich   Susan   Peter   Al   Patricia   Danny

grandparents
grandmother
grandfather

grandchildren
granddaughter
grandson

aunt	uncle
niece	nephew
cousin	

How old is this person?
Who do you think he (she) is?

• Play the audio several times and have students repeat.

• Talk about the relationships in this family. For example: *Susan and Al are brother and sister. Rose is a grandmother. She has four grandchildren. She is Matt's grandmother.*

• Discuss who the people are. Help students match each word in Exercise B with a person in the picture. Then, have students label all the people in the picture. You may wish to draw arrows from people at the left to people at the right to show the difference between a *nephew* (adult at right to child at left) and a *cousin* (child at right to child at left).

C. Listen and complete.

1. Susan is Rich's <u>wife</u>.
2. Rich is Susan's <u>husband</u>.
3. Caroline is Rich and Susan's <u>daughter</u>.
4. Matt is Rich and Susan's <u>son</u>.
5. Caroline is Matt's <u>sister</u>.
6. Susan and Rich are Caroline and Matt's <u>parents</u>.
7. Caroline and Matt are Susan and Rich's <u>children</u>.

D. Read and answer.

1. How many grandchildren does Rose have? <u>four grandchildren</u>
2. Who is Caroline's uncle? <u>Al</u>
3. Who are Rich's nephews? <u>Peter and Danny</u>
4. Who is Al's father? <u>Fred</u>
5. Who is Matt's aunt? <u>Patricia</u>
6. Who are Fred's grandsons? <u>Matt, Peter, and Danny</u>
7. How many cousins does Danny have? <u>two</u>

E. Listen and repeat. Then, complete the sentences below.

| mother-in-law | daughter-in-law | sister-in-law |
| father-in-law | son-in-law | brother-in-law |

1. Fred is Patricia's **father-in-law.**
   Who is Patricia's **mother-in-law?** <u>Rose</u>

2. Rich is Patricia's **brother-in-law.**
   Who is Patricia's **sister-in-law?** <u>Susan</u>

3. Susan is Al's **sister.**
   Who is Al's **brother-in-law?** <u>Rich</u>

The Family   **47**

Audio Script

C. Listen and complete. (CD1, Track 23)

1. Susan is Rich's wife.
2. Rich is Susan's husband.
3. Caroline is Rich and Susan's daughter.
4. Matt is Rich and Susan's son.
5. Caroline is Matt's sister.
6. Susan and Rich are Caroline and Matt's parents.
7. Caroline and Matt are Susan and Rich's children.

C. Listen and complete.
(CD 1, Track 23)

Explain that the missing words are the family member names from page 46. Play the audio as many times as necessary for students to complete and check their work.

D. Read and answer.

Tell students to use the picture at the bottom of page 46 to answer these questions. Have them complete the exercise on their own and compare answers with a partner. Suggest that they point to people in the picture to show each other how they arrived at each answer.

E. Listen and repeat.
(CD 1, Track 24)

• Explain the concept of an *in-law: an* in-law *is a relative that comes into the family through marriage.*

• First, have the whole class listen and repeat the vocabulary. Next, have them read the statements and the questions in Exercise E. Then, have them write the answers in the blanks. Check the answers as a class.

Suggestion

Play Word Bingo using the names for family members. (1) Each student chooses five of the terms introduced on page 46 and writes them on a piece of paper. (2) You call out the names of family members at random. Students cross out each word they hear if it appears on their own paper. (3) The first student to cross out all five of his or her words is the winner. (4) Have the student read aloud the five words and check that they are the same five words you called out.

Active Grammar:
Possessive Adjectives and Possessive Nouns

A. Listen and repeat.
(CD1, Track 25)

- Point out the CD player in each of the pictures. Explain that the possessive pronouns under each picture refers to who possesses the player.

- Point to the pictures and have students listen and repeat the words.

- Ask students to make up simple sentences about actual classroom objects using each of the possessive adjectives. For example: *This is my notebook. Those are our books.*

B. Listen and complete, using *she* or *her*, *he* or *his*, or *they* or *their*. (CD1, Track 26)

- Discuss the pictures with the students. Ask:

  How old is he/she?
  Where is he/she?
  What do you think he/she is doing?
  Who are these people?

- Play the audio and have students fill in the missing subject pronouns (*she, he, they*) and possessive adjectives (*her, his, their*).
- Review the correct answers with the class. To help explain any incorrect answers you can ask these questions:

  Does the word name a person?
  Does the word describe something that belongs to the person?

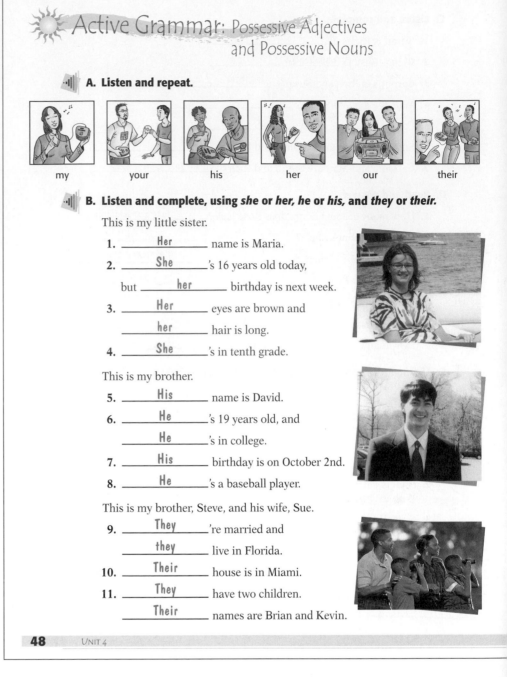

Active Grammar: Possessive Adjectives and Possessive Nouns

A. Listen and repeat.

my   your   his   her   our   their

B. Listen and complete, using *she* or *her*, *he* or *his*, and *they* or *their*.

This is my little sister.

1. ___Her___ name is Maria.
2. ___She___'s 16 years old today, but ___her___ birthday is next week.
3. ___Her___ eyes are brown and ___her___ hair is long.
4. ___She___'s in tenth grade.

This is my brother.

5. ___His___ name is David.
6. ___He___'s 19 years old, and ___He___'s in college.
7. ___His___ birthday is on October 2nd.
8. ___He___'s a baseball player.

This is my brother, Steve, and his wife, Sue.

9. ___They___'re married and ___they___ live in Florida.
10. ___Their___ house is in Miami.
11. ___They___ have two children. ___Their___ names are Brian and Kevin.

48   UNIT 4

Audio Script

B. Listen and complete, using *she* or *her*, *he* or *his*, and *they* or *their*. (CD1, Track 26)

This is my little sister.
1. Her name is Maria.
2. She's sixteen years old today, but her birthday is next week.
3. Her eyes are brown and her hair is long.
4. She's in tenth grade.

This is my brother.
5. His name is David.
6. He's nineteen years old, and he's in college.
7. His birthday is on October 2nd.
8. He's a baseball player.

This is my brother, Steve, and his wife, Sue.
9. They're married and they live in Florida.
10. Their house is in Miami.
11. They have two children. Their names are Brian and Kevin.

☀ Personal Information

A. Read the license. Answer the questions.

DRIVER'S LICENSE
NEW MEXICO
NM2079 51562 6855

Angelica Ortega
4000 South Meadows Road
Santa Fe, New Mexico 87507

09/15/82	5'3"	Brown	10/2010
DOB	Height	Eyes	Exp. Date

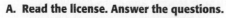

Culture Note

Every driver's license has an expiration date. Your license is good for two, three, four, or more years. Then, you must renew your license.

1. What's her first name? **Angelica.**
2. What's her last name? **Ortega.**
3. What's her address? **400 South Meadows Road.**
4. What's her date of birth? **9/15/82.**

(Answer will vary depending on year activity is done.)
5. How old is she?
6. What is her height? **5'3".**
7. What color are her eyes? **Brown.**
8. What is the expiration date? **10/2010.**

B. My classmates. Write the name of a classmate who matches the description. Then complete the sentence, using *his* or *her*. **(Answers will vary.)**

long hair   short hair   wavy hair   curly hair

1. ____Maria's____ hair is black.   ____Her____ hair is black.
2. _____ eyes are brown.   _____ eyes are brown.
3. _____ hair is brown.   _____ hair is brown.
4. _____ eyes are blue.   _____ eyes are blue.
5. _____ eyes are large.   _____ eyes are large.
6. _____ hair is long.   _____ hair is long.
7. _____ hair is curly.   _____ hair is curly.
8. _____ hair is wavy.   _____ hair is wavy.
9. _____ hair is short.   _____ hair is short.

The Family   **49**

☀ Personal Information

A. Read the license.

• Point out the Culture Note and explain the meaning of the words *expiration date* and *renew*.

• Answer the questions with the whole class.

Suggestion

Have students take turns reading aloud one of the questions at random and calling on another class member to answer the question.

S1: *How old is she?*
S2: *She's _____ years old.*

B. My classmates.

• Point out the four different types of hair. Say the words and ask students to repeat.

• Students complete the exercise on their own. Allow them to stand up and move around the room if they need to see the other students more clearly. When they finish, review the items one by one. Call on several students to read what they wrote for each item.

☀ Occupations

A. Read the occupations.

Say the name of each occupation aloud and invite students to point to the corresponding picture in Exercise B. If they aren't sure, show them the answer.

Suggestion

If students have difficulty pronouncing any of the words, write them on the board, separating the syllables and using capital letters to show the stressed syllables. Then, point to the words and ask students to repeat them. For example:

ac COUN tant
FAC to ry WOR kers
en gi NEER

B. Write the occupations under the correct pictures.

• Ask students to identify as many of the occupations as they can. Ask:

What is this (man) wearing?
What is (he) doing?
What do you think his job is?

• Have students complete this activity on their own and check their answers with a partner.

C. *A* and *An.*

• Ask a volunteer to summarize the basic rule for using *a* and *an.* (The article *a* comes before words that begin with consonant sounds, whereas the article *an* comes before words that begin with vowel sounds.)

• Have students complete the activity on their own. Review the correct answers with the whole class.

☀ Occupations

A. Read the occupations. Ask your teacher about any new words.

| an accountant | a cook | an engineer | landscapers |
| an auto mechanic | a custodian | factory workers | a waiter / a waitress |

B. Write the occupations under the correct pictures.

1. __landscapers__   2. __a waiter__   3. __a cook__

4. __factory workers__   5. __a waitress__   6. __an auto mechanic__

7. __a custodian__   8. __an accountant__   9. __an engineer__

C. *A* and *An.* Put *a* or *an* before each occupation.

1. __a__ nurse   4. __a__ doctor   7. __a__ busy accountant

2. __a__ landscaper   5. __a__ teacher   8. __a__ tired waitress

3. __an__ excellent cook   6. __a__ student   9. __an__ electrical engineer

A. Read the occupations. Ask your teacher about any new words.

an architect	a farmer	a nurse
an artist	a home health aide	a secretary
a bus driver	a housewife	a security guard
a computer programmer	a lawyer	a taxi driver
a dentist	a machine operator	a travel agent

B. Write three occupations under each workplace. (Answers will vary. Possible responses below.)

Factory
a machine operator
a security guard
a computer programmer

Office
a lawyer
a secretary
an architect

Hospital
a doctor
a nurse
a home health aide

Restaurant
a cook
a waiter
a waitress

School
a teacher
a student
a bus driver

Outdoors
a landscaper
a farmer
an artist

C. Complete the sentences about your family. (Answers will vary.)

1. My __brother__ (family member), __Massimo__ (name), is __a__ (a / an) __dentist__ (occupation).
2. My _____, _____, is ___ _____.
3. My _____, _____, is ___ _____.
4. My _____, _____, is ___ _____.
5. My _____, _____, is ___ _____.

A. Read the occupations.

- Ask students to read the names of the occupations to themselves and then to a partner. Have them circle any words they don't understand or have difficulty pronouncing.
- Read the list and ask students to raise their hands if they have difficulty with a particular word. Write these words on the board. Explain what they mean and practice the pronunciation with the class.

Suggestion

Separate the words into syllables and use capital letters to indicate stress as on page 50 of the Teacher's Guide.

B. Write three occupations under each workplace.

- Ask students to write three occupations from pages 50 and 51 under the appropriate headings in Exercise B.
- Ask different students to read one of the six lists aloud. As each student reads, copy the list on the board. Discuss differing opinions.

C. Complete the sentences about your family.

- Ask students to complete the activity on their own. As they work, move around the room supplying additional names of occupations if necessary.
- Ask several students to read one or two of their sentences to the class.

A. Pronunciation: *What's.* Listen and repeat.

(CD1, Track 27)

• Point out that Americans usually connect the contraction *What's* with the following pronoun. For example:

What's her sounds like *Whatser*
What's his sounds like *Whatsiz*
What's your sounds like *Whatsyur*

• Have students follow along in the book as they listen and repeat the sentences.

B. Listen and complete.

(CD1, Track 28)

Play the audio several times so students can complete and check their work.

Practice the questions with a partner.

Have students take turns repeating the questions in A and B with a partner.

Working Together: Student to Student

A. Student A and Student B

• Read the instructions. Then ask a student to explain how to do the exercise in his or her own words.
• Students work in pairs. After Student A has answered the questions, have the pairs switch roles and repeat the activity.
• Check students' work by calling on different pairs to read each question and answer.

A. Pronunciation: *What's.* Listen and repeat.

1. What's her name?
2. What's her address?
3. What's your name?
4. What's your last name?
5. What's his name?
6. What's his address?
7. What's her job?
8. What's your job?
9. What's her first name?
10. What's his name?

B. Listen and complete.

1. What's ___her___ name?
2. What's ___his___ name?
3. What's ___your___ address?
4. What's ___her___ address?
5. What's ___your___ job?
6. What's ___his___ job?

Practice the questions with a partner.

Working Together: Student to Student

A. STUDENT A: Cover the questions. Look at the picture of the family. Then, listen to Student B and answer the questions.

STUDENT B: Read the questions about the family to Student A. Student A will answer the questions.

Masa Yoko Hiro Julia Loretta

Eddie Yoshiko

1. Who is Julia's husband?
2. Who is Yoshiko's brother?
3. Who is Masa's daughter-in-law?
4. Who is Eddie's grandmother?
5. Who is Julia's mother-in-law?
6. Who is Loretta's niece?
7. Who is Masa's grandson?
8. Who is Hiro's daughter?
9. Who is Eddie's aunt?

52 UNIT 4

Audio Script

B. Listen and complete. (CD1, Track 28)

1. What's her name?
2. What's his name?
3. What's your address?
4. What's her address?
5. What's your job?
6. What's his job?

Working Together

B. Photographs. Two students, Beata and Olga, are talking about their photographs. With a partner, read and practice the conversation.

Beata: These are my children, Peter and Zofia. Peter is 6 and Zofia is 5.

Olga: Are they in school?

Beata: Peter is in first grade, and Zofia is in kindergarten. And, how about you?

Olga: I have a little girl. This is her picture. Her name is Maria.

Beata: She's beautiful. How old is she?

Olga: She's four years old.

Beata: She looks like you. She has your eyes and nose.

C. Your family. Bring in one or two photographs of your family. Write a conversation with a partner. Use these questions and expressions.

Who's this?	Who's this?
What's his name?	What's her name?
How old is he?	How old is she?
Is he in school?	Is she in school?
What's his occupation?	What's her occupation?
He looks like you.	She looks like you.
He looks like his father.	She looks like her father.
He has your eyes / nose / hair.	She has your eyes / nose / hair.

B. Photographs.

- Discuss the photos. Ask:

  Who (are they)?
  How old are they?
  What (are they) doing?

- Ask students to practice reading the conversation together. Have them switch roles so that both of them have a chance to practice both parts.

- Ask students to circle any expressions they don't understand. Write these items on the board and explain what they mean. For example: *She has your eyes and nose* means *Her eyes and nose are the same as your eyes and nose.*

C. Your family.

- Ask students to review the list of questions and expressions. Then, write these expressions on the board, underlining the words as shown:

  What's his name?
  He looks like you.
  She looks like her father.

Help students substitute other words for the underlined items. For example:

  What are their names?
  She looks like her mother.
  He looks like his sister.

- Students work in pairs to write a conversation about one of their pictures. Then, they both work together on a conversation about the other partner's picture.

- Invite pairs of students to present one of their conversations to the class.

The Big Picture: A Family Reunion

A. Talk about the picture.

- Ask students to take turns pointing out details in the picture and commenting on them. You might ask:

  How old is this person?
  What (is she) wearing?
  What (is she) doing?

- Discuss the questions in the text.
- Invite students to comment on anything else they see in the picture. Answer any questions they may have.

Suggestion

Ask students if their families ever have family reunions. If so, what time of year do they get together? Where do they meet? How many people attend? What do they do while they are together? What favorite foods do people eat?

B. Listen and label the family members. (CD1, Track 29)

The first time students listen to the story, ask them to just look at the picture. The second time through, you might have pairs of students point to the people as they are mentioned. The third time through, students can write the name of each family member in the correct place on the picture. Pause the audio so that students have time to write their answers.

The Big Picture: A Family Reunion

A. Talk about the picture.

1. Where is the family?
2. What is the occasion?
3. What do you think the family relationships are?

Culture Note

Family reunion — a meeting of many family members one time a year or every other year, etc.

B. Listen and label the family members.

| Betty | Frank | Erika |
| Julia | Bobby, Jr. | Valerie |

Audio Script

B. Listen and label the family members. (CD1, Track 29)

A: Oh, Victoria, this is a great picture. Is this your family?

B: Yes, it is. It's our family reunion at the park.

A: Are these your children?

B: Yes, I have three daughters and a son: Barbara, Betty, Benita, and that's Bobby next to the tree. And, that's my daughter-in-law, Julia. She's talking with my daughters.

A: Where's your husband?

B: There he is. That's Frank over there. He's with Bobby, of course.

A: Oh, look at the babies. They're so cute. Are they your grandchildren?

B: Yes, those are my grandbabies. That's Bobby, Jr. He's two. And that's Erika. She's four. They're Bobby and Julia's children.

A: Are those your grandchildren, too?

B: Yes, they're Benita's children. They're twins. That's Victor and Valerie.

A: Well, this is a wonderful picture. Did you have a good time?

B: We had a wonderful time.

C. Read and complete about the family in Exercise A.

1. Victoria has four children, ___Barbara___, ___Betty___, ___Benita___, and ___Bobby___.

2. Bobby and ___Julia___ are married. They have two children, ___Bobby, Jr.___ and ___Erika___.

3. Benita's children are ___Victor___ and ___Valerie___.

4. Victor and Valerie are ___twins___.

5. Bobby is holding his ___daughter___, Erika. Erika is Victor and Valerie's ___cousin___.

D. Match each person with an occupation.

1. Julia works in a hospital.
2. Betty works with food. (f.)
3. Bobby works for the post office. (a.)
4. Benita drives a bus. (b.)
5. Victoria is 70 years old. She doesn't work. (g.)
6. Barbara stays at home with her children. (c.)
7. Frank is 73. He doesn't work. (d.)

a. He's a mail carrier.
b. She's a bus driver.
c. She's a homemaker.
d. He's retired.
e. She's a doctor.
f. She's a cook.
g. She's retired.

E. Complete the sentences. Use the possessive 's form.

1. Frank is ___Victoria's___ husband.
2. Frank is ___Bobby's___ father.
3. Bobby, Jr. is ___Frank's___ grandson.
4. Erika is ___Bobby, Jr.'s___ sister.
5. Victor and Valerie are ___Benita's___ children.
6. Barbara, Betty, and Benita are ___Bobby's___ sisters.
7. Julia is ___Victoria and Frank's___ daughter-in-law.
8. Barbara is ___Julia's___ sister-in-law.
9. Bobby, Jr. and Erika are ___Victor and Valerie's___ cousins.

C. Read and complete about the family in Exercise A.

Remind students to look back at the names they wrote on the picture on page 54 as they do this exercise. Review the correct answers orally with the whole class.

D. Match the person with an occupation.

Ask students to complete the exercise on their own. Then, have a student write the matches on the board and go over the answers with the class.

E. Complete the sentences.

Students can use the labels on the picture on page 54 to find the correct name to go in each blank. Then, they add the correct possessive ending.

Suggestion

Ask students to sit in pairs and write five more sentences about the relationships in the picture.

Suggestion

Ask students to sit in pairs and write a short (4–6 line) conversation between two people at the family reunion.

A. Before You Read.

• Invite several different students to answer the questions at the top of the exercise. Encourage them to add information. For example, *I'm married and I have two children.*

• Point to the pictures and invite students to comment. Ask:

Who are these people?
How old is each one?
Where was the picture taken?

• Ask students to read the stories to themselves. Explain that it isn't important for them to understand every single word, but that they should try to understand the main ideas in each passage.

• When they finish, invite students to ask about anything they don't understand and to make any comments they wish about the readings.

B. Read and check what is true about the families in Exercise A.

• Ask students to answer the questions on their own.

• Review the answers with the whole class. When a student gives an answer, ask him or her to point out and read aloud the sentence that contains the information that answers the question.

Reading: Families

A. Before You Read.

How many people are in your family? Are you married or single?

Family 1: A Nuclear Family

This is my family. I live with my husband and my two children. My husband's parents live an hour away. We visit the grandparents on holidays, in the summer, and sometimes on the weekends.

Family 2: An Extended Family

This is my family. I live with my parents, my wife and my two children. My parents are both 70 years old. They're retired. My children are in high school. My sons are 15 and 16.

Family 3: A Blended Family

This is my family. I was married before, and my wife, Linda, was too. Her first husband died. My first wife and I divorced. Linda has two children from her first marriage. I have one child from my first marriage.

B. Read and check (✓) what is true about the families in Exercise A.

	Family 1	Family 2	Family 3
1. There are three children in this family.			✓
2. The children live with their parents and grandparents.		✓	
3. The daughter-in-law lives with her mother-in-law.		✓	
4. The grandparents live in a different house.	✓		✓
5. The parents have children from different relationships.			✓
6. My family is similar to . . .			

A. Read.

My name is Luis. This is a photo of me, my wife, and some of our grandchildren. My wife and I have 11 grandsons and three granddaughters. The oldest is 15 years old, and the youngest is nine months old. Ten of our grandchildren live here in the United States. One of our sons still lives in Colombia. He's married and has one child. We visit them once a year.

B. Complete. (Answers will vary.)

1. I am **single / married / divorced.**

2. My **wife's / husband's** name is _____.

   He's / She's a / an _____.

3. I have _____ children. **My daughter's name / My son's name**

   is _____.

4. My mother's name is _____. She's _____ years old.

5. My father's name is _____. He's _____ years old.

6. I am a / an _____.

C. In your notebook, write about your family.

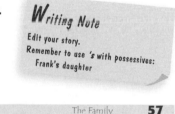

Writing Note

Edit your story.
Remember to use 's with possessives:
Frank's daughter

The Family   **57**

☀ Writing Our Stories: My Family

A. Read.

• Discuss the picture with the class. Have the students to cover the reading. Ask:

How many people are in the picture?
What do you think their relationships are?

• Read the passage aloud to the class. Then, ask students to point to the people mentioned as you read it a second time.

• Ask questions about the story such as:

Where is Luis from?
Where does he live now?
How many grandchildren does he have?
Who lives in Colombia?

B. **Complete.**

Have each student complete the information about his or her own family.

C. **In your notebook, write about your family.**

Less advanced writers can just copy Exercise B into their notebooks, being careful to spell the possessives correctly. Encourage more advanced writers to add further information, like that in Exercise A. For example, they might write specific information about the ages, locations, and marital status of various relatives.

☀ Practicing on Your Own

A. Answer the questions about yourself.

Have students do the activity individually. Students can use then the questions and answers for conversation practice with a partner.

Suggestion

Have students circle all the examples of 's in items 7 and 8. Ask them to explain the difference between the 's in *What's* and the 's in *mother's* and *father's*. (The 's in *What's* is a contraction of the verb *is*; The 's in *mother's* and *father's* is a possessive ending.)

B. The Campbell family.

Have students fill in the blanks on their own. When they finish, ask a volunteer to read the paragraph aloud, emphasizing the answers as he/she reads. Encourage the class to listen carefully.

☀ Practicing on Your Own

A. Answer the questions about yourself. (Answers will vary.)

1. What's your first name? <u>My first name is . . .</u>
2. What's your last name? _____
3. What's your date of birth? _____
4. What's your occupation? _____
5. What color is your hair? _____
6. What color are your eyes? _____
7. What's your mother's name? _____
8. What's your father's name? _____

B. The Campbell family. Read carefully and complete the story. Use *he, she, they, their, his, her,* and *is* or *are*.

The Campbell family lives in Chicago, Illinois. The father's name <u>is</u> Robert, and the mother's name <u>is</u> Ginger. Robert's job is interesting. <u>He</u> <u>is</u> a police officer. <u>His</u> wife has an unusual job for a woman. She <u>is</u> an auto mechanic. <u>They</u> have three children, Leslie, Louis, and Melanie. Leslie <u>is</u> 10 years old, Louis <u>is</u> 9 years old, and Melanie <u>is</u> 6 years old. <u>They</u> <u>are</u> elementary school students. <u>Their</u> grandmother lives in the house, too. <u>Her</u> name is Matilda. The family has a dog, too. <u>Their</u> dog's name is Friendly.

Looking at Graphs: American Households

A. Talk about the graph.

> household — the people who live together in one home

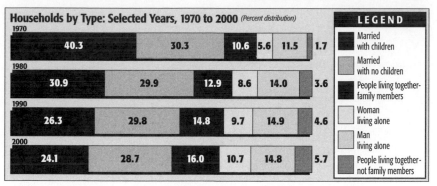

Households by Type: Selected Years, 1970 to 2000 (Percent distribution)

1970						
40.3	30.3	10.6	5.6	11.5	1.7	

1980
30.9 | 29.9 | 12.9 | 8.6 | 14.0 | 3.6

1990
26.3 | 29.8 | 14.8 | 9.7 | 14.9 | 4.6

2000
24.1 | 28.7 | 16.0 | 10.7 | 14.8 | 5.7

LEGEND
- Married with children
- Married with no children
- People living together-family members
- Woman living alone
- Man living alone
- People living together-not family members

Source: U.S. Census 2000.

B. Where do you belong in the graph?

Grammar Summary

1. Possessive nouns Add apostrophe **s** (**'s**).

David is **Olga's** husband.

That is **Tom's** book.

David is **Tom and Kathy's** father.

2. Possessive adjectives Use a possessive adjective before a noun.

I	→	**My** class is at 9:00.
You	→	**Your** hair is long and wavy.
He	→	**His** eyes are brown.
She	→	**Her** eyes are blue.
We	→	**Our** teacher is friendly.
They	→	**Their** classroom is large.

The Family **59**

Looking at Graphs: American Households

A. Talk about the graph.

- Point to the dates over each bar of the graph and explain that the graph gives information for these years.

- Point out the legend at the right of the graph. Read each classification aloud and ask students to repeat. Explain any of the legends that students don't understand.

Married with no children also includes older couples. Their children are adults now.
People living together-family members includes a single parent with a child or children.

- Help students make comments about the information in the graph. Don't be concerned about grammar. For example:

Many people live alone.
Only 24.1 percent of homes are a husband and wife and children.

B. Where do you belong in the graph?

Ask students to take turns describing who they live with and then telling which label on the legend applies to them.

Grammar Summary

- Review the summary with the class. Invite students to make up alternate sentences for each example in the chart. For example, in place of *My class is at 9:00,* a student might say, *My appointment is at 2:00.* In place of *Their classroom is large,* a student might say, *Their car is red.*

- See the Grammar Summary Expansion on page 233 for a more complete explanation of these grammar points.

Unit 5
Home and Neighborhood

Discuss the unit title art. Ask: *What is the man doing?* (He's leaning on a little house. He's relaxing.)

☀ Dictionary:
Rooms, Furniture

▖ A. Listen and repeat.
(CD 1, Track 30)

- Before playing the audio, ask students to talk about the four pictures. Find out how many of the words they already know by pointing to items and asking questions such as:

   Is this a stove or a sink?
   Is this a lamp?
   What is this?
   What are these?
   What do you call this room?
   Can you point to an end table?

- Play the audio once or twice as students just listen. Then play the audio again, pausing it so that students can repeat.

B. Label the furniture in this house.

Ask students to work in small groups of three and label the items in this house. Walk around the classroom and answer any questions.

Suggestion

Bring in pictures of various rooms from home decorating magazines. Divide the class into groups and give each one a picture to discuss. Model statements such as *There's an armchair in the living room* and *There are night tables in the bedroom*. After several minutes, have the groups exchange pictures and continue the activity.

☀ Dictionary: Rooms, Furniture

▖ **A. Listen and repeat.**

living room	kitchen	bedroom	bathroom
sofa	table	bed	bathtub
television/TV	chairs	dresser	toilet
armchair	stove	night table	sink
coffee table	sink	light / lamp	shower
end table	refrigerator	pillows	
picture	cabinets		
	counter		

B. Label the furniture in this house.

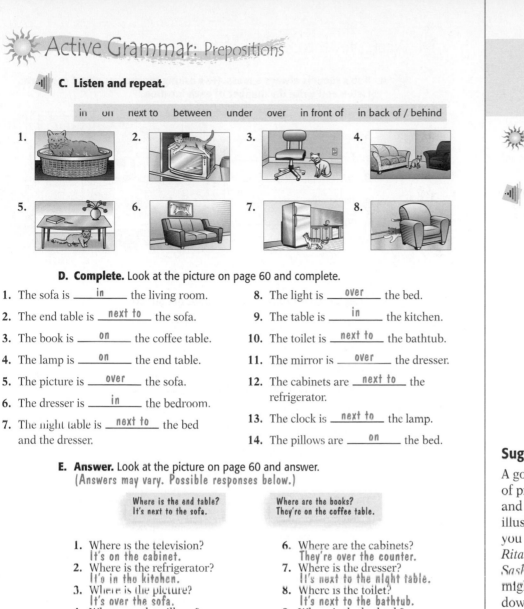

Active Grammar: Prepositions

C. Listen and repeat.

in	on	next to	between	under	over	in front of	in back of / behind

1.
2.
3.
4.
5.
6.
7.
8.

D. Complete. Look at the picture on page 60 and complete.

1. The sofa is ____in____ the living room.
2. The end table is ___next to___ the sofa.
3. The book is ____on____ the coffee table.
4. The lamp is ____on____ the end table.
5. The picture is ___over___ the sofa.
6. The dresser is ____in____ the bedroom.
7. The night table is ___next to___ the bed and the dresser.

8. The light is ___over___ the bed.
9. The table is ____in____ the kitchen.
10. The toilet is ___next to___ the bathtub.
11. The mirror is ___over___ the dresser.
12. The cabinets are ___next to___ the refrigerator.
13. The clock is ___next to___ the lamp.
14. The pillows are ____on____ the bed.

E. Answer. Look at the picture on page 60 and answer.
(Answers may vary. Possible responses below.)

> Where is the end table?
> It's next to the sofa.

> Where are the books?
> They're on the coffee table.

1. Where is the television?
   It's on the cabinet.
2. Where is the refrigerator?
   It's in the kitchen.
3. Where is the picture?
   It's over the sofa.
4. Where are the pillows?
   They're on the bed.
5. Where is the night table?
   It's next to the bed and dresser.

6. Where are the cabinets?
   They're over the counter.
7. Where is the dresser?
   It's next to the night table.
8. Where is the toilet?
   It's next to the bathtub.
9. Where is the bathtub?
   It's in the bathroom.
10. Where is the stove?
    It's under the cabinets.

Home and Neighborhood   **61**

Active Grammar:
Prepositions

C. Listen and repeat.
(CD 1, Track 31)

- Review vocabulary in the pictures by asking:
  Is this a basket or a bed?
  Is this a sofa?
  What's this?
- Play the first part of the audio and ask students to repeat the prepositions. Then play the rest and ask students to repeat each sentence. Answer any questions about the meaning of the prepositions.

Suggestion

A good way to clarify the meaning of prepositions is by using people and objects in the classroom. To illustrate *in front of* and *in back of*, you can point to students and say: *Rita is sitting in front of Sasha. Sasha is sitting in back of Rita.* You might use a bookcase and a window to illustrate *over* and *under*: *The bookcase is under the window. The window is over the bookcase.* Ask students to give the location of other classroom objects.

D. Complete.

Have students complete the fill-ins on their own and check their work with a partner. Check the correct answers with the whole class.

E. Answer.

- Read the sample questions and answers and ask the class to repeat. Answer any questions.

- Select two students and have one ask a question in the exercise, and the other answer it. Repeat exercise items until everyone has had a chance to speak.

Audio Script

C. Listen and repeat. (CD 1, Track 31)

The cat is in the basket.
The cat is on the TV.
The cat is next to the chair.
The cat is between the sofa and the chair.
The cat is under the coffee table.
The cat is over the sofa.
The cat is in front of the refrigerator.
The cat is in back of the chair.
The cat is behind the chair.

☀ Where's my soccer ball?

◁|| A. Bob's room is always a mess. (CD 1, Track 32)

- Ask students to identify as many items in the picture as they can. Ask:

  Whose room is this?
  How old do you think he is?
  What's in his room?

- Read and discuss the instructions. Go over the sample answer with the class. Then, play the audio and have students complete the activity on their own. Review the correct answers with the class.

B. Complete these conversations about the picture.

- Read aloud the questions and the partial answers. Explain the meaning of *I think it's . . .* and *Look . . . ,* if necessary.
- Ask students to look back at the picture of Bob's room and complete the answers on their own. Review the correct answers with the class.

Suggestion

Have students use the questions and answers for conversation practice with a partner.

👥 C. The classroom.

- Have pairs complete this activity on their own. As they work, move around the room, helping as needed.
- Ask a different pair to present each question and answer to the class.

☀ Where's my soccer ball?

◁|| A. Bob's room is always a mess. He's asking his mother about each item. Listen and write the number of each location.

a. telephone   __4__
b. wallet   __3__
c. keys   __5__
d. soccer ball   __1__
e. backpack   __6__
f. sneakers   __2__

B. Complete these conversations about the picture.

1. **Bob:** Mom, where's my tennis racquet?
   Mom: I think it's __in the closet__ .

2. **Bob:** Mom, where__'s__ my radio?
   Mom: I think it's __under the bed__ .

3. **Bob:** Mom, where__'s__ my baseball hat?
   Mom: Look __in your dresser__ .

4. **Bob:** Mom, where __are__ my books?
   Mom: Look __next to the dresser__ .

👥 C. The classroom. Look around your classroom and answer these questions with a partner.

1. Where is the door?
2. Where are the windows?
3. Where is the clock?
4. Where is the chalkboard?
5. Where is the map?
6. Where is the wastepaper basket?
7. Where is the pencil sharpener?
8. Where is the teacher?
9. Where is the teacher's desk?
10. Where are you?

Audio Script

A. Bob's room is always a mess. He's asking his mother about each item. Listen and write the number of each location. (CD 1, Track 32)

a. A: Mom, where's my telephone?
   B: I think it's under your bed.
b. A: Mom, where's my wallet?
   B: I think it's on your desk.
c. A: Mom, where are my keys?
   B: I think they're on your night table.
d. A: Mom, where's soccer ball?
   B: Look in your closet.
e. A: Mom, where's backpack?
   B: I think it's in front of your dresser.
f. A: Mom, where is my other sneaker?
   B: Look under your desk.

A. Megan's new apartment. Megan is moving into her first apartment today. What does she have? What does she need?

| She has a computer. | She needs a desk. |

B. Interview. Ask your partner these questions. (Circle) the answer.

1. Do you have a stereo?   Yes, I do.   No, I don't.
2. Do you have a computer?   Yes, I do.   No, I don't.
3. Do you have a desk?   Yes, I do.   No, I don't.
4. Do you have a VCR or a DVD?   Yes, I do.   No, I don't.
5. Do you have a microwave?   Yes, I do.   No, I don't.
6. Do you have a cell phone?   Yes, I do.   No, I don't.
7. Do you have a pager?   Yes, I do.   No, I don't.
8. Do you have a fax machine?   Yes, I do.   No, I don't.

C. Complete. (Answers will vary.)

1. My partner has a _____.
2. My partner has a _____.
3. My partner needs a _____.
4. I have a _____.
5. I have a _____.
6. I need a _____.

> **Have/Has**
> I **have** a computer.
> He **has** a computer.
> She **has** a computer.

☀ Furniture

A. Megan's new apartment.

• Discuss the objects in the picture. Ask:

Is this a table?
Where is the computer?
Is there a bed?

• Do the activity with the whole class. Read the sample sentences and ask students to repeat.

• Call on volunteers to tell what Megan has and what she needs. Repeat each correct sentence and ask students to repeat after you.

B. Interview.

Have students interview partners and circle the answers they receive.

C. Complete.

Ask students to complete the first three sentences using the information they found out in Exercise B. Then, have them complete the other three sentences using information about themselves. Invite several students to read their sentences to the class.

Suggestion

Write the pronouns *I, You, He, She, It, We,* and *They* in a column on the board. Point out the *Have/Has* box on page 63 and read the sentences aloud. Ask different students to go to the board and write *has* or *have* after each pronoun. Correct any errors as you go along. Then, ask students to take turns making up original sentences using each pronoun plus the correct form of the verb *have.*

Dictionary: My Neighborhood

A. Listen and repeat.
(CD 1, Track 33)

- Play the audio once or twice as students just follow along and listen. Then, present the words again and have students repeat each one. Spend extra time on words with pronunciation problems.
- Review the words one by one and ask students to give simple definitions or make up sentences that show they know what each one means. For example: *You can buy clothes and furniture in a department store. You take books from a library. You can get a cheap meal at a diner.* You may also have them give the names of specific stores and businesses of each type whenever possible.

B. Write the names of six more stores or buildings in a town.

- Brainstorm a few ideas with the class and write their responses on the board. Then, have students complete their lists individually.
- As you review students' responses with the whole class, make a master list on the board. It might include places such as *clinic, museum, bagel shop,* and *hardware store.*

C. Complete with the name of a store or a building.

Have students complete the sentences and compare answers with a partner.

A. Listen and repeat.

department store	drugstore	bank	diner
supermarket	library	jewelry store	police station
laundromat	post office	barber shop	bookstore
car wash	parking lot	City Hall	hospital

B. Write the names of six more stores or buildings in a town.

(Answers will vary.) _____   _____

_____   _____

_____   _____

C. Complete with the name of a store or building.

1. I can mail a letter at the <u>post office</u>.
2. I can wash my car at the <u>car wash</u>.
3. I can get a prescription at the <u>drugstore</u>.
4. I can eat lunch at the <u>diner</u>.
5. I can borrow a book at the <u>library</u>.
6. I can get emergency medical help at the <u>hospital</u>.
7. I can wash my clothes at the <u>laundromat</u>.
8. I can buy a coat at the <u>department store</u>.
9. I can buy food at the <u>supermarket</u>.
10. I can get a marriage license at <u>City Hall</u>.
11. I can get help at the <u>police station</u>.
12. I can get a haircut at the <u>barber shop</u>.
13. I can buy a book or a magazine at <u>the bookstore</u>.
14. I can park my car in the <u>parking lot</u>.
15. I can <u>(answers will vary)</u>.

64   Unit 5

D. Read.

The drugstore is on Park Avenue.
Jenny is **in** the drugstore.
The drugstore is **next to** the post office.
The drugstore is **between** the post office and the bank.
The bank is **on the corner of** Park Avenue and South Street.
The drugstore is **across from** the library.
The parking lot is **in back of** the drugstore.
The mailbox is **in front of** the post office.

E. Read the sentences below and write each store or building on the map.

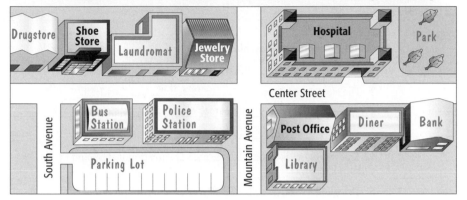

1. The laundromat is between the shoe store and the jewelry store.

2. The park is next to the hospital.

3. The bank is across from the park.

4. The bus station is on the corner of Center Street and South Avenue.

5. The diner is between the post office and the bank.

6. The drugstore is next to the shoe store.

7. The police station is next to the bus station.

8. The library is on Mountain Avenue, next to the post office.

9. The parking lot is in back of the bus station.

D. Read.

Ask students to take turns reading sentences aloud as the rest of the class locates the items on the map.

E. Read the sentences below and write each store or building on the map.

• Point out the map. Ask students to describe the locations of as many of the buildings as they can. For example:

T: *Where is the post office?*
S1: *It's on the corner of Mountain Avenue and Center Street.*
T: *Where is the park?*
S2: *It's next to the hospital.*

• Have students read the sentences at the bottom of the page and write the names on the map independently. Review the completed maps with the whole class.

Suggestion

You can team up a less advanced student with a more advanced student to do this activity. The less able students benefit from the guidance they receive. The more able students get a valuable review as well as extra practice speaking English.

☀ Downtown

☀ Downtown

A. Complete about the map above.

• Ask students to point out stores on the map based on your description of their locations. Ask questions such as:

What is next to the donut shop?
What is across the street from the library?

• Have students complete the activity individually and check their answers with a partner. Then, have students read one sentence each to the class.

B. Complete these conversations about the map above.

Ask students to look at the map and write their own answers to the questions. Check the answers with the whole class.

C. Talk about the location of each building on the map above.

• Ask students to practice the conversations in Exercise B in pairs. Walk around the room offering help as needed.
• Have students continue to talk about the map, asking and answering questions about the rest of the buildings on the map. Move around the room as they work offering help as needed.
• Review the answers by pointing to the buildings one by one and eliciting sentences from different students. Have each student give both versions of an answer wherever possible. For example: *The drugstore is across from Tony's Pizza* and *Tony's Pizza is across from the drugstore.*

A. Complete about the map above.

1. The library is _____next to_____ the post office.
2. The elementary school is _____across from_____ City Hall.
3. The drugstore is _____on the corner of_____ Pine Avenue and Main Street.
4. The parking lot is _____behind_____ the library.
5. The shoe store is _____between_____ the donut shop and the laundromat.
6. The mailbox is _____in front of_____ the post office.
7. Jason is _____in_____ the parking lot.
8. The donut shop is _____on_____ Main Street.

B. Complete these conversations about the map above.
(Answers may vary. Possible answers below.)
1. **A:** Where's the bank?
   B: It's _on the corner of Main St. and Broad St._ .
2. **A:** Where's the supermarket?
   B: It's _across from the movie theater._ .
3. **A:** Where's Debbie?
   B: She's _in front of the library._ .

C. Talk about the location of each building on the map above.

66   UNIT 5

D. Pronunciation. Prepositions: *in back of, in front of.* Listen and repeat.

1. The pizza shop is in back of the supermarket.
2. The mailbox is in front of the post office.
3. The parking lot is in back of the school.
4. The flag is in front of City Hall.
5. The children are in front of the school.

> in front of — in front_of
> in back of — in back_of

Practice these sentences with a partner.

Working Together: Student to Student

A. STUDENT A: Look at the map below. Ask Student B about the location of the places in the box. Complete the map.

STUDENT B: Do not look at your partner's map! Turn to page 68.

| the Mexican restaurant | the supermarket | the diner |
| the bus station | the police station | the bakery |

> Where's the Mexican restaurant?

> It's on the corner of River Road and Second Street.

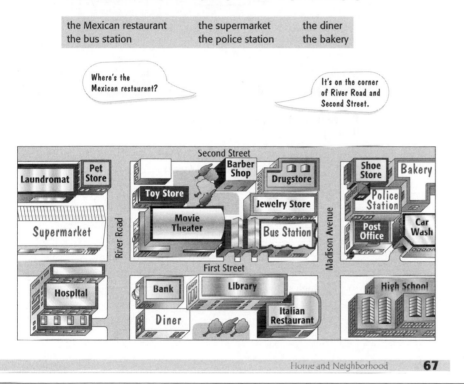

D. Pronunciation. Prepositions: *in back of, in front of.*
(CD 1, Track 34)

• Point out the pronunciation note showing that the next to last sound in the words *front* and the last sound in *back* are connected to the word *of*. Ask students to make this connection as they repeat the two phrases after you.
• Ask students to listen only the first time you play the audio. Then, have them repeat each sentence.

Teacher Note

The word *of* is shortened. It sounds almost like *uh*. The word *of* is also connected to the last sound in the previous word. *In front of* sounds like *in front of*. Drop the /t/ sound.

Practice these sentences with a partner.

Model the pronunciation again, if necessary. Then, have pairs take turns saying the sentences to each other. Encourage them to give each other feedback.

Working Together: Student to Student

A. Student A.

• Ask students to look at the maps on pages 67 and 68. State that they are the same area. Then, explain that students are going to work in pairs. One student will look at the map on page 67 and one will look at the map on page 68.
• Read the instructions. Then, ask a student to explain how to do the exercise in his or her own words.
• Students work in pairs. Remind them not to look at each other's map. After Student A has asked the questions and Student B has answered, Student B will ask the questions as Student A gives the locations.

B. Student B.

- Now Student B asks questions about the map on this page and Student A answers.
- Check students' work on both versions of the map by calling on different pairs to read each question and answer.

C. Figure it out!

- Ask students to work alone as they read the sentences and fill in the names of the stores on the map. Move around the room offering help as needed.
- Draw the map grid on the board and have several students fill it in together. Review the finished map with the whole class.

Suggestion

List the names of stores on the board and ask students to take turns coming to the board and writing an actual name of a store in their area next to each word on the board. For example: *Laundromat—Lacey's Quick Wash.*

B. STUDENT B: Look at the map below. Ask Student A about the location of the places in the box. Do not look at your partner's map! Complete the map.

the laundromat	the barber shop	the hospital
the car wash	the jewelry store	the Italian restaurant

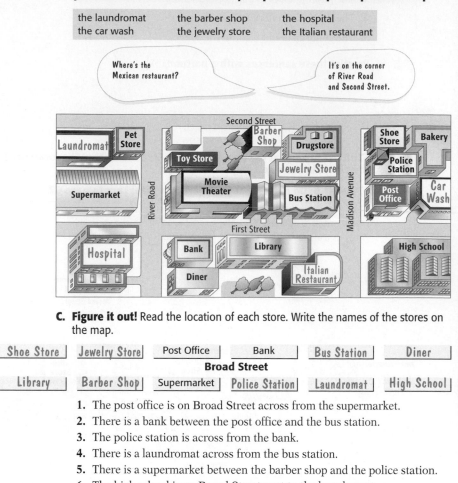

Where's the Mexican restaurant?

It's on the corner of River Road and Second Street.

C. Figure it out! Read the location of each store. Write the names of the stores on the map.

Shoe Store	Jewelry Store	Post Office	Bank	Bus Station	Diner

Broad Street

Library	Barber Shop	Supermarket	Police Station	Laundromat	High School

1. The post office is on Broad Street across from the supermarket.
2. There is a bank between the post office and the bus station.
3. The police station is across from the bank.
4. There is a laundromat across from the bus station.
5. There is a supermarket between the barber shop and the police station.
6. The high school is on Broad Street next to the laundromat.
7. There's a jewelry store across from the barber shop.
8. The shoe store is next to the jewelry store and across from the library.
9. The bus station is between the bank and the diner.

D. Downtown. Sit with a partner. Plan a town. Include the stores and buildings in the box. Add more stores and buildings. Name the streets.

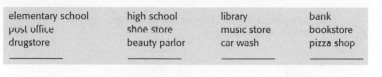

elementary school	high school	library	bank
post office	shoe store	music store	bookstore
drugstore	beauty parlor	car wash	pizza shop
_____	_____	_____	_____

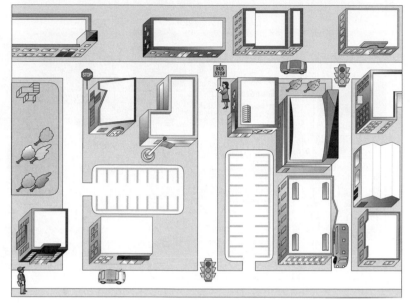

E. Write five sentences about the locations of the buildings on your map.

1. (Answers will vary.) _____

2. _____

3. _____

4. _____

5. _____

D. Downtown.

• Ask students to read through the list of stores and buildings and circle any they don't understand. Write these words on the board and ask other students to define what they mean and give examples. For example: *A woman gets her hair cut at a beauty parlor. Hairmasters is a beauty parlor.*

• Point to different parts of the map and ask students to identify them. For example:

 (pointing to parking lot)
 Is this a stadium?
 (pointing to a park)
 Is this a car wash or a park?

• Have students form pairs and plan their town together. When they finish, ask them to exchange books with another pair and study each other's maps. Invite them to ask questions and make comments about the maps.

E. Write five sentences about the locations of the buildings on your map.

Have each partner write the sentences separately. Then ask them to share their sentences with their partner and check each other's work.

A. Talk about the location of the buildings in this neighborhood.

- Point out the note about *neighbor* and *neighborhood*. Explain that some neighborhoods have an informal name. Ask students to say the name of their neighborhood, if it has one. For example, *The East Village, The South Side, The Hills,* etc.
- Discuss the locations of the buildings in the picture. Ask:

  Is the grocery store next to 234 Pine Street?
  Is the cleaners across from the laundromat?

- Invite students to describe the locations of all the buildings shown on the map.

Suggestion

Ask a student to make three statements about the location of items on the map. Then, call on a second student to repeat as many of the statements as he or she can remember. Repeat the activity several times.

B. Listen to the Story.
(CD 1, Track 35)

Play the audio once and have students listen for general information. Then read through the questions with the class. Check that they understand what each one means. Play the audio again several times as students record and check their answers.

Suggestion

You may wish to pause the audio after key sentences to give students time to record their answers.

---

neighbor — a person who lives near you
neighborhood — the area where you live

A. Talk about the location of the buildings in this neighborhood.

B. Listen to the story. Then, read and circle.

1. Magda lives at 238 Pine Street.	Yes	(No)
2. She lives in a one-bedroom apartment.	Yes	(No)
3. She has two children.	(Yes)	No
4. Her children go to the school across the street.	(Yes)	No
5. Her sister lives in the same building.	Yes	(No)
6. There is a laundry room on the first floor of the building.	Yes	(No)
7. Her husband drives to work.	Yes	(No)
8. The neighbors are friendly.	(Yes)	No

70 UNIT 5

Audio Script

B. Listen to the story. Then, read and circle.
(CD 1, Track 35)

My name is Magda Santos. I live in an apartment building on Pine Street, between Second Street and Third Street. My address is 232 Pine Street, Apartment 4G. My apartment is on the fourth floor. I live in a two-bedroom apartment with my husband and my two daughters. My sister lives in the next building, at 234 Pine Street. She's in Apartment 3A. I like my apartment and my neighborhood.

The elementary school is very near my building, it's across the street, on the corner of Pine Street and Third Street. My daughters can walk to school. There's a small park next to the school. My daughters play there on Saturday and Sunday. The grocery store is on the corner of Pine and Third Street. There's a coffee shop across the street from our apartment buildings. Sometimes my sister and I get a cup of coffee and sit and talk. My building doesn't have a laundry room, but that isn't a problem. There is a laundromat next to our apartment building. There are many restaurants in the neighborhood–Mexican, Italian, Chinese, and Indian.

(Continued on page 71.)

C. Complete with a preposition.

1. I live ___in___ a small apartment building on Pine Street.
2. My sister lives in the building ___next to___ me.
3. The coffee shop is ___across the street from___ the apartment building.
4. The Mexican restaurant is ___across from___ the Chinese restaurant.
5. The bus stop is ___in front of___ the laundromat.
6. The cleaners is ___between___ the coffee shop and the school.
7. The park is ___next to___ the school.
8. The parking lot is ___behind___ the apartment buildings.
9. The school is ___on the corner of___ Pine Street and Third Street.
10. The grocery store is ___next to___ my sister's apartment building.

D. Complete. Use *can* and a verb from the list.

1. My husband ___can get___ the bus on the corner.
2. My daughters ___can walk___ to school.
3. I ___can buy___ a cup of coffee across the street.
4. I ___can visit___ my sister every day.
5. I ___can wash___ my clothes at the laundromat.
6. I ___can park___ in back of the building.
7. My daughters ___can play___ in the park.

play
buy
visit
wash
✓get
park
walk

E. Listen and respond to each statement. Use *That's good* or *That's too bad.*

1. That's good.
2. That's too bad.
3. That's good.
4. That's good.
5. That's good.
6. That's too bad.
7. That's good.
8. That's too bad.
9. That's good.
10. That's too bad.

C. Complete with a preposition.

Remind students to refer back to the map on page 70. Have them fill in the prepositions on their own.

D. Complete.

Have students complete the sentences and check their answers with a partner. Review the completed sentences with the class, focusing on any sentences that students had difficulty with.

E. Listen and respond to each statement. (CD 1, Track 36)

• Say the expressions *That's good* and *That's too bad* and have students repeat. Emphasize the positive tone of voice and rising intonation on *That's good.* Emphasize the sympathetic tone of voice and the falling intonation on *That's too bad.*
• Play the audio and ask the class to respond in unison. If there are differences of opinion, pause and repeat that item. Write the statement on the board and discuss why the situation is positive or negative.

(Continued from page 70.)
I like to try different food. There's a parking lot in back of the apartment buildings. Each apartment has only one space.

My husband takes the bus to work. The bus stop is on the corner of Pine and Second Street, in front of the laundromat. Sometimes, Pine Street is busy and noisy, and there is a lot of traffic, but that's OK. Everything is convenient and the neighbors are friendly.

E. Listen and respond to each statement. Use *That's good* or *That's too bad.* (CD 1, Track 36)

1. The apartment is large.
2. The neighborhood is noisy.
3. The neighbors are friendly.
4. The school is near my apartment building.
5. My sister lives in the next building.
6. The traffic is heavy.
7. The bus stop is on the corner.
8. There's no laundry room in the building.
9. The laundromat is next to my building.
10. Each apartment only has one parking space.

A. Before You Read.

- Invite students to comment on the picture. Ask:

  Have you ever seen a house like this?
  What is special about it?

- Read aloud the list of possible amenities and ask students to repeat. For each amenity they are not familiar with, give a brief definition and an example of what the feature is used for. For example, for *spa* you might say, *A* spa *is a room where you can relax. It has a very big bathtub. Sometimes two or three people can sit in the bathtub. It has soft colored lights and soft music.*

- Ask students to read the passage to themselves. When they finish, invite them to ask about any sentences they don't understand. Try to avoid spending a lot of time defining and discussing individual words. Explain that they only need to understand the main idea of each sentence. Restate problem sentences in simple English.

B. Write the name of the room.

Have students complete the exercise on their own and compare answers with a partner. Review the answers with the class.

C. Underline these words in the story.

Have students locate and underline the words individually. Then, ask a student to read aloud each sentence that contains an underlined word and tell what they think it means. Write a synonym or brief definition of each word on the board.

Suggestion

Show students how to use the sentence context to figure out the meaning of the words. For example, *lake* is found in a sentence where a *boat house* is mentioned. This gives a clue to the meaning of *lake*.

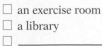

Reading: The Big House

A. Before You Read. Imagine that you are very rich. You are going to build a house. What will you put in your house?

- ☐ a swimming pool
- ☐ an office
- ☐ an exercise room
- ☐ a spa
- ☐ a guest room
- ☐ a library
- ☐ a five-car garage
- ☐ _____

Bill Gates is the president of Microsoft, the largest computer software company in the world. He is the richest person in the United States. Microsoft is located in Seattle, Washington. In 1990, Bill Gates decided to build a house on Lake Washington, near Seattle.

At first, Bill Gates wanted a small house. He was single. He wanted a house with a kitchen, a dining room, a living room, and three bedrooms. But, in planning, Gates had many ideas. Also, in 1994, Gates got married. His wife, Melinda, had more ideas.

It took seven years to build the Gates' house. It doesn't have six rooms. It has 20 rooms! There is an indoor swimming pool; the pool is 60 feet long. You can listen to music <u>underwater</u> when you swim. You can watch a movie in the 20-seat theater. One hundred people can sit in the dining room. There is a library, an exercise room, two spas, and a sauna. In the main <u>reception</u> room, there is a 24-monitor video wall. The garage is very large; there are spaces for 30 cars! There is a <u>guest</u> house for friends. And, there is a boat house on the <u>lake</u>.

Bill and Melinda Gates now have two children. They need more room, so it's time to <u>expand</u> the house!

B. Write the name of the room.

1. One hundred people can eat in the <u>dining room</u> .
2. You can swim in the <u>indoor swimming pool</u> .
3. You can read a book in the <u>library</u> .
4. You can relax in the <u>spa and sauna</u> .
5. You can park your car in the <u>garage</u> .
6. You can watch a movie in the <u>theater</u> .
7. Friends can stay in the <u>guest house</u> .

C. Underline these words in the story. What is the meaning of each word?

(See above. Meanings found in context.)

| lake | underwater | reception | guest | expand |

☀ Writing Our Stories: My Neighborhood

A. Read.

I live in Oakland, California. I am from China, and there are many people from China in my neighborhood. I live in an apartment near the town. There are many Chinese stores on my street. There is a Chinese grocery store across from my apartment building. I can buy my favorite kinds of Chinese fruit, such as lichee and duran. Every Friday I buy the Chinese newspapers there. There is a good video store on the corner. I can rent movies from the United States and from China. There are many Chinese restaurants. Some of the restaurants have very good food. There is a bank next to my apartment building. The tellers speak English and Chinese. My street is always busy, but on Saturday and Sunday, it is very busy.

B. Name six buildings or stores in your neighborhood.
(Answers will vary.)

_____   _____

_____   _____

_____   _____

C. Write about your neighborhood. (Answers will vary.)

I live in _____, _____. I live
                  city   state
in **a house / an apartment** on _____ Street. My neighborhood
is quiet / busy.

_____

_____

_____

_____

_____

Writing Note
Street names begin with capital letters: Main Street.

☀ Writing Our Stories: My Neighborhood

A. Read.

- Discuss the picture with students. Ask:

  How many stores do you see?
  What kind of lettering is on the signs?
  Where do you think this picture was taken?

- Ask students to read the story all the way through without stopping. Then read the story to the students. Ask: *Do you have any questions about the story?*

B. Name six buildings or stores in your neighborhood.

Students will have different answers depending on where they live. Invite students to share their lists with the class.

C. Write about your neighborhood.

- Students fill in the blanks and circle either *a house* or *an apartment* in the first three sentences. They can use Exercise A as a model for the rest of their writing.
- Review students' writing and copy on the board some of the original sentence they wrote at the end of their stories. Ask other students to read these sentences aloud.

Suggestion

Have students copy some of the sentences from the board into their notebooks. For homework, they can rewrite these sentences to fit their own stories.

☀ Practicing on Your Own

A. Prepositions.

Students can complete the activity for homework. Have students put the answers on the board and review them with the whole class.

B. Complete.

Write the word *get* on the board. Ask students to suggest as many words as they can that can follow *get*. (In addition to the ones in the lesson, they may suggest *get an A, get a cold, get mail, get a phone call*, etc.)

Suggestion

Divide the class into teams and see which group can come up with the most examples of *get* + a noun. Allow only one example for each type of item. For example, *get shoes* would be the only *get* + clothing item you would allow a group to list. Then, ask the groups to present their examples in sentence form using *can*. For example: *You can get shoes in a department store.*

☀ Practicing on Your Own

A. Prepositions. Look at this map. Complete the sentences.

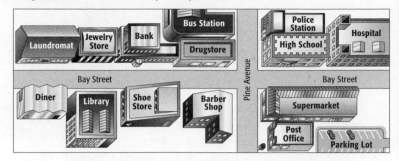

1. The bank is ___between___ the jewelry store and the drugstore.
2. There is a bus station ___across from___ the police station.
3. The high school is ___on the corner of___ Pine Avenue and Bay Street.
4. The library is ___on___ Bay Street.
5. The barber shop is ___on the corner of___ Pine Avenue and Bay Street.
6. The parking lot is ___behind/in back of___ the supermarket.
7. There is a jewelry store ___next to___ the laundromat.
8. The hospital is ___next to___ the high school.
9. There is a shoe store ___across from___ the bank.
10. The shoe store is ___between___ the barber shop and the library.

B. Complete. Use *can* and a verb from the list.

1. I ___can get___ a prescription at the drugstore.
2. I ___can buy___ sneakers at the shoe store.
3. I ___can get___ a haircut at the barber shop.
4. I ___can mail___ a letter at the post office.
5. I ___can cash___ a check at the bank.
6. I ___can borrow___ a book at the library.
7. I ___can eat___ breakfast at the diner.

> can mail
> can eat
> can buy
> can get
> ✓can get
> can cash
> can borrow

Looking at Charts: Electronic Equipment

A. Look at the chart. It shows the percentage of homes in the United States with different kinds of electronic equipment. Look at the chart and complete the sentences. (Answers may vary.)

1. Most homes have a _television, a radio, and a telephone_.
2. Many homes have a _VCR and an answering machine_.
3. Half of the homes have a _computer_.
4. Not many homes have a _fax machine_.
5. I have a _____.
6. I would like a _____.

Electronic Equipment	
Television	98%
Radio	98%
Telephone	96%
VCR	88%
Answering machine	60%
Computer	50%
Cell phone	33%
Camcorder	23%
Fax machine	8%

Grammar Summary

---

1. Prepositions

The keys are **in** the desk.

The keys are **on** the table.

The keys are **next to** the telephone.

The keys are **between** the telephone and the lamp.

The keys are **under** the chair.

The jewelry store is **on** Park Avenue.

The bank is **next to** the drugstore.

The supermarket is **across from** the police station.

The bakery is **between** the shoe store and the post office.

The diner is **on the corner of** Main Street and Park Avenue.

The parking lot is **in back of** / **behind** the supermarket.

The mailbox is **in front of** the post office.

2. Can

I **can wash** my clothes at the laundromat.

I **can buy** stamps at the post office.

Looking at Charts: Electronic Equipment

A. Look at the chart.

- Model the language as you read some of the information from the chart. For example: *Ninety-eight percent of the homes in the United States have a television.* Ask students to repeat five model statements like this. Then, call on different students to read the rest of the information from the chart without your model.

- Have students complete the sentences on their own. Review the exercise and discuss the different possible answers.

Grammar Summary

- Review the summary with the class. Invite students to make up alternate sentences for each example in the chart. For example, in place of *The keys are **in** the desk*, a student might say *I am **in** the classroom*. In place of *I can buy stamps **at** the post office*, a student might say *I can borrow money **at** a bank*.

- See the Grammar Summary Expansion on page 233 for a more complete explanation of these grammar points.

Unit 6
A Typical Day

Discuss the unit title art. Ask: *What is the person doing?* (She is chasing a clock.)

☀ Dictionary:
Daily Activities

A. Listen and repeat.
(CD1, Track 37)

• Use questions like these to get students to talk about the activities in the pictures:

Is he waking up or getting up?
What is he doing here?

• Play the audio once or twice while students just listen. Then, play or read the list again, pausing after each verb to give students time to repeat and to complete the sentences in their books.

Suggestion

Point out that the verb *washes* ends in an /əz/ sound. Pronounce the sound by itself (/əz/) and then pronounce the whole word, *washes*. Ask students to repeat the sound and the word.

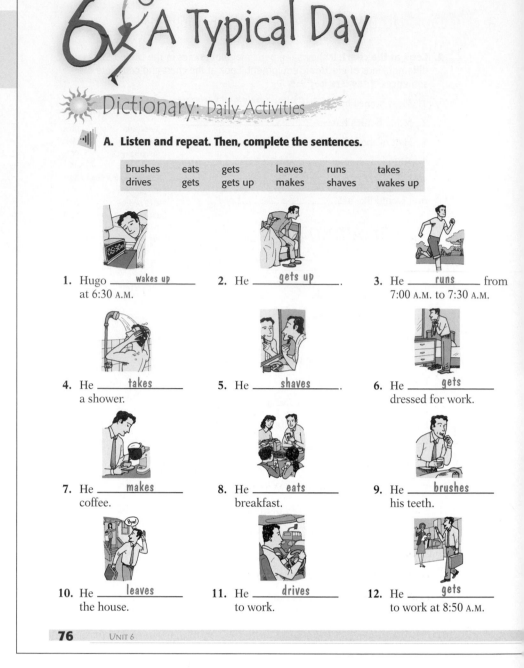

6 A Typical Day

☀ Dictionary: Daily Activities

A. Listen and repeat. Then, complete the sentences.

brushes	eats	gets	leaves	runs	takes
drives	gets	gets up	makes	shaves	wakes up

1. Hugo __wakes up__ at 6:30 A.M.

2. He __gets up__.

3. He __runs__ from 7:00 A.M. to 7:30 A.M.

4. He __takes__ a shower.

5. He __shaves__.

6. He __gets__ dressed for work.

7. He __makes__ coffee.

8. He __eats__ breakfast.

9. He __brushes__ his teeth.

10. He __leaves__ the house.

11. He __drives__ to work.

12. He __gets__ to work at 8:50 A.M.

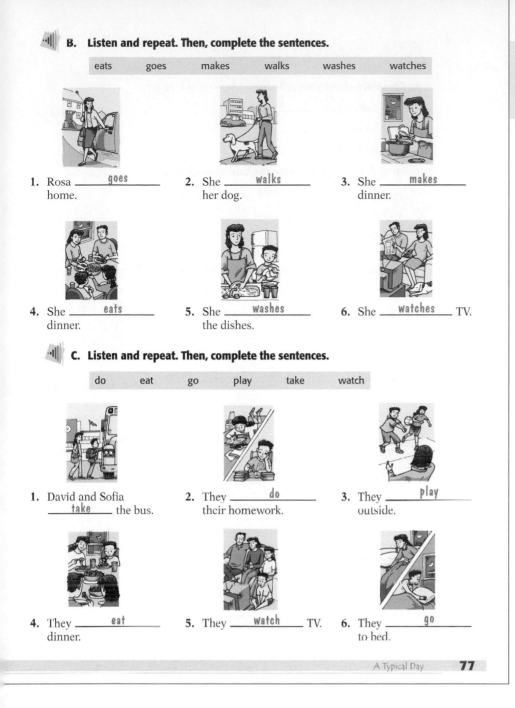

B. Listen and repeat. Then, complete the sentences.

eats	goes	makes	walks	washes	watches

1. Rosa _____goes_____ home.

2. She _____walks_____ her dog.

3. She _____makes_____ dinner.

4. She _____eats_____ dinner.

5. She _____washes_____ the dishes.

6. She _____watches_____ TV.

C. Listen and repeat. Then, complete the sentences.

do	eat	go	play	take	watch

1. David and Sofia _____take_____ the bus.

2. They _____do_____ their homework.

3. They _____play_____ outside.

4. They _____eat_____ dinner.

5. They _____watch_____ TV.

6. They _____go_____ to bed.

(CD1, Track 38)

Do this activity orally with the whole class. Call on different students to complete one sentence each. Repeat each correct response and ask the class to repeat after you.

Suggestion

Ask students questions like these about their schedules.

What time do you wake up?
What time do you eat breakfast?
What do you eat for breakfast?
Do you drink coffee?

C. Listen and repeat.
(CD1, Track 39)

Introduce and practice these verbs as you did in Exercises A and B.

Active Grammar: Present Tense

A. Complete about your schedule.

- Have students look over the sentences. Answer any questions they may have.
- Ask students to complete the activity individually and then compare answers with a partner. Call on individuals to tell the class about their schedules.

B. Complete with verbs from the list.

- Point out the chart in the green box at the right of the exercise and have a student read it aloud. Point out the *s* ending on the verb in the sentences that start with *he* and *she*. Remind them to watch for this as they complete the exercise.
- Have students complete the sentences on their own using the verbs from the list in the yellow box. Check the answers by calling on different students to read one answer each to the class.

Suggestion

Ask students to work in pairs. Have them take turns dictating five different sentences from Exercises A and B to each other. Have them use the completed exercises in their books to check their work.

Active Grammar: Present Tense

A. Complete about your schedule. (Answers will vary.)

1. I wake up at _____.
2. I get up at _____.
3. I eat breakfast at _____.
4. I **drive / walk / take the bus** to work at _____.
5. I arrive at **work / school** at _____.
6. I go home at _____.
7. I do homework at _____.

> I wake up at 6:30.
> I go to bed at 11:00.

B. Complete with verbs from the list. (Answers may vary. Suggested responses below.)

1. Hugo _____gets up_____ at 6:30.
2. His children _____get up_____ at 7:00.
3. Hugo _____runs/walks_____ in the park every morning.
4. Hugo _____walks/drives_____ to work at 8:00.
5. David and Sofia _____take_____ the bus at 8:10.
6. Rosa _____walks/drives_____ to work.
7. David and Sofia _____watch_____ TV from 8:00 to 9:30.
8. Rosa _____watches_____ TV from 9:00 to 10:30.
9. The family _____eats_____ dinner together every night.
10. The children _____eat_____ lunch at school.

I We They You	work	on Monday.
He She	works	

drive
drives
eat
eats
get up
✓ gets up
run
runs
take
takes
watch
watches
walk
walks

A. Look at the chart. Use your imagination. Talk about Hugo and his family's schedules. Then, talk about your schedule.

I Hugo and Rosa	exercise eat dinner go to work watch the news visit friends	at ___ : ___ . on weekends. in the morning. in the evening. every day. from Monday to Friday.
Sofia David	does homework eats lunch plays outside watches TV goes to bed	

B. More time expressions. Ask and answer questions with a partner. (Answers will vary.)

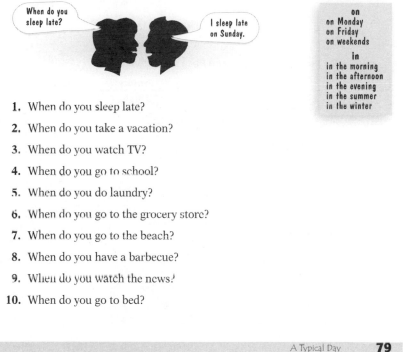

When do you sleep late?

I sleep late on Sunday.

on
on Monday
on Friday
on weekends

in
in the morning
in the afternoon
in the evening
in the summer
in the winter

1. When do you sleep late?

2. When do you take a vacation?

3. When do you watch TV?

4. When do you go to school?

5. When do you do laundry?

6. When do you go to the grocery store?

7. When do you go to the beach?

8. When do you have a barbecue?

9. When do you watch the news?

10. When do you go to bed?

A Typical Day **79**

※ Time Expressions

A. Look at the chart.

• Review the meanings of the time expressions in the third column of the chart. Invite students to suggest other similar time expressions they know. For example: *every night, on Sundays,* and *in the afternoon.*

• Invite students to take turns making up sentences using the information in the chart. As each student says a sentence, listen carefully for the correct verb endings. Be sure they add the *s* ending when they talk about Sofia (she) and David (he).

B. More time expressions.

• Ask a pair of students to read the sample dialogue to the class. Then, have students review the list of time expressions in the box. Answer any questions they may have.

• Have students take turns asking and answering the questions with a partner. Move around the room checking progress and offering help as needed.

• Call on different pairs of students to ask and answer the questions as the rest of the students listen.

Suggestions

• Write on the board headings taken from Exercise B. The headings might look like this: *Sleep late, Take a vacation,* etc.

• Have students form groups and ask each other about these activities. Ask each group to appoint a secretary to record the results.

• Read each heading aloud and ask the groups to report on when most people do each activity. For example: *Five people sleep late on Saturday. Two people sleep late on Sunday.*

Suggestion

Discuss the chart at the top of the page. Explain that we use the contractions *don't* and *doesn't* very often in speech but in writing we use *do not* and *does not*.

A. Complete the sentences, using a time expression.

Ask students to complete the sentences on their own. Then, call on different students to read their sentences to the class.

👥 **Compare your sentences with a partner.**

Ask students to form pairs and look at each other's answers to Exercise A. Then, have each pair join another pair. Ask each person to tell the new pair about his or her partner's habits.

Suggestion

You may want to review A.M. and P.M. with the students before beginning Exercise B.

B. Talk about Hugo's and Rosa's schedules.

• Ask about the various activities shown on the schedule. For example:

Who's this?
Where is (he)?
What does Hugo do on Thursday mornings?
When does he go to school?
What do Hugo and Rosa do on Saturday evening?

• Have students study the schedule. Answer any questions they may have.

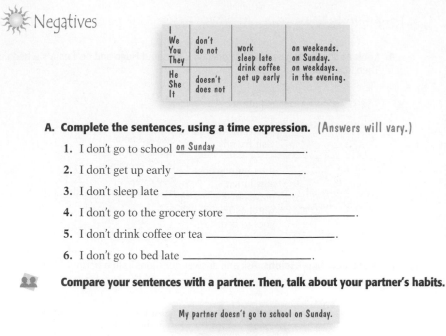

| I We You They | don't do not | work sleep late drink coffee | on weekends. on Sunday. on weekdays. |
| He She It | doesn't does not | get up early | in the evening. |

A. Complete the sentences, using a time expression. (Answers will vary.)

1. I don't go to school _on Sunday_____.
2. I don't get up early _____.
3. I don't sleep late _____.
4. I don't go to the grocery store _____.
5. I don't drink coffee or tea _____.
6. I don't go to bed late _____.

👥 **Compare your sentences with a partner. Then, talk about your partner's habits.**

> My partner doesn't go to school on Sunday.

B. Talk about Hugo's and Rosa's schedules.

C. Complete the sentences about Hugo and Rosa.

eat
✓work
study
stay
go

1. Rosa _____works_____ on Wednesday.

2. Hugo ____doesn't work____ on Thursdays.

3. Hugo _____goes_____ to the gym on Thursdays.

4. Hugo _____studies_____ on Thursday evenings.

5. Rosa and Hugo _____go_____ to school on Wednesday evenings.

6. Rosa ____doesn't study____ on Friday mornings.

   She _____goes_____ to the gym.

   (Answers may vary. Sample responses above.)

With a partner, write eight more sentences about Hugo's and Rosa's schedules. Four sentences must be negative.

D. Cultural differences. Read the statements about American culture. Then, talk about your culture.

> Americans drive everywhere.
> Russians don't drive everywhere. They use public transportation.
> or
> In Russia, we do, too.

1. Americans use credit cards.

2. Americans use babysitters.

3. Americans shop at shopping malls.

4. Americans move many times.

5. Americans watch many hours of TV.

6. Americans like football.

7. American teenagers wear jeans to school.

8. Americans eat a large meal in the evening.

Write five more cultural differences.

Writing Note

Countries and nationalities begin with capital letters: **R**ussia, **B**razilians.

C. Complete the sentences about Hugo and Rosa.

Point out the verbs in the box that students will use to complete the sentences. Ask students to complete the sentences on their own and compare answers with a partner.

With a partner, write eight more sentences about Hugo's and Rosa's schedules.

Remind students to write four affirmative sentences and four negative sentences about Hugo and Rosa. As they work, move around the room offering help as needed.

Suggestion

Have students who finish first put one sentence each on the board. Ask each person to check the sentences already there so that they don't write the same thing. Review the sentences with the class and correct any errors.

D. Cultural differences.

Read the sample sentences and explain the meaning of *We do, too.* Then, read each statement about American culture. Encourage students to speak about their cultures, explaining how each item is the same or different. Example: *Americans use credit cards. In Italy, many people use credit cards. In Honduras, most people pay cash.*

Write five more cultural differences.

Call on some students to read their list to the class.

Suggestion

Ask two or three students from the same country to work together and list five more differences or similarities. Provide spelling of countries or nationalities as needed.

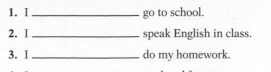
How often?

A. Adverbs of frequency.

Review the meaning of the adverbs of frequency in the box. Call on individual students to complete each sentence orally. Then have students write their own answers in the blanks.

Suggestion

Ask students to look at the eight sentences in Exercise A and tell where the adverb of frequency appears in the sentence. (It comes before most verbs but after the verb *be*.)

B. Ask your partner these questions.

• Review the meaning of *how often, once, twice,* and the other time expressions in the yellow box. Explain as necessary.

• Ask a pair of students to read the sample exchange. Then, have pairs take turns asking and answering the questions. Encourage them to tell the truth.

C. Work with a partner.

Have each pair write three questions to ask you. Then, invite students to ask you questions.

A. Adverbs of frequency. Complete the sentences with adverbs. (Answers will vary.)

1. I _____ go to school.
2. I _____ speak English in class.
3. I _____ do my homework.
4. I _____ eat breakfast.
5. I am _____ late for an appointment.
6. I am _____ on time for class.
7. I am _____ nervous before an exam.
8. I am _____ relaxed.

100%	always
80%	usually
50%	sometimes
0%	never

B. Ask your partner these questions. (Answers will vary.)

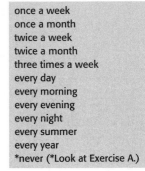

How often do you exercise?

I exercise three times a week.

once — one time

twice — two times

1. How often do you exercise?
2. How often do you play a sport?
3. How often do you wash your car?
4. How often do you visit your native country?
5. How often do you go to the park?
6. How often do you eat out?

once a week
once a month
twice a week
twice a month
three times a week
every day
every morning
every evening
every night
every summer
every year
*never (*Look at Exercise A.)

C. Work with a partner. Write three more *How often* questions, and ask the teacher your questions.

A. Pronunciation: Final *s*. Listen and repeat.

/ s /	/ z /	/ əs /
wakes	drives	fixes
walks	arrives	relaxes
takes	does	washes
drinks	goes	brushes
likes	knows	watches
eats	plays	
gets	wears	
sleeps		
shops		

B. Read the verbs. Pronounce them. Put them in the correct columns.
Add two or more verbs to each column.

/ s /	/ z /	/ əs /
stops	cleans	finishes
cooks	studies	teaches
speaks	leaves	practices
visits	buys	

cleans
studies
finishes
leaves
stops
cooks
teaches
speaks
buys
visits
practices

Practice saying the verbs with a partner.

A. Pronunciation: Final *s*. Listen and repeat.
(CD1, Track 40)

Point out the pronunciation symbols at the top of the three columns and have students listen to the sounds. Then, pause the tape after each word and ask students to repeat.

Suggestion

After students have listened once or twice, demonstrate the three different sounds of the present tense *s* ending. Write these three symbols on the board: /s/, /z/, and /əs/. Place your fingers on your voice box and make the three different sounds. Ask students to do the same thing, repeating the sounds after you. Point out that:

• /s/ is a continuing *s* sound that doesn't use the voice box.
• /z/ is a continuing *z* sound. It uses the voice box and you can feel the vibrations in your throat.
• /əs/ is a syllable that you hear at the end of the word *washes*. It makes the word *wash* into the two-syllable word *washes*. The /əs/ sound ends with the /z/ sound.

B. Read the verbs.

Put the chart on the board and have students come up to fill it in. Review the chart and make corrections if necessary. Then, have students take turns reading one column each.

Practice saying the verbs with a partner.

Students practice in pairs. Remind them to listen carefully and try to help each other pronounce the verbs correctly.

☀ Working Together

Suggestion

Review the use of *at* and *from . . . to . . .* with clock time. *At* indicates a specific clock time. *From . . . to . . .* shows how long an activity lasted.

A. Interview.

Ask students to complete their own columns first. Students then complete this activity in pairs.

B. More about the interview.

Have students circle answers on their own. Then, ask them to check some answers with their partner from Exercise A.

☀ Working Together

A. Interview. Work with a partner. Ask and answer these questions. Write the time. (Answers will vary.)

Question	You	Your partner
What time do you get up?		
What time do you leave for school?		
What time do you get home from school?		
What hours do you work?		
What time do you eat dinner?		
What time do you do your homework?		
What time do you go to sleep?		
What time do you get up on weekends?		

B. More about the interview. Look at your chart. Circle the correct information about the schedules. (Answers will vary.)

1. My partner gets up **early / late**.

2. I **get up / don't get up** early.

3. My partner **leaves / doesn't leave** for school early in the morning.

4. I **leave / don't leave** for school at about the same time.

5. My partner **works / doesn't work**.

6. I **work / don't work**.

7. My partner does homework in **the morning / the afternoon / the evening**.

8. I do my homework in **the morning / the afternoon / the evening**.

9. My partner **goes / doesn't go** to bed before midnight.

C. My day. The teacher will give each student 10 small pieces of paper. On each piece of paper, write an activity that you do on a typical day, such as:

brush my teeth

take a shower

eat breakfast

study

exercise

Then, give the pieces of paper to a partner. Describe your typical day. Your partner will listen and arrange your papers in the correct order. You cannot touch the papers!

First,
Next,
Then,
After that,

First, I exercise from 6:30 to 7:00. Then, I take a shower. I eat breakfast at 7:30 in the morning. Next, I brush my teeth. After that, I study.

D. A day in the life. In a small group, think of a famous person. Choose an athlete, an actress, a politician, a singer, a writer, etc. What is a typical day for this famous person? Write six sentences describing a day in the life of this person. Use your imagination!

1. Michael Jordan gets up at 10:00.

2. He goes to the gym.

3. He plays basketball.

4. He talks to his family.

1. ___(Answers will vary.)___
2. _____
3. _____
4. _____
5. _____
6. _____

Tell your classmates about _A day in the life of (the famous person)._

C. My day.

- Before class, prepare ten slips of paper for each student. Students can write about activities they have discussed in class. Suggest that each student puts the slips in the order they do the activities and quietly rehearse what they will say.
- Divide the class into pairs. Students take turns describing their typical day.
- You may want to demonstrate this activity with a student. Have students check the reordered slips for accuracy.

Suggestion

Encourage students to add some new activities. For example, students may already know expressions such as *walk the dog, take out the trash,* and *go shopping.*

D. A day in the life.

Read and discuss the instructions and the sample sentences with the class. Then, help them form small groups, choose a person to write about, and make their lists. Set a time limit (15 minutes).

Tell your classmates about *A day in the life of (the famous person).*

Call on each group to report on what the person they chose does on a typical day.

Suggestion

- Bring in five to ten magazine or newspaper photos of famous people, such as the president, the president's spouse, well-known actors, singers, and so on. Groups can choose a picture and write about him or her.
- Tape the pictures to the board. Each group can write about one person, not mentioning the name. One person from the group reads the sentences and the class can guess which person they are describing.

The Big Picture:
A Daily Schedule

A. Listen to Susan's and Peter's schedules.

(CD1, Track 41)

• Invite students to look at the pictures and make any comments or ask any questions they wish. Ask questions such as:

> Do they wake up at the same time?
> Who exercises in the morning?
> Do you think Susan drives to work?
> Where do you think Peter works?

• Play the audio once or twice as students just listen.

• Point out the blank clock faces and tell students these are the places where they will write the time they hear on the audio. Play the audio several more times as students fill in the answers.

• Ask the class what they think about Susan's and Peter's schedules.

Suggestion

You may wish to pause the audio after key sentences to give students time to record their answers.

The Big Picture: A Daily Schedule

A. Listen to Susan's and Peter's schedules. Write the correct time on each clock. Then, talk about their schedules.

6 : 00 6 : 30 7 : 30

8 : 00 9 : 00 - 5 : 00 6 : 00

7 : 00 - 9 : 00 9 : 30 - 11 : 00

86 UNIT 6

Audio Script

A. **Listen to Susan's and Peter's schedules. Write the correct time on each clock. Then, talk about their schedules.**
(CD1, Track 41)

Susan and Peter have busy schedules during the week. At 6:00, the alarm rings, and Susan and Peter wake up. Susan exercises for half an hour–she runs from 6:30–7:00. Peter takes a shower and gets dressed. At 7:30, they are in the kitchen. Susan and Peter eat breakfast. Susan eats yogurt, fruit, and drinks water. Peter eats

toast and eggs. He always drinks coffee. At 8:00, they leave for work. Peter drives to work, and Susan walks. Susan works in an office. She's a secretary. Peter works for a construction company. They both work from 9:00 to 5:00. They eat dinner together at 6:00. At 7:00, they go to classes at the community college. They have classes from 7:00 to 9:00 two times a week. From 9:30 to 11:00, they relax. Susan likes to read. Peter usually watches TV. At 11:00, they go to bed.

86 ENGLISH IN ACTION 2

B. Complete the sentences about Susan's and Peter's schedules. Use the simple present tense.

drink	drive	eat	✓get	go	run	walk	watch	work

1. Susan and Peter _____get_____ up early.
2. Susan _____runs_____ for 30 minutes.
3. They _____eat_____ breakfast together.
4. Susan _____eats_____ a healthy breakfast.
5. Peter always _____drinks_____ coffee.
6. Peter _____drives_____ to work.
7. Susan _____walks_____ to work.
8. Susan and Peter _____work_____ from 9:00 to 5:00.
9. They _____go_____ to classes twice a week.
10. Peter _____watches_____ TV in the evening.

C. Correct it! The information is not correct. Find the mistakes. Then, say the sentences correctly.

Susan takes a shower first.
Susan **doesn't take** a shower first.
Peter **takes** a shower first.

They leave for work at 9:00.
They **don't leave** for work at 9:00.
They **leave** for work at 8:00.

1. Susan and Peter get up at 8:00. **(6:00)**
2. They eat breakfast at 7:00. **(7:30)**
3. Peter drinks tea for breakfast. **(coffee)**
4. Peter runs in the morning. **(Susan)**
5. Peter eats yogurt for breakfast. **(Susan)** or **(toast and eggs)**
6. Susan drives to work. **(Peter)** or **(Walks)**
7. Susan works at a construction company. **(Peter)**
8. They go to bed at midnight. **(11:00)**

D. A daily schedule. Look at the pictures of Susan's and Peter's schedules. In your notebook, write a story about their schedules.

A Typical Day   **87**

B. Complete the sentences about Susan's and Peter's schedules.

• Remind students about the use of the *s* ending on present tense verbs when using *he, she,* or a person's name. You might have students look back at the chart on page 78.

• Ask students to complete the sentences on their own. Then review the answers with the whole class.

C. Correct it!

• Read and discuss the instructions. Ask volunteers to read aloud the two sample answers at the top. Then, ask students to rehearse the answer to each question by themselves.

• Read the incorrect sentences aloud and call on a student to give the negative sentence. Then, call on another student to give the correct version of each one.

D. A daily schedule.

Ask students to complete the activity on their own. Tell them that they can use the sentences they completed in the previous exercises as models and even copy some exactly as they appear.

Suggestion

Students can follow the pictures and include the activities in the order they happened. Encourage students to write something different about the pictures. For example, *Susan is very healthy. She likes to exercise. She wants Peter to run with her or join a gym. He isn't interested.*

☀Reading: A Day at the Bakery

A. Before You Read.

- Discuss the picture. Ask:

  Who is this person?
  Where does she work?
  Do you ever shop at a bakery?

- Invite several students to answer the questions at the top. Encourage them to add information. For example, *Sometimes I stop at the bakery after school. I buy bread for dinner.*

- Ask students to read the story to themselves. When they finish, invite them to ask about anything they don't understand. Also invite them to add their comments about the reading.

B. Circle the answer.

- Ask students to reread the story and answer the questions individually. Suggest that they choose a key word from each question as they look back to find the answer. For example, for question 1 they might look for the word *Angela*. It appears four times in the story. The answer to the first question item appears the first time the name *Angela* appears.

- As you review the answers, have students go back to the story and point out the sentence or sentences where they found each answer.

☀Reading: A Day at the Bakery

A. Before You Read.

1. Where do you buy bread?
2. What do you buy at a bakery?
3. Where is the best bakery in your neighborhood?

It's 3:00 A.M. Angela is ready to start the day at the family bakery. She has three children, and they all help at the bakery. Vincent and Angela are the owners of his family's bakery. Vincent's father owned the bakery, and before that, Vincent's grandfather owned the bakery. Now, Vincent and his wife, Angela, own and manage the bakery.

Everyone in the family works in the bakery. The oldest daughter, Claire, decorates many of the special cakes. Maria is the middle child. She works at the counter, and sometimes she makes cookies. Paul is only 14, but he makes bread. Vincent says, "Paul has good hands for bread." The whole family works in the bakery, but the children only work there before or after school.

Mr. Martino is a regular customer. He visits the bakery every morning. He always buys the round loaf of bread with no seeds. He says that it's good. Mrs. Salerno is also a regular customer. Every Friday, she buys two loaves of Italian bread and a large box of cookies. Her six-year-old daughter, Laura, always gets one free cookie. Mrs. Salerno says that Vincent's bakery is the best in the area.

The bakery is open from 6:30 A.M. to 3:00 P.M. every day except Monday. The bakery sells cookies, cakes, and bread. For special holidays, such as Easter and Christmas, Vincent keeps the bakery open until 6:00 P.M., and Angela always prepares fresh coffee for their customers.

B. Circle the answer.

1. Angela goes to work at 6:00 A.M.	Yes	(No)
2. Angela and her husband manage the bakery.	(Yes)	No
3. The children work in the bakery all day.	Yes	(No)
4. Claire usually makes bread.	Yes	(No)
5. Paul makes bread and cakes.	Yes	(No)
6. Mr. Martino goes to the bakery every day.	(Yes)	No
7. Mrs. Salerno buys cakes and cookies every week.	Yes	(No)
8. The bakery is open every day.	Yes	(No)

A. Read.

I am from Colombia. I came to the United States eight years ago. In Colombia, I had a deli. I made all kinds of sandwiches, hamburgers, hot dogs, and Colombian dishes. Now, I have a job in a Cuban bakery. A friend told me about the job. I didn't have any experience, but now I have a lot of experience.

I have a difficult schedule. On Saturday, Sunday, and Monday, I work from 4:00 A.M. to 3:00 P.M. I bake all kinds of breads: garlic bread, butter bread, bread with cheese, and special bread with pork inside. On Tuesday, Wednesday, and Thursday I work from 10:00 A.M. to 7:00 P.M. I help customers at the counter. From 7:30 P.M. to 10:00 P.M., I study English four nights a week. I get home at about 10:30 P.M. Then, I take a shower and do my homework. I'm very busy, but I like my job. In the future I would like to have my own bakery.

Patricia, Colombia

B. Complete the sentences with information about yourself. (Answers will vary.)

1. I get up at _____.
   <small>time</small>
2. I **drive / walk / take public transportation** to work.
3. I get to work at _____. I work at _____.
   <small>time</small>   <small>company name</small>
4. I work from _____ to _____.
   <small>time</small>   <small>time</small>
5. I go to school on _____.
   <small>days of the week</small>
6. I get home from school at _____.
   <small>time</small>

C. In your notebook, write a story about your typical day.

Writing Note

Put **time expressions** at the beginning or at the end of a sentence.

On Monday, I don't go to work.
I don't go to work **on Monday.**

☀ Writing Our Stories: My Day

A. Read.

- Discuss the photo with students. Ask:

  What kind of store is this?
  Can you identify any of the foods?

- Read the story aloud to the class. Then ask questions such as:

  What is her name?
  Where is she from?
  Where does she work?
  How did she find the job?
  What does she do at work?
  What is her schedule?
  How often does she go to class?

B. Complete the sentences with information about yourself.

Students complete the sentences individually. Invite some students to share their sentences.

C. In your notebook, write a story about your typical day.

- Students should use the information from Exercise B as they complete this activity.

- The story at the top of the page can serve as a model for their writing. Show how they can adapt sentences to fit their own needs. For example: *On Saturday, Sunday, and Monday, I work from 4:00 A.M. to 3:00 P.M.* can become *On Thursdays and Fridays, I work from 9:00 A.M. to 12:00 P.M.*

- Point out the Writing Note and remind students to check where they put the time expressions in their sentences.

Suggestion

Write and type up a story that contains several errors in the verbs, time expressions, and adverbs of frequency. (*I works on Monday. I don't work in weekends. I go never to work on Sunday.*) Distribute copies and have students correct the errors. Go over the errors and corrections together.

Practicing on Your Own

A. Put the words in the correct order.

Ask students to complete the sentences on their own. Then, have students write the correct answers on the board so you can review them with the class.

B. Read the sentences.

• Read the original sentence and the corrected version aloud. Remind students to write two sentences for each answer–one negative sentence and one affirmative sentence.
• Review the corrected sentences orally with the whole class.

C. There is <u>one</u> mistake in each sentence.

Ask students to correct the errors and check their answers with a partner.

Practicing on Your Own

A. Put the words in the correct order. Write the sentences.
(Placement of time expressions may vary. Suggested answers below.)

1. in the morning / I / drink / orange juice / always
   I always drink orange juice in the morning.

2. every / Mrs. Salerno / her / go / to the bakery / and / daughter / Friday
   Every Friday Mrs. Salerno and her daughter go to the bakery.

3. holidays / to school / don't / the students / on / go
   The students don't go to school on holidays.

4. twice / takes / an / a / she / class / week / English
   She takes an English class twice a week.

5. exercise / gym / to / 6:00 A.M. / they / at / from / 7:30 A.M. / the
   They exercise at the gym from 6:00 A.M. to 7:30 A.M.

B. Read the sentences. Then, correct the information that is not true for you.
(Answers will vary. Sample answers below.)

1. I drink cola for breakfast.
   I don't drink cola for breakfast. I drink milk.

2. I go to work every Sunday.
   I don't go to work every Sunday. I work every weekday.

3. My teacher gives a test every day.
   My teacher doesn't give a test every day. She gives a test once a week.

4. I go to school in the afternoon.
   I don't go to school in the afternoon. I go to school in the evening.

5. I take a long vacation every winter.
   I don't take a long vacation every winter. I take a vacation every summer.

C. There is <u>one</u> mistake in each sentence. Correct the mistakes.

1. He ~~take~~ the bus to school. takes
2. She ~~don't drink~~ coffee in the evening. doesn't drink
3. They ~~eat out never~~ on Monday evenings. never eat out
4. My friends and I always ~~goes~~ to the movies on Saturday nights. go
5. I usually work from 7:00 A.M. ~~at~~ 3:00 P.M. to

Grammar Summary

1. Simple present tense Use the simple present tense to talk about everyday actions. These actions happen every day, every weekend, every year, etc.

2. Statements

I **work** from Monday to Friday.	He **works** from Monday to Friday.
We **study** on Tuesday and Thursday.	She **studies** on Tuesday and Thursday.
You **get** up early.	The train **arrives** on time.
They **drive** to work every day.	

3. Negatives

I **do not work** on Saturday.	I **don't work** on Saturday.
We **do not study** on Wednesday.	We **don't study** on Wednesday.
You **do not get** up early.	You **don't get** up early.
They **do not drive** in the winter.	They **don't drive** in the winter.
He **does not work** on Saturday.	He **doesn't work** on Saturday.
She **does not study** on Wednesday.	She **doesn't study** on Wednesday.
The train **does not stop** here.	The train **doesn't stop** here.

4. Time expressions and *How often . . . ?*

Put these time expressions at the end of the sentence.

How often do you work overtime?	I work overtime **once a month.**
How often do you take the bus?	I take the bus **every morning.**
How often do you go on vacation?	We go on a vacation **every summer.**
How often does she go to the gym?	She goes to the gym **three times a week.**

5. Adverbs of frequency

Adverbs of frequency come <u>before</u> all verbs except the verb *to be.*	Adverbs of frequency come <u>after</u> the verb *to be.*
I **always** go to school.	I am **always** on time.
I **usually** speak English in class.	I am **usually** quiet.
I **sometimes** arrive early.	I am **sometimes** late for work.
I **never** eat breakfast.	I am **never** at home in the afternoon.

A Typical Day **91**

Grammar Summary

• Review the summary with the class. Invite students to make up alternate sentences for each example in the chart. For example, in place of *She **studies** on Tuesday and Thursday,* a student might say *She **works** on Monday and Wednesday.* In place of *How often do you **take** the bus?,* a student might ask *How often do you **drive** to work?*

• See the Grammar Summary Expansion on page 234 for a more complete explanation of these grammar points.

Unit 7
Airport Jobs

Discuss the unit title art. Ask: *What do you see?* (There is a woman flying in the sky and some airplanes flying around her.)

☀ Dictionary:
Jobs at the Airport

📶 A. Listen and repeat.
(CD1, Track 42)

• See how many of the jobs in the pictures students can identify. Ask:

Is this woman a pilot or a caterer?
Is this woman carrying luggage or food?
What is this man doing?

• The first time through, have students listen as you play the audio. The second time through, pause after each job and have students repeat. Have students repeat the names of the airport jobs several times until they seem comfortable pronouncing them.

• Discuss each job in the list. Ask students to define as many of the jobs as they can and give specific examples of the duties it involves. For example:

S1: *The pilot drives the plane. The pilot also manages the other workers on the plane.*

S2: *The caterer makes food for people on planes. The caterer makes thousands of meals every day.*

B. Match the pictures and the airport jobs from the box.

Ask students to complete the matching activity on their own. Then, have them check their answers with a partner.

7 Airport Jobs

☀ Dictionary: Jobs at the Airport

📶 **A. Listen and repeat.**

pilot	caterer	baggage handler
parking lot attendant	flight attendant	air traffic controller
cabin cleaner	ticket agent	aircraft mechanic
security screener	skycap	electric cart driver

B. Match the pictures and the airport jobs from the box.

1. caterer
2. baggage handler
3. electric cart driver
4. pilot
5. ticket agent
6. flight attendant
7. aircraft mechanic
8. parking lot attendant
9. security screener

C. Complete. (Answers may vary. Suggested answers below.)

1. A pilot _____*flies*_____ a plane.
2. A baggage handler _____*puts*_____ luggage on the plane.
3. A security screener _____*checks*_____ passengers and their luggage.
4. An aircraft mechanic _____*repairs*_____ the planes.
5. An electric cart driver _____*helps*_____ people who can't walk far.
6. A flight attendant _____*serves*_____ beverages and meals on a flight.
7. A parking lot attendant _____*collects*_____ parking fees from drivers.
8. A caterer _____*prepares*_____ meals for flights.
9. A ticket agent _____*sells*_____ tickets.
10. An air traffic controller _____*guides*_____ planes in and out of the airport.

repairs
helps
✓ flies
collects
guides
puts
sells
checks
serves
prepares

D. *Who* questions. Answer these questions about airport jobs. (Answers will vary.)

Who flies a plane?	Who repairs the planes?
A pilot does.	An aircraft mechanic does.
Pilots do.	Aircraft mechanics do.

1. Who wears a uniform?
2. Who uses a computer?
3. Who speaks English at work?
4. Who stands all day?
5. Who works outside?
6. Who has an interesting job?
7. Who has a boring job?
8. Who has a dangerous job?
9. Who has a stressful job?
10. Who has a high-paying job?

Write the opposites.

interesting	boring
safe	dangerous
high-paying	low-paying
relaxing	stressful

Airport Jobs   **93**

C. Complete.

Point out the list of present tense verbs at the right. Say the verbs and ask students to repeat. Then complete the sentences with the whole class.

Suggestion

As you go along, ask students to raise their hands if they want some additional help understanding what one of the words means. Define the verb in simple terms and give some additional sample sentences. For example:

S1: *I don't understand* guides.
T: To guide *means to show someone where to go, to give somebody directions. You might guide a new student to the main office. An air traffic controller guides planes.*

D. *Who* questions.

• Read aloud the sample *Who* questions and short answers. Ask students to explain why some answers use *do* and others use *does*. (*Does* is used with words that can take the place of *he, she,* and *it. Do* is used with words that can take the place of *I, you, we,* and *they. A pilot [he] does. Pilots [they] do.*)
• Tell students they can look back at the list of jobs on page 92 to answer these questions. Then read each question and call on different students to answer. There is more than one correct answer for many questions. For example, the answer to the question *Who wears a uniform?* could be pilot, security screener, flight attendant, skycap, and so on. Elicit as many answers as possible for each question.
• Point out the opposites exercise at the right and ask students to complete it on their own. Go over the answers with the whole class.

Active Grammar:
Present Tense
Questions

A. Listen and complete the information about Alberto's job. (CD1, Track 43)

- Invite students to comment on the picture. Ask questions such as:

  Where is this man?
  What is he wearing?
  What is his job?
  What is he doing?

- Play the audio once as students just listen. Then, present the dialogue again and ask students to record their answers. Present the dialogue once more so they can check their own work. Review the correct answers with the whole class.

B. Circle Alberto's answers.

- Ask students to complete the answers on their own. Present the dialogue again if students seem to need additional help. Review answers 1–5 with the whole class.
- Ask students to write three more questions and answers on their own and then check their work with a partner. Call on different students to read a question and answer to the class.

Suggestion

Write examples of useful new questions students came up with and answers on the board and invite the rest of the class to copy them into their notebooks.

C. Match.

Students complete the matching activity individually and then practice the conversation with a partner.

Active Grammar: Present Tense Questions

A. Listen and complete the information about Alberto's job.

Airport:	Atlanta Airport
Job:	Mechanic
Days:	Wednesday to Sunday
Hours:	5 A.M. to 1 P.M.
Overtime:	(Yes) No
Uniform:	(Yes) No

B. Circle Alberto's answers. Then, write three more questions and answers.

1. Do you work at JFK Airport?   Yes, I do.   (No, I don't.)
2. Do you work at Atlanta Airport?   (Yes, I do.)   No, I don't.
3. Are you a pilot?   Yes, I am.   (No, I'm not.)
4. Do you work on Monday?   Yes, I do.   (No, I don't.)
5. Do you work on weekends?   (Yes, I do.)   No, I don't.
6. Do __(Answers will vary.)_____? _____
7. _____? _____
8. _____? _____

C. Match. Then, read the conversation with a partner.

1. Where do you work? — I work from Wednesday to Sunday.
2. What do you do? — Yes, I put in a lot of overtime.
3. What's your schedule? — I work at Atlanta Airport.
4. Do you work overtime? — Yes, I do.
5. Do you wear a uniform? — I'm a mechanic.
6. Do you like your job? — Yes. I wear a blue uniform.

Audio Script

A. Listen and complete the information about Alberto's job. (CD1, Track 43)

A: Alberto, where do you work?
B: I work at Atlanta Airport.
A: What do you do?
B: I'm a mechanic. I repair passenger planes and cargo planes.
A: What's your schedule?
B: I work from Wednesday to Sunday, from 5:00 A.M. to 1:00 P.M.

A: You get up early! Do you work overtime?
B: Oh, yes. I put in lots of overtime.
A: Do you wear a uniform?
B: Yes, we all wear company uniform: blue pants and a blue shirt.
A: Do you like your job?
B: Yes, I do. I like it a lot.

D. Read.

Ellen is a flight attendant. She works for Dove Airlines. She works at the Denver Airport. She makes passengers comfortable. She serves beverages and meals on the plane. She gives safety instructions. Ellen usually works from Monday to Thursday. Her schedule is from 7:00 A.M. to 4:00 P.M. But there are often delays, so sometimes she works from 7:00 A.M. to 7:00 P.M. She usually flies from Denver to Seattle. Ellen has a stressful job, but she likes her job a lot.

E. Circle. Then, write three more questions and answers.

1. Does Ellen work at Denver Airport? (Yes, she does.) No, she doesn't.
2. Is she a pilot? Yes, she is. (No, she isn't.)
3. Does she work for Universal Airlines? Yes, she does. (No, she doesn't.)
4. Does she work on the weekends? Yes, she does. (No, she doesn't.)
5. Does she fly from Denver to Miami? Yes, she does. (No, she doesn't.)
6. Does _she serve beverages on the plane_ ? _Yes, she does._
7. _Does she work on Fridays_ ? _No, she doesn't_
8. _Does Ellen like her job_ ? _Yes, she does._

(Questions may vary. Sample questions above.)

F. Listen and complete. Then, answer the questions.

1. Where _does_ Ellen _work_ ?
2. What _does_ she _do_ ?
3. What airline _does she work_ for?
4. What _'s_ her schedule?
5. _Does she work_ on weekends?
6. What route _does she fly_ ?
7. _Does she like_ her job?

Audio Script

F. Listen and complete. Then, answer the questions. (CD1, Track 44)

1. Where does Ellen work?
2. What does she do?
3. What airline does she work for?
4. What's her schedule?
5. Does she work on the weekends?
6. What route does she fly?
7. Does she like her job?

D. Read.

- Invite students to comment on the picture. Ask questions such as:

  Where is this woman?
  What is she wearing?
  What's her job?
  What is she doing?

- Have students read the passage silently. Answer any questions they may have.

E. Circle.

- Students complete the answers on their own. Review answers 1–5 with the whole class.
- Students write three more questions and check their work with a partner. Call on different students to read a question and answer to the class.

F. Listen and complete. (CD1, Track 44)

- Before playing the audio, ask student to guess what the missing words might be. Give them one or two tries on each sentence and then go on. Explain that they will hear the answers on the audio.
- Play the audio and have students fill in the missing words. Repeat the presentation as many times as necessary. Have students write the completed sentences on the board so you can review the correct answers with the class.

G. Circle.

Have students complete the
exercise on their own. Review
the correct answers with
the class.

H. Complete this conversation.

Ask students to fill in the blanks
individually. Check the correct
answers with the whole class.

Suggestion

Have students use the dialogue for
conversation practice with a partner.

I. Ask and answer questions about these employees.

• Review the names of the jobs
in the pictures by asking different students to identify each one.
• Suggest that students use the
dialogues in Exercise H as models as they make up questions
and answers about the people
in the pictures. Begin by doing
the activity with the whole class.
Write key questions and answers
on the board.
• Divide the class into groups of
three students. Ask one student
to be the employee in the first
picture, and have the rest of the
group ask him or her questions.
Change roles so that all three
students get a chance to ask and
answer questions.

G. Circle.

A: What **do** / **does** your sister **do** / **does** ?

B: She's an air traffic controller.

A: Where **do** / **does** she **work** / **works** ?

B: She **work** / **works** at Logan Airport.

A: What airline **do** / **does** she **work** / **works** for?

B: She doesn't work for an airline. She **work** / **works** for the airport.

H. Complete this conversation.

A: Where _____ does _____ your brother _____ work _____ ?

B: He works at Logan Airport.

A: What _____ does _____ he _____ do _____ ?

B: He's a skycap.

A: _____ Does _____ he wear a uniform?

B: Yes, he does.

A: Which airline _____ does _____ he _____ work _____ for?

B: He works for World Airlines.

A: How much _____ does _____ he _____ make _____ an hour?

B: He makes $8 an hour plus tips.

I. Ask and answer questions about these employees. (Questions and answers will vary.)

1.

2.

3.

4.

Looking at the Classified Ads

A. Match.

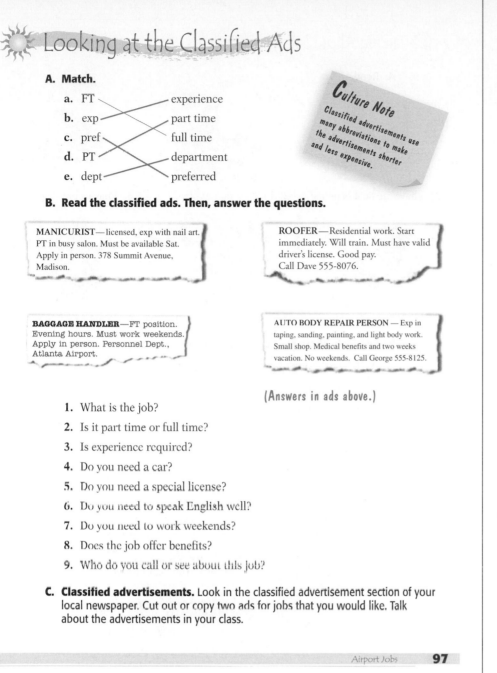

a. FT
b. exp
c. pref
d. PT
e. dept

experience
part time
full time
department
preferred

Culture Note
Classified advertisements use many abbreviations to make the advertisements shorter and less expensive.

B. Read the classified ads. Then, answer the questions.

MANICURIST—licensed, exp with nail art. PT in busy salon. Must be available Sat. Apply in person. 378 Summit Avenue, Madison.

ROOFER—Residential work. Start immediately. Will train. Must have valid driver's license. Good pay. Call Dave 555-8076.

BAGGAGE HANDLER—FT position. Evening hours. Must work weekends. Apply in person. Personnel Dept., Atlanta Airport.

AUTO BODY REPAIR PERSON — Exp in taping, sanding, painting, and light body work. Small shop. Medical benefits and two weeks vacation. No weekends. Call George 555-8125.

(Answers in ads above.)

1. What is the job?
2. Is it part time or full time?
3. Is experience required?
4. Do you need a car?
5. Do you need a special license?
6. Do you need to speak English well?
7. Do you need to work weekends?
8. Does the job offer benefits?
9. Who do you call or see about this job?

C. Classified advertisements.
Look in the classified advertisement section of your local newspaper. Cut out or copy two ads for jobs that you would like. Talk about the advertisements in your class.

Looking at Classified Ads

A. Match.

Have students make the matches on their own. Answer any questions students may have.

B. Read the classified ads.

• Begin by reading through the list of questions with the class. Explain any questions students don't understand.
• Work with each ad separately. Begin by saying the name of the job and any other new words in the ad and asking students to repeat. Provide pronunciation practice as needed. For example, in the first ad you might focus on the words *manicurist, licensed, salon,* and *available*. Explain the meaning of any new words students don't understand.
• Go through the ads one at a time, calling on different students to answer each of the questions in the list.

C. Classified advertisements.

• Ask students to find ads for jobs that they might actually be able to get some day. Suggest that that use the questions in Exercise B to prepare to talk about the jobs in class.
• During class, ask students to read the ads and then give as much information as they can about the job in their own words. Invite students to ask questions about each job.
• Collect the job ads that students have brought to class a make a handout with six or seven of the ads.

☀ Talking About Salary and Benefits

A. Read.

Point to each picture and read the sentence below it aloud. Ask students to repeat the sentences.

Suggestion

Focus on the pronunciation of the benefit programs. Write key words on the board using capital letters to point out the stressed syllables. For example:

DEN tal plan,
pre SCRIP tion plan,
re TIRE ment plan.

B. Complete about your benefits.

• Ask students to complete the exercise using information about their own current jobs. If a student isn't working at the moment, have him or her use information about a past job.
• Conduct a whole-class discussion.

Suggestion

Read and discuss the Culture Note with the class. If several students are working at different places, help them make a chart on the board comparing the benefit programs at the various companies.

☀ Talking About Salary and Benefits

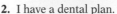

A. Read.

1. I have medical benefits. **2.** I have a dental plan. **3.** I have a prescription plan.

4. I have five sick days. **5.** I have two weeks' vacation. **6.** I have a retirement plan.

B. Complete about your benefits. (Answers will vary.)

1. I **have / don't have** medical benefits.
2. I **have / don't have** a dental plan.
3. I **have / don't have** a prescription plan.
4. I have _____ sick days.
5. I have _____ weeks' vacation.
6. I also have _____.

> ### Culture Note
>
> Many companies pay overtime. Sometimes the overtime pay is two or three dollars more per hour. In some companies, overtime pay is time and a half. For example, if your salary is $10 an hour, overtime pay is $15 an hour.
>
> Many companies pay double time for work on national holidays. What is your company's policy for overtime and holiday pay?

Audio Script

(Refer to page 99, Exercise C.)

C. Listen and write the salary and benefits.
(CD1, Tracks 45, 46, 47, 48)

Karina (Track 45)
Manager: Your salary is $8 an hour. Overtime pay is $10 an hour.
Karina: What are the benefits?
Manager: You have medical benefits after six months. You have three sick days and one week vacation the first year.

Mohammed (Track 46)
Mohammed: What is the salary?
Manager: The salary is $6 an hour plus tips.

Mohammed: And the benefits?
Manager: For part-time employees, there are no benefits.

Li-Ping (Track 47)
Manager: The starting salary is $9 an hour.
Li-Ping: And the overtime pay?
Manager: The overtime pay is the same, $9 an hour.
Li-Ping: Are there medical benefits?
Manager: Yes, there are medical benefits and a prescription plan. You have two sick days and two weeks' vacation.

(Continued on page 99.)

C. Listen and write the salary and benefits.

Employee	Salary	Overtime	Medical benefits	Dental plan	Sick days	Vacation
Karina	$8	$10	After 6 months		3	1 week
Mohamed	$6 plus tips		No	No	No	No
Li-Ping	$9	$9	Yes and prescription plan		2	2 weeks
Juan	$14/$16		Yes and prescription plan	Yes	5	2 weeks 3 weeks

D. Ask and answer questions about the chart above.

1. What is _____'s salary?

2. How much is his/her overtime pay?

3. Does she have medical benefits / a dental plan / a prescription plan?

4. How many sick days does he/she have?

5. How many weeks' vacation does he/she get?

Working Together: Student to Student

A. STUDENT A: Ask your partner about Lena's job.

STUDENT B: Turn to page 100.

Job: Ticket agent

Airport: San Jose Airport

Days: Tuesday to Saturday

Hours: 6:00 A.M. to 2:00 P.M.

Salary: $600 a week

Medical benefits: (Yes)   No

Dental plan: Yes   (No)

Sick days: 7 days

Vacation: 2 weeks

> What does Lena do?
> Where does she work?
> What days does she work?
> What's her schedule?
> What's her salary?
> Does she have _____ ?

Airport Jobs   **99**

• Explain that students will hear a conversation about the salary and benefits of four workers. Play the part of the audio (or read the Audio Script) that describes Karina's situation. Point out the answers in the chart.

• Present the rest of the information about Mohamed, Li-Ping, and Juan and have students fill in the chart on their own. Play the audio several times if necessary.

D. Ask and answer questions about the chart above.

This exercise can be used to check students' answers to Exercise C and also provides oral practice. Call on different students to answer each of the questions.

Working Together: Student to Student

A. Student A.

• Read the instructions. Point out the model language in the box. Explain that Student A can use these questions to find out the necessary information. Student A then writes the answers in the blanks on this page. Move around the class and help students with this activity. Be sure that Student B is looking at page 100.

• When Student A finishes, the pair can change roles and repeat the activity.

(Continued from page 98.)

Juan (Track 48)

Manager: The salary is $14 an hour. After six months, it's $16 an hour.

Juan: And the benefits?

Manager: We have a good benefit package here. There's medical and dental and prescription. You have five sick days and two weeks' vacation the first year. The second year, you have three weeks vacation.

Working Together: Student to Student

B. Student B.

These are the answers to Student A's questions.

Suggestion

If the class is small, tape record or videotape pairs of students as they interview each other. Play the tapes back privately for each pair and have them make suggestions for improving their own work and the other person's work. If the class is large, have students tape record or videotape their conversations outside of class and bring in the tapes on the next class meeting. Give the students feedback on the interviews.

Interview.

Ask students to form groups of three to complete this activity. As they work, move from group to group, checking their progress and offering help as needed.

Teacher Note

Have the students read the Culture Note. Ask students what other kinds of information they think people in the United States don't like to share in public (their ages, how much rent they pay, how much money they have in the bank, etc.).

Working Together: Student to Student

B. STUDENT B: Answer your partner's questions about Lena's job.

Job:	Ticket agent
Airport:	San Jose Airport
Days:	Tuesday to Saturday
Hours:	6:00 A.M. to 2:00 P.M.
Salary:	$600 a week
Medical benefits:	(Yes) No
Dental plan:	Yes (No)
Sick days:	__7__ days
Vacation:	__2__ weeks

Culture Note

In the United States, people consider it impolite to ask their friends or co-workers about their salaries.

Interview. Sit in a group of three students. Ask your partners about their jobs or the jobs they would like to have.

(Questions and answers may vary. Sample questions below.)

Questions	Student 1	Student 2
Where do you work?		
What do you do?		
How many days a week do you work?		
What hours do you work?		
Do you ever work overtime?		
Do you speak English at work?		
Do _you wear_ a uniform?		
Do _you have medical benefits_ ?		
Do you have a vacation ?		

C. Work facts. These statements are true about work in the United States. Check the statements that are true about your country. Sit in a group and discuss your responses. (Answers will vary.)

1. ☐ Full-time work is between 35 and 40 hours a week.

2. ☐ Most people drive to work.

3. ☐ There is a minimum wage.

4. ☐ Most full-time workers receive medical benefits.

5. ☐ Many high school students have part-time jobs.

6. ☐ 75% of women with children work outside the home.

7. ☐ Men and women sometimes receive the same salary for the same work.

8. ☐ Most service workers wear uniforms.

9. ☐ The standard retirement age is 67.

10. ☐ Most companies offer retirement plans.

D. Pronunciation: *Does he / Does she.*

Listen and repeat.

1. a. Does he work at the airport?   b. Does she work at the airport?

2. a. Does he like his job?   b. Does she like her job?

3. a. Does he wear a uniform?   b. Does she wear a uniform?

Listen and complete.

1. Does _____she_____ work full time?

2. Does _____he_____ work on weekends?

3. Does _____she_____ use a computer at work?

4. Does _____he_____ speak English at work?

5. Does _____he_____ need a driver's license?

6. Does _____she_____ get good benefits?

7. Does _____he_____ have a dental plan?

Practice the sentences above with a partner.

Audio Script

Listen and complete. (CD1, Track 50)

1. Does she work full time?
2. Does he work on weekends?
3. Does she use a computer at work?
4. Does he speak English at work?
5. Does he need a driver's license?
6. Does she get good benefits?
7. Does he have a dental plan?

C. Work facts.

- As students discuss the statements, ask them to make notes about important differences between work in the United States and work in their home countries.
- Conduct a whole-class discussion about the differences students have discovered. Write some statements about important differences on the board. For example: *In China, most people ride bicycles to work. In Japan, everyone receives medical benefits, not just workers.*

D. Pronunciation: *Does he / Does she.* (CD1, Track 49)

- Demonstrate the pronunciation of *Does he*. Point out that the *h* sound is dropped and that the letter *s* at the end of *does* sounds like a *z*. (*does he = duzee*)
- Demonstrate the pronunciation of *Does she*. Point out that the *s* at the end of *does* is dropped and that the two words are connected together. (*does she = dushee*)
- Have students just listen as you play the audio. The second time through, pause after each line and ask students to repeat. Do the repetition step several times.

Listen and complete. (CD1, Track 50)

Play the audio and have students fill in *he* or *she*. Review the correct answers with the whole class.

Practice the sentences above with a partner.

After students have practiced the sentences, call on volunteers to demonstrate the correct pronunciation to the class.

A. Listen. (CD1, Track 51)

• Ask questions about the people in the big picture:

Who are these two people?
Where are they?
What are they doing?
Which person is nervous?
Why?

Accept all reasonable responses and rephrase one-word answers or incomplete sentences into full-sentence form.
• Play the audio once or twice. Then, ask students more questions about the picture. For example:

What is his/her name?
What is his/her job right now?
When did Mr. Chan start to work at the airport?

B. Answer.

Point out the sample answers. Then ask the questions and call on individuals to answer.

Suggestion

Divide the class into small groups and have students take turns asking other group members the questions. Suggest that they ask the questions in random order. If appropriate for your class, invite students to make up some original questions to ask other people in their group.

The Big Picture: The Interview

A. Listen. Mr. Chan is in the personnel office of a major airport. He is applying for a position as an electric cart driver.

B. Answer.

> Yes, he does.
> No, he doesn't.

1. Does Mr. Chan work at the airport now?	Yes, he does.
2. Does he drive an electric cart?	No, he doesn't.
3. Does he make $8 an hour?	Yes, he does.
4. Does he have any violations on his license?	No, he doesn't.
5. Does he have a good letter of reference?	Yes, he does.
6. Does he have experience with elderly people?	Yes, he does.
7. Does he have medical benefits now?	Yes, he does.
8. Does he have a dental plan now?	No, he doesn't.
9. Does he speak English well?	Yes, he does.
10. Does he have the new job?	No, he doesn't.

102 UNIT 7

Audio Script

A. Listen. (CD1, Track 51)

Mr. Chan is in the personnel office of a major airport. He is applying for a position as an electric cart driver. An electric cart driver assists elderly passengers or passengers who need assitance.

A: Good morning, Mr. Chan. I'm Ms. Ross.
B: Good morning, Ms. Ross.
A: Mr. Chan, I have your application in front of me. I see that you work at the airport now. You are a parking lot attendant.

B: Yes, Ms. Ross. I collect tolls. Sometimes I help passengers find their cars.
A: And why are you interested in a job as an electric cart driver?
B: I started to work at the airport two years ago. I didn't speak much English. Now, I speak English much better. This job is a promotion for me. I make eight dollars an hour now. The salary for this job is one dollar more an hour.
A: Do you have a driver's license?
B: Yes.

(Continued on page 103.)

C. Complete with the interview vocabulary.

position	recommendation	available
personnel	✓interview	benefits
applicants	promotion	experience

Mr. Chan is on an _____interview_____ with Ms. Ross, the director of _____personnel_____. He is applying for a _____position_____ as an electric cart driver. This job would be a _____promotion_____ for him because the salary is higher and the job has more responsibility. Mr. Chan knows he has a good chance to get the job. He has a good letter of _____reference_____ from his supervisor. He has _____experience_____ with people in wheelchairs. He is _____available_____ to work any hours. Mr. Chan would like this job because the salary is higher and it offers more _____benefits_____ than his current job. Ms. Ross is going to interview two more _____applicants_____. After that, she will call Mr. Chan.

D. Complete these questions about Mr. Chan.

(Answers may vary. Sample answers below.)

1. Where _does he work_ ?   At the airport.
2. What _does he do_ ?   He's a parking lot attendant.
3. Why _does he want this job_ ?   Because the salary is higher.
4. What benefits _does he receive_ ?   He receives medical benefits.
5. How much vacation _does he have_ ?   Two weeks.

E. Interview. Sit with a partner. Write a job interview. One student is the personnel director and the other student is the applicant. Use these questions to help you.

1. What do you do now? What are your responsibilities?
2. Why do you want this job?
3. Do you have any experience? Do you have a license or special training?
4. Can you _____?

(Examples: drive/speak English/type/work on weekends)

(Continued from page 102.)

A: Do you have any tickets? Any accidents?
B: No, I don't. I have a clean driving record.
A: You have a good letter of recommendation from your supervisor. When are you available to work?
B: I can work any hours.
A: Many of the passengers who need assistance are elderly. Do you have any experience with older people?
B: Yes. My grandfather is in a wheelchair. I often help him. I'm a friendly person and comfortable with everyone.

A: Do you have any questions?
B: Do I receive the same benefits?
A: You still get medical benefits. But in this job you also have a prescription plan. Your vacation is the same, two weeks. Anything else?
B: No, that's all.
A: I'm going to interview two more applicants. I will call you on Friday about the position.
B: Thank you for the interview, Ms. Ross.

C. Complete with the interview vocabulary.

• Ask students to complete as many of the fill-ins as they can individually. Then, have them work with a partner to complete the rest.
• Read the completed passage to the class so students can check their answers. Invite them to ask about any words or sentences they don't understand. Help them use context clues to guess the meaning of words such as *director, responsibility,* and *current.*

D. Complete these questions about Mr. Chan.

Have students complete the questions with a partner. Review the correct answers with the class. Then, ask pairs to use the questions and answers for conversation practice.

E. Interview.

• Read and discuss the instructions. Then, ask students to read through the questions and ask about anything they don't understand. Ask students to write down in their interviews specific examples of *licenses* (driver's license, chauffeur's license, etc.) and *special training* (a word-processing class, a cooking class, etc.).
• As the pairs write their interviews, move around the room offering support as needed.

Suggestion

Ask different pairs to act out their interviews for the class. After each pair speaks, write two sentences from their dialogue on the board. The sentences should have no errors. Ask the class to repeat the sentences.

☀ Reading:
A Job Posting

A. Before You Read.

• Ask students where they can learn about job openings (on bulletin boards at work, in company publications, from friends who work for a certain company, in newspapers, etc.).

• Read through the job posting with students. As you go along, pause and discuss any new words or expressions that students might not know. For example: *ramp, load, unload, GED, repetitively, shifts, authorized, personal days, resume,* and *reference*. Ask students to repeat the words and explain in their own words what each one means, if possible. If no one knows a particular word, provide your own definition and examples.

B. Circle *True* or *False.*

Ask students to complete the exercise on their own. Then, review the answers with the whole class. For any items that several students missed, help them locate the phrase that contains the correct answer.

☀ Reading: A Job Posting

A. Before You Read.

Where can you find job postings?

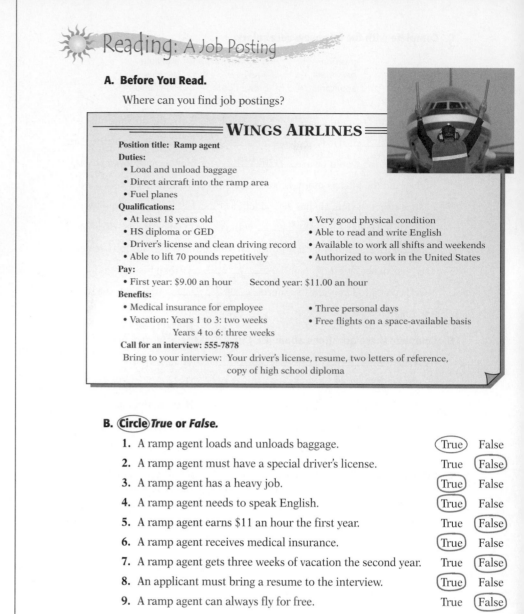

WINGS AIRLINES

Position title: Ramp agent
Duties:
• Load and unload baggage
• Direct aircraft into the ramp area
• Fuel planes

Qualifications:
• At least 18 years old
• HS diploma or GED
• Driver's license and clean driving record
• Able to lift 70 pounds repetitively

• Very good physical condition
• Able to read and write English
• Available to work all shifts and weekends
• Authorized to work in the United States

Pay:
• First year: $9.00 an hour   Second year: $11.00 an hour

Benefits:
• Medical insurance for employee
• Vacation: Years 1 to 3: two weeks
              Years 4 to 6: three weeks

• Three personal days
• Free flights on a space-available basis

Call for an interview: 555-7878

Bring to your interview: Your driver's license, resume, two letters of reference,
                          copy of high school diploma

B. Circle *True* or *False.*

1. A ramp agent loads and unloads baggage. — (True) False
2. A ramp agent must have a special driver's license. — True (False)
3. A ramp agent has a heavy job. — (True) False
4. A ramp agent needs to speak English. — (True) False
5. A ramp agent earns $11 an hour the first year. — True (False)
6. A ramp agent receives medical insurance. — (True) False
7. A ramp agent gets three weeks of vacation the second year. — True (False)
8. An applicant must bring a resume to the interview. — (True) False
9. A ramp agent can always fly for free. — True (False)

☼ Writing Our Stories: My Job

A. Read.

My name is Nelson. I'm a security screener at New Orleans Airport. I sit at the scanner. I check people when they walk through the gate. If there is a problem, I call my supervisor. I work full time. My schedule is always different. I work different days each week. I usually work in the afternoon and in the evening. I don't have good medical benefits. I have five sick days and two weeks' vacation. I like my job at the airport. It is busy and exciting. There are many jobs here. I hope to get a promotion in the future.

B. Write. Complete this information about your job. Write a few more sentences about your work. (Answers will vary.)

I am a _____ at _____ .
              position   company

I _____ and _____ .
        responsibility   responsibility

I work _____ . I work from _____ to _____ ,
       full time / part time   day   day

from _____ to _____ . I _____
      time   time   have / don't have

good job benefits. I have _____
                             benefits

_____

_____

_____

_____

_____

Writing Note

Use a colon when you write the time: 6:00, 4:30.

You can use capital or lowercase letters for A.M. and P.M.: 6:00 A.M. or 6:00 a.m.

☼ Writing Our Stories: My Job

A. Read.

Ask students to read the story all the way through without stopping. Then, read the story aloud to the students. Ask: *Do you have any questions about the story?*

B. Write.

• Students fill in the blanks and write several of their own sentences at the end. They can use Exercise A as a model.
• Review students' writing and copy on the board some of the original sentences they wrote at the end of their stories. Ask other students to read these sentences aloud.

Suggestion

Have students copy some of the sentences from the board into their notebooks. Draw students' attention to the Writing Note if they need a review of how to punctuate time in their writing. For homework, they can rewrite these sentences to fit their own stories.

Practicing on Your Own

A. Complete with *Do* or *Does*.

Students write the answers and check their work with a partner.

B. Read this story.

• Read the story aloud to the class and invite students to ask about anything they don't understand. Then, have them complete the questions on their own.

• Review the correct answers by having different students put one sentence each on the board. Elicit several possible questions for items 7 and 8.

Practicing on Your Own

A. Complete with *Do* or *Does*. Write the short answer. (Responses may vary.)

1. __Do__ pilots travel a lot? Yes, they do.
2. __Does__ an air traffic controller have a stressful jobs? Yes, he/she does.
3. __Do__ many flight attendants speak two languages? Yes, they do.
4. __Does__ a baggage handler lift heavy bags and boxes? Yes, he/she does.
5. __Does__ a personnel director interview job applicants? Yes, he/she does.
6. __Do__ ticket agents stand all day? Yes, they do.
7. __Do__ passengers often wait many hours in airports? Yes, they do.
8. __Does__ a passenger need ID in an airport? Yes, he/she does.
9. __Do__ all airport employees speak English? No, they don't.
10. __Does__ an aircraft mechanic need special training? Yes, he/she does.

B. Read this story. Then, complete the questions.

Jeff Miller is a pilot. He lives in Boston and works at Logan Airport. He flies international routes, usually from Boston to London. He works four days a week. On Monday, he flies from Boston to London. He stays overnight in London. Then, he flies back on Tuesday. He has two days off, and then he repeats this schedule on Friday and Saturday. Jeff earns about $150,000 a year and he has excellent benefits. He loves to fly, and he travels all over the world. He doesn't like the headaches at the airport. Air traffic is always heavy, and there are often long delays. His days are often 10 to 12 hours long.

1. What _does Jeff Miller do_ ? He's a pilot.
2. Where _does he work_ ? At Logan Airport.
3. What route _does he fly_ ? From Boston to London.
4. How many days _does he work_ ? Four.
5. How much _does he earn_ ? $150,000 a year.
6. _Where does he travel_ ? All over the world.

(Answers for 7 and 8 may vary.)

7. _Does he like to fly_ ? Yes, he does.
8. _Does he like air traffic and long delays_ ? No, he doesn't.

Looking at Numbers: Salaries

A. Figure out the salaries.

1. Kathy works part time. She makes $8 an hour. She works 20 hours a week. What is her salary? **$160 a week**

2. Ivan works 25 hours a week. His earns $11 an hour. What is his salary? **$275 a week**

3. Vinh works full time, 40 hours a week. His salary is $15 an hour. What is his weekly salary? **$600 a week**

4. Dorota works full time. She makes $10 an hour. She makes $14 an hour overtime. She usually works 50 hours a week. What is her salary? **$540 a week**

5. Roya likes to work holidays because she makes double time. She makes $14 an hour. If she works eight hours on Thanksgiving, what is her pay for that day? **$224 for that day**

6. Mustafa works 40 hours a week, plus eight hours on Sunday. His salary is $12 an hour plus time and a half for Sunday. What is his weekly salary? **$624 a week**

Grammar Summary

▶ **1. Yes/No questions**

Do I work?	Yes, you do.	No, you don't.
Do you work?	Yes, I do.	No, I don't.
Do we work?	Yes, you do.	No, you don't.
Do they work?	Yes, they do.	No, they don't.
Does he work?	Yes, he does.	No, he doesn't.
Does she work?	Yes, she does.	No, she doesn't.
Does it work?	Yes, it does.	No, it doesn't.

▶ **2. Wh- questions**

Where do I work?	**Where** does he work?
When do you work?	**When** does she work?
What hours do we work?	**Why** does it work?
What days do they work?	

▶ **3. Who questions (Who as subject)**

Who works full time?	Alberto does.	Alberto and Ela do.

Looking at Numbers: Salaries

A. Figure out the salaries.

- Demonstrate how to figure out Kathy's salary. Write on the board *8 × 20 = 160. $8 (an hour) × 20 (hours a week) = $160 a week.*

- Ask students to complete the activity with a partner. As they work, walk around the classroom and check students' work.

- Have a different student write the math they used to figure out each payment on the board. Then have the class check their own answers.

Grammar Summary

- Review the summary with the class. Point out the special meaning for the question *Does it work?* We use this question to ask about whether or not a machine, such as a refrigerator or a car, is in good condition. For example:

A: That's a big air conditioner. Does it work?
B: No, it doesn't. It's broken.
A: Does your computer work?
B: Yes, it does. I just got it fixed.

- See the Grammar Summary Expansion on page 235 for a more complete explanation of these grammar points.

Unit 8
A College Campus

Discuss the unit title art. Ask: *What do you see?* (There is a person wearing a cap and gown. He or she is holding a diploma. The person is graduating from college.)

☀ Dictionary:
The Campus

📢 A. Listen and repeat.
(CD1, Track 52)

- Talk about the picture with the class. Encourage them to name the things they see and tell what the various people are doing. Ask questions such as:

> *What's this?*
> *What are these?*
> *What is he/she doing?*
> *Where are they going?*

- Have students just listen the first time through. The second time through, have them point to the item in the picture as they hear the word. Pause and point out any items students are not sure of. The third time through, ask students to repeat each word. You can repeat this last step several times.

B. Label each person, place, or thing on the campus.

If students seem to have a good grasp of the new words, have them label the items on their own. If not, say each word, have the class repeat, and then do the labeling activity together.

Suggestion

Have groups of students collaborate in making similar maps of their own campus or the area around their own school building. Have a representative from each group display the map and describe it to the rest of the class.

---

8 A College Campus

☀ Dictionary: The Campus

📢 A. Listen and repeat.

benches	mailbox	lights
garbage cans	bus stop	statue
dogs	students	security guards
cars	pay telephone	security booth
flag	parking lot	

B. Label each person, place, or thing on the campus.

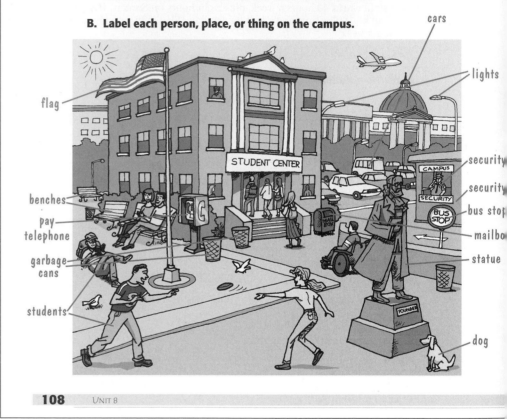

STUDENT CENTER

cars
lights
flag
security
security
bus stop
mailbo
statue
benches
pay telephone
garbage cans
students
dog

Active Grammar: *There is/There are*

A. Listen and complete with *Is* or *are* and a quantity expression. (Answers may vary.)

a	a few	several	some	a lot of	many	any

1. There ___are___ ___a few___ benches outside.

2. There ___are___ ___many___ students outside the building.

3. There ___is___ ___a___ statue in front of the building.

4. There ___are___ ___several___ garbage cans outside.

5. There ___is___ ___a___ pay telephone next to the building.

6. There ___is___ ___a___ bus at the bus stop.

7. There ___are___ ___a lot of___ cars in the parking lot.

8. There ___aren't___ ___any___ students at the bus stop.

a few	a small number, for example, three or four
several	more than a few, for example, five, or six, or seven

B. Write seven sentences about your classroom. Do not use a number. Use a quantity expression.

C. *How many* questions. Ask and answer questions about the picture on page 108.

How many flags are there?	There is one.
How many cars are in the parking lot?	There are a lot.
How many trees are next to the building?	There aren't any.

(Answers may vary.)

1. How many students are outside the building? There are a lot. There are ten.

2. How many dogs are outside? (1) There is one.

3. How many mailboxes are next to the building? (1)

4. How many cars are in front of the building? (0)

5. How many windows are in the building? We can see 20 windows.

6. How many security guards are in the booth ?

7. How many flags are on the campus ?

8. How many lights are in the parking lot ?

A College Campus **109**

Audio Script

A. Listen and complete with *is* or *are* and a quantity expression. (CD1, Track 53)

1. There are a few benches outside.
2. There are many students outside the building.
3. There is a statue in front of the building.
4. There are several garbage cans outside.
5. There is a pay telephone next to the building.
6. There isn't a bus at the bus stop.
7. There are a lot of cars in the parking lot.
8. There aren't any students at the bus stop.

Active Grammar:
There is/There are

A. Listen and complete with *is* or *are* and a quantity expression. (CD1, Track 53)

- Use the explanations in the box at the right as you review the meaning of the six quantity expressions. Help students understand that *a lot of* and *many* have very similar meanings. Tell students that *any* is used in questions and in negative statements.
- The first time you play the audio, pause after each expression and have students fill in the answers. The second time through, pause after each sentence and ask a student to repeat the expression.

B. Write seven sentences about your classroom.

- Students write sentences in pairs. Ask them to use a different quantity expression in each sentence.
- Review the sentences with the whole class by calling on several pairs to read aloud the sentences they wrote for *a*, for *a few*, and the like.

C. *How many* questions.

- Read and discuss the instructions and the sample questions and answers. Answer any questions students may have.
- Call on one student to read (or complete) each question and another to answer the question.

Teacher's Guide, Unit 8 **109**

D. Is there . . . ? / Are there . . . ?

Ask each sample question and call on a student to give the true answer. Then, call on students at random to answer the rest of the questions.

Suggestion

Have the class repeat each correct response. If a student makes a mistake, explain why the first response was wrong and help the student find the correct response. Then, ask the class to repeat the correct response.

E. With a partner, write five more questions about your classroom or your building.

Discuss the instructions and make sure students know how to proceed. As they work, move from group to group checking for accuracy and helping as needed.

F. Polite questions.

• Point out the picture and ask students to look at the list of eight items and say which one the picture applies to (Number 6). Discuss what *broke your foot* means. Answer any other questions students may have.

• As you complete this activity with the whole class, encourage students to find several possible questions for each situation. For example:

T: *You would like something to eat.*

S1: *Is there a snack bar in this building?*

S2: *Are there any restaurants near here?*

S3: *Are there any vending machines on this floor?*

D. Is there . . . ? / Are there . . . ? Answer these questions about your classroom or your building. (Answers will vary.)

> Is there a television in your classroom?
> Yes, there is.
> No, there isn't.

> Are there any maps on the walls?
> Yes, there are.
> No, there aren't.

1. Is there a television in your classroom?
2. Are there any computers in your classroom?
3. Is there a world map in your classroom?
4. Is there a map of the United States in your classroom?
5. Is there a pencil sharpener in your classroom?
6. Are there any restrooms on your floor?
7. Are there any escalators in your building?
8. Is there an elevator in your building?
9. Are there any computer labs in your building?
10. Are there any vending machines in your building?

E. With a partner, write five more questions about your classroom or your building. Then, combine groups and ask other students your questions.

F. **Polite questions.** Read the situations. Ask questions with *Is there* or *Are there*.

> You need to make a telephone call.
> Is there a public telephone in this building?

(Questions may vary.)
1. You want to mail a letter.
   Is there a mailbox?
2. You need to wash your hands.
   Is there a bathroom?
3. You want to sharpen your pencil.
   Is there a pencil sharpener?
4. You would like a drink of water.
   Is there a water fountain?
5. You need to make a copy of a paper.
   Is there a copy machine?
6. You broke your foot and you can't walk up the stairs.
   Is there an elevator?
7. You would like a can of soda.
   Are there vending machines?
8. You would like something to eat.
   Is there a cafeteria or restaurant?

G. College information. Complete these questions.

1. There are many colleges in the United States.

   A: How many <u>colleges are there in the United States</u>?

   B: There are more than 4,000 colleges in the United States.

2. There are many four-year colleges in the United States.

   A: How many <u>four-year colleges are there in the United States</u>?

   B: There are about 2,300 four-year colleges in the United States.

3. There are many two-year colleges in the United States.

   A: How many <u>two-year colleges are there in the United States</u>?

   B: There are more than 1,700 two-year colleges in the United States.

4. There are many colleges in California.

   A: How many <u>colleges are there in California</u>?

   B: There are about 400 colleges in California.

5. There are not many colleges in Alaska.

   A: How many <u>colleges are there in Alaska</u>?

   B: There are eight colleges in Alaska.

6. There are many students in college in the United States.

   A: How many <u>students are there in college in the United States</u>?

   B: There are about 15 million students in college.

7. There are many women in college in the United States.

   A: How many <u>women are there in college in the United States</u>?

   B: There are about 8,500,000 women in college.

College Information

How many colleges are there in your state?
Name four colleges in your state.
Which college is the closest to your home?
Is it a two-year college or a four-year college?

Teacher Note

You will probably need to use an almanac or a college guidebook to find out information about colleges in your state. If possible, display the book where students can look through it before or after class. Encourage them to locate information that interests them in the book and share it with the class.

G. College Information.

• Do the activity orally once or twice through with the class. Then have students complete the questions.

• Ask different students to write one question each on the board. Correct as necessary and have the rest of the class check their own work.

• Read the questions in the College Information box. Call on volunteers to answer.

Suggestion

Extend this grammar practice by writing cue words on the board and eliciting *How many* questions and *There is* and *There are* answers from students. For example, the cue words *Brazilian students* might elicit the question *How many Brazilian students are there in this class?* The answer might be *There are six* or *There is one Brazilian student in this class.*

H. Pronunciation: *there, they.*
(CD1, Track 54)

- Read through the sentences with students and ask them to point out the sentences with *They* and the ones with *There*. Then, play the audio as students listen for the difference between the two words. Explain that the ending of each of these words is connected to the following word in spoken English.
- Explain and demonstrate that *They + are* sounds like *They* (with *ey* pronounced like long *a*) followed by *yar*. *There + are* sounds like *There* followed by *rar*. Have students repeat *yar* and *rar* first by themselves, and then combined in *They are* and *There are*.
- Present the sentences several more times, pausing after each for students to repeat.

I. Listen and complete these sentences. (CD1, Track 55)

Students listen two or three times and complete the sentences on their own. Review the correct answers with the class.

Practice the sentences above with a partner.

As pairs practice the sentences, move around the room helping with pronunciation as needed.

J. Circle.

Students complete the activity individually and check their answers with a partner.

Suggestion

Have students use the sentences for pronunciation practice with a partner.

H. Pronunciation: *there, they.* Listen and repeat.

1. They are here.
2. There are four here.
3. They aren't here.
4. There aren't any here.
5. They are in class.
6. There are many students in class.
7. They aren't in class.
8. There aren't any students in class.

I. Listen and complete these sentences.

1. _____There_____ _____are_____ many cars on campus.
2. _____They_____ _____are_____ in the parking lot.
3. _____There_____ _____aren't_____ any buses.
4. _____They_____ _____aren't_____ on the bus.
5. _____There_____ _____aren't_____ any students in the cafeteria.
6. _____They_____ _____are_____ in class.
7. _____There_____ _____are_____ many students in the gym.
8. _____They_____ _____aren't_____ in the pool.

Practice the sentences above with a partner.

J. Circle.

1. (There) / They are four students walking into the building. (They) / There are early.
2. (There) / It is a bus stop on campus. (There) / They aren't any students waiting for the bus. There / (They) are in class.
3. (There) / It is a mailbox in front of the building. There / (It) is full.
4. (There) / They are several lights in the parking lot. There / (They) aren't on now because it's daytime. There / (They) are only on at night.
5. (There) / They are many cars in the parking lot. There / (They) are not students' cars because this is a faculty parking lot. (There) / They are four parking lots for students.
6. (There) / It is a pay telephone booth next to the building. There / (It) is empty.

Audio Script

I. Listen and complete these sentences.
(CD1, Track 55)

1. There are many cars on campus.
2. They are in the parking lot.
3. There aren't any buses.
4. They aren't on the bus.
5. There aren't any students in the cafeteria.
6. They are in class.
7. There are many students in the gym.
8. They aren't in the pool.

A. STUDENT A: Listen to Student B. Write each sentence next to the correct picture.

> **STUDENT B: Turn to page 114. Read the eight sentences to your partner.**

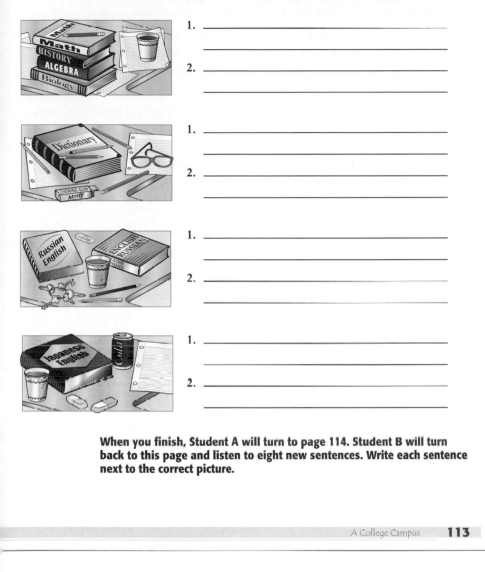

1. _____
   _____
2. _____
   _____

1. _____
   _____
2. _____
   _____

1. _____
   _____
2. _____
   _____

1. _____
   _____
2. _____
   _____

When you finish, Student A will turn to page 114. Student B will turn back to this page and listen to eight new sentences. Write each sentence next to the correct picture.

Suggestion

Ask students to name all the objects shown in the four pictures. Write any words students are unfamiliar with on the board and practice pronouncing them.

A. Student A: Listen to Student B. Student B: Turn to page 114.

• Read the instructions. Explain that Student B will read eight sentences from page 114 to Student A. Student A will write each one next to the picture it describes. Remind Student A not to look ahead to page 114 while doing the exercise.

• The pair can correct Student A's work together.

☀ Working Together:
Student to Student

B. Read these sentences to your partner.

• Student A now reads the sentences in the second column to Student B who writes each one next to the picture on page 113 that it describes. Remind Student B not to look ahead to page 114 while doing the exercise.
• The pair can correct Student B's work together.

👥 C. Our classroom.

• Ask students to find a new partner and complete the sentences together. Suggest that they look back at the explanations and examples on pages 109 and 110 if they need help completing any items.
• Review the answers with the class. Elicit multiple correct answers whenever possible. For example:

T: *Number 1.*
S1: *There are a lot of students in my class.*
S2: *There are 14 students in my class.*
S3: *There are several students in my class.*

☀ Working Together: Student to Student

B. Read these sentences to your partner.

STUDENT B	STUDENT A
a. There are two dictionaries on this desk.	a. There are two pencils on this desk.
b. There are two erasers on this desk.	b. There aren't any pencils on this desk.
c. There is one pencil on this desk.	c. There aren't any dictionaries on this desk.
d. There's a can of soda on this desk.	d. There isn't any coffee on this desk.
e. There are several pencils on this desk.	e. There are several keys on this desk.
f. There isn't any paper on this desk.	f. There's a lot of paper on this desk.
g. There is a pair of glasses on this desk.	g. There is a piece of paper on this desk.
h. There are a few books on this desk.	h. There is a pack of gum on this desk.

👥 C. Our classroom. Complete these sentences about your class and your school.
(Answers will vary.)

1. There _____ _____ students in my class.
2. There _____ _____ man / men.
3. There _____ _____ woman / women.
4. There _____ _____ student(s) from Mexico.
5. There _____ _____ student(s) from Japan.
6. There _____ _____ student(s) from _____.
7. There _____ _____ teenager(s)
8. There _____ _____ teacher.
9. There _____ _____ married students.
10. There _____ _____ single students.
11. There _____ _____ maps in our classroom.
12. There _____ _____ computers in our classroom.
13. There _____ _____ desks in our classroom.
14. There _____ _____ clock(s) in our classroom.
15. There _____ _____ electrical outlets in our classroom.

D. A blueprint. Work in groups of three or four students. Go to different rooms or areas in your school building: for example, the cafeteria, library, lobby, main floor, lounge, etc. Draw a detailed blueprint of the area. Only include large items in your drawing, such as desks, tables, bookshelves, and other furniture. Write 10 sentences about the room. Come back to class, and draw your blueprint on the chalkboard or a large piece of paper. Describe the room or area to your classmates.

E. *How many* questions. Ask the question for each pair of words. Match each question with the correct number.

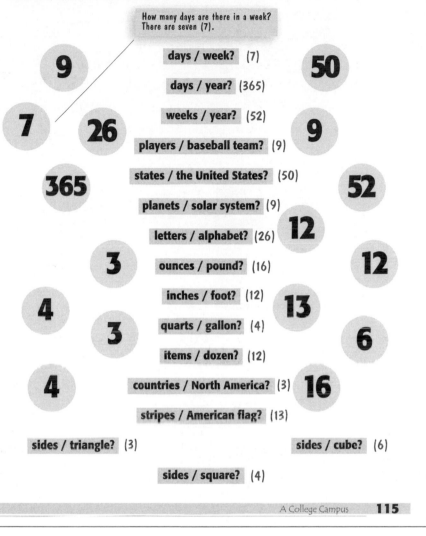

How many days are there in a week?
There are seven (7).

days / week? (7)
days / year? (365)
weeks / year? (52)
players / baseball team? (9)
states / the United States? (50)
planets / solar system? (9)
letters / alphabet? (26)
ounces / pound? (16)
inches / foot? (12)
quarts / gallon? (4)
items / dozen? (12)
countries / North America? (3)
stripes / American flag? (13)
sides / triangle? (3)
sides / cube? (6)
sides / square? (4)

Suggestion

Demonstrate how to make a blueprint. On the board, draw a floor plan of the classroom as if you were looking down from above. Explain what you are doing as you go along. Draw lines for walls and put breaks in the lines to indicate windows and doors. Then, add a rectangle for the teacher's desk. Invite students to come to the board and add shapes indicating student desks, chairs, and other items in the room.

D. A blueprint.

• Read and discuss the instructions. Invite students to suggest additional items they may wish to include on their blueprints. Ask volunteers to add them to the floor plan on the board.

• Give each group a time limit for presenting their blueprint–perhaps ten minutes. Ask each member of the group to make at least one statement about their blueprint. Encourage other students to ask questions. For example: *Is there a computer in the room? Are there any CD-ROMs?*

Suggestion

If possible, have each group actually visit the room they are drawing. If they can't, ask them to work from memory and share what they remember about the room.

E. *How many* questions.

Students complete this activity in pairs. Review the answers orally with the whole class.

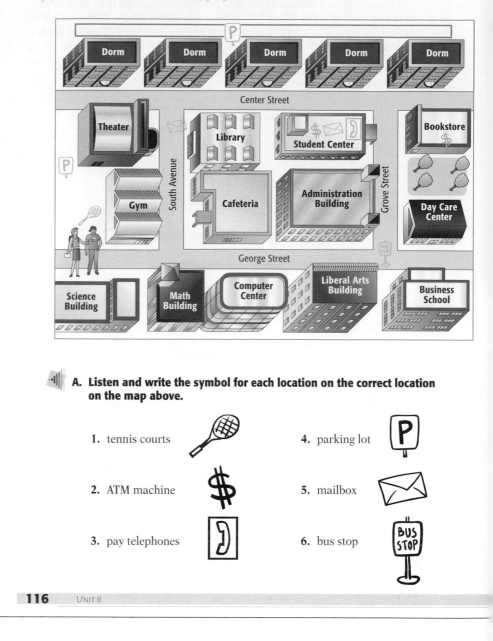

☀ The Big Picture: Campus Information

⊪ A Listen and write the symbol for each location on the correct location on the map above. (CD1, Track 56)

• Point to the people in the picture. Ask:

Where are these people?
Who are they?
What are they doing?

• Read the names of the streets and buildings on the map and ask students to point to each one. Then, say the names of new items such as *Liberal Arts Building* and *Day Care Center* again and ask students to repeat. Help students define any new terms.

• Read aloud the names of the six locations and point out the symbol for each. Explain that students will hear short conversations describing the location of each of these items. Then, play the audio as students look at the map and try to find the locations mentioned. Present the conversations again, pausing after each, giving students enough time to mark the locations on the map. Review the correct answers with the class.

⊪ A. Listen and write the symbol for each location on the correct location on the map above.

1. tennis courts
2. ATM machine
3. pay telephones
4. parking lot
5. mailbox
6. bus stop

Audio Script

A. Listen and write the symbol for each location on the map above. (CD1, Track 56)

Conversation 1
A: I love tennis. Are there any courts on campus?
B: Yes. There are four tennis courts in back of the gym.

Conversation 2
A: I need some cash. Is there an ATM machine on campus.

B: Yes, there are several. I know that there's one in the Student Center and there's another one in the bookstore.
A: Thanks.

Conversation 3
A: Are there any public telephones on campus?
B: Not many. Most students have cell phones. I think there's one in the Student Center.

Conversation 4
A: This parking lot is for faculty. Where are the student parking lots?

B: There are some student parking lots in back of the dorms. And there's a big student parking lot in back of the theater.

Conversation 5
A: I'm looking for a mailbox.
B: There's one in front of the library. And there's a small post office in the Student Center.

Conversation 6
A: Is there a bus stop around here?
B: Yes, there's one across the street, in front of the Administration Building.

B. Answer these questions about the campus.

1. Are there any tennis courts on campus?

   <u>There are four tennis courts in back of the gym.</u>

2. Are there any pay telephones on campus?

   <u>There's one in the Student Center.</u>

3. Are there any mailboxes on campus?

   <u>There's one in front of the library.</u>

4. Are there any ATM machines on campus?

   <u>There's one in the Student Center and one in the bookstore.</u>

5. Is there a bus stop on campus?

   <u>There's one in front of the Administration Building.</u>

C. Complete with *it, they,* or *there.*

1. <u>There</u> are five dormitories on campus. <u>They</u> are on Center Street.

2. <u>There</u> is a day care center on campus. <u>It</u> is on the corner of George Street and Grove Street.

3. <u>There</u> is a large library. <u>It</u> has books on every subject.

4. <u>There</u> are many parking lots for students, but <u>they</u> are usually full.

5. <u>There</u> are four tennis courts in back of the gym. <u>There</u> are four more in back of the liberal arts building.

6. <u>There</u> are only two pay phones on campus. Students don't need pay phones because <u>they</u> have cell phones.

7. <u>There</u> is an active theater on campus. <u>There</u> are music and art performances every week. <u>There</u> are free movies every Monday night.

D. Write a paragraph about this campus. Describe the location of the buildings and the facilities.

B. Answer these questions about the campus.

Complete the activity orally with the whole class.

Suggestion

Ask students to take turns making up other questions about the map using *Is there . . .* and *Are there . . . .* Allow them to choose a classmate to answer the question. For example:

Binh: *Are there any dorms on campus, Carlos?*

Carlos: *Yes, there are. There are five dorms on Center Street.*

C. Complete with *it, they, or there.*

Ask students to complete the sentences individually and check their answers with a partner. Go over the correct answers with the class.

D. Write a paragraph about this campus.

Ask students to work individually or in pairs to describe the campus on page 116.

Suggestion

Choose some sentences from student papers that contain errors in the use of *it, they,* and *there* and write them on the board. Ask the class to rewrite each sentence correctly on a piece of paper. Then, ask different students to write the correct version of each sentence on the board. Go over the corrections with the whole class.

☀️Reading: College 101

A. Before You Read.

• Ask students to list some of the rules they follow in your class. For example:

> *Don't be late.*
> *Bring a dictionary every day.*
> *Do your homework.*

• Ask students to read the opening paragraph to themselves. When they finish, invite them to ask about anything they don't understand. Restate some sentences in different words if necessary. Then, ask a student what the main idea of the paragraph is. (College is different from high school.)

• Ask students to read the numbered list. When they finish, read aloud the list of expectations one item at a time and explain anything they don't understand.

Suggestion

Help students use sentence context to figure out the meaning of any words they don't know. For example, they can figure out what *sharpen* means by noting that it is what a person does to a pencil before class begins. You can use this method for other words, such as *regularly, from time to time, participate,* and *tutoring center.*

B. Which information is true about colleges in the United States?

Ask students to answer the questions on their own. Review the answers orally with the whole class.

C. Which expectations are the same in your native country?

After students have marked their answers, conduct a class discussion about the similarities and differences in schools in different countries.

☀️ Reading: College 101

A. Before You Read.

What are some of your class rules?

In high school, students learn how to study. Students have classes every period and follow a regular schedule. In college, students have free periods during the day. Their schedules may be different each day. In college, students are adults. They are responsible for their schedules and studying. What are some of the expectations of college students?

1. Attend the first day of class. Get all first day notes, which may include a list of assignments, test information, syllabus, calendar, class rules, and so on.
2. Get to class on time. Turn your cell phones and beepers off! Bring your books with you. Sharpen your pencil <u>before</u> class.
3. Attend your classes regularly. You are responsible for the information in your books, assignments, and class notes.
4. Find one or two partners the first week or two of class. Study together. Share your notes. If one of you is absent, get the homework from your partner.
5. Look at the professor from time to time. This shows that you are listening. When you speak, look directly at your teacher.
6. Ask questions. Participate in class discussions.
7. Do your homework. Hand in all papers and reports on time.
8. Find the tutoring center. Most colleges have study centers with tutors, computer programs, and writing help.

B. Which information is true about colleges in the United States? Circle *T* or *F*.

1. Your teacher will understand if you hand in a paper late.   T   F
2. You should never look directly in your teacher's eyes.   T   F
3. Always do your homework alone. Do not work with another student.   T   F
4. Students are only responsible for the information in the book.   T   F
5. College teachers often hand out important papers during the first class.   (T)   F
6. If you ask a question, the teacher will think you are not studying.   T   F
7. You are alone at college. You must succeed by yourself.   T   F

C. Which expectations are the same in your native country? Which are different?

Writing Our Stories: My School

A. Read.

I attend UCSD, the University of California San Diego. The campus is very big. There are many buildings. There are dormitories, classroom buildings, libraries, theaters, and cafeterias. There is an indoor pool and an outdoor pool.

I am a student at the English Language Program. There are about 1,000 students in English classes during the year. Our program is in a small group of buildings. There are about twenty classrooms and two computer labs. In the center, there is a large patio. The weather in San Diego is warm and sunny all year, so we are often outside. We sit on the patio and talk and study and work in small groups. There is only one problem with our campus. It is too big! It is a fifteen-minute walk from here to the pool.

B. Check (✓) some of the buildings or facilities at your school.

(Answers will vary.)

☐ library ☐ cafeteria
☐ study center ☐ gym
☐ day care center ☐ parking lot
☐ student center ☐ dormitory
☐ bookstore
☐ computer center
☐ theater
☐ _____

Writing Note

Use a comma in a list of people, places, or things: There are dormitories, classroom buildings, libraries, theaters, and cafeterias.

C. In your notebook, describe your school.

Writing Our Stories: My School

A. Read.

- Discuss the picture. Ask:
  Who are these people?
  What are they doing?

- Read the passage to the class. Then, ask a student to read aloud the sentence that describes the picture. ("We sit on the patio and talk and study and work in small groups.")

- Ask simple comprehension questions about the story such as:
  Where is this college?
  Is it big or small?
  What are some of the buildings?

- Ask students to read the story all the way through on their own.

B. Check (✓) some of the buildings or facilities at your school.

Students check the facilities that they have at their school. Point out the blank at the bottom of the list and encourage each student to add one new item.

C. In your notebook, describe your school.

- Read and discuss the writing note. Then ask students to read the story once more, this time circling all the commas. Ask them which commas are used in lists. Then, explain that the other commas are used to make it easier to read long sentences.

- Students can use the information from Exercise B as they complete this activity. If possible, display a map of your campus or school.

- They can also use the story at the top of the page as a model. Show how they can adapt sentences to fit their own needs. For example: *There is an indoor pool and an outdoor pool.* can become *There is a faculty parking lot and a student parking lot.*

Practicing on Your Own

A. Circle the correct words in these questions and answers.

Have students complete the activity individually and check their answers with a partner.

B. Complete these questions about time.

Have students complete the activity on their own.

Suggestion

You might ask students to work in pairs. They can take turns asking and answering the questions before they write them in the book.

Practicing on Your Own

A. Circle the correct words in these questions and answers.

1. A: **Is** / **Are** there any students from China in your class?
   B: Yes, there **is** / **are** five students from China. **They** / There are from Beijing.

2. A: Is there **an** / **any** elevator in this building?
   B: Yes, **there** / it is. There / **It** is at the end of the hall.

3. A: **Is** / Are there a ladies room on this floor?
   B: No, there **isn't** / aren't. **There** / It is one on the second floor.

4. A: Are there any vending **machine** / **machines** on this floor?
   B: Yes, they / **there** are. There / **They** are in the student lounge.

5. A: Is there a copy **machine** / machines for student use?
   B: Yes, **there** / it is one in the library. It costs ten cents a copy.

6. A: Are there many **computer** / **computers** in the library?
   B: Yes, there are one / **a lot of** computers in the library.

7. A: **Is** / Are there a fax machine in the library?
   B: No, there **isn't** / aren't. There is **a** / some fax machine in the student center.

B. Complete these questions about time. Write the answers.

1. How many seconds ____are____ ____there____ in a minute?
   There are 60 seconds in a minute.

2. How many minutes ____are____ ____there____ in an hour?
   There are 60 minutes in an hour.

3. How many hours ____are____ ____there____ in a day?
   There are 24 hours in a day.

4. How many months ____are____ ____there____ in a year?
   There are 12 months in a year.

5. How many days ____are____ ____there____ in a year?
   There are 365 days in a year.

6. How many years ____are____ ____there____ in a decade?
   There are 10 years in a decade.

Looking at Forms: Registration Form

A. Answer these questions about Adam's registration form.

Registration Form

Last name	First name	Student ID Number			
Wojik	Adam	152 — 15 — 1515			

Course / Number	Section	Credit Hours	Day	Time	Room
English 102	136	3	M-W	9:00	N317
Math 203	251	3	M-W	11:00	M305
Comp Sc. 210	204	4	T-R	10:00	T406
BIO 105	131	4	T-R	2:00	S112
Bio LAB 105	107	1	F	12:00	S102

Student Signature ___Adam Wojik___   Advisor's Signature ___R. Dewey___   Date __8/15__

1. What classes is Adam taking? English, Math, Computer Science, Biology, and a Biology Lab.
2. What days does Adam's computer class meet? What time is the class?
   Tuesday and Thursday   10:00
3. What days does his math class meet? What time is the class? What's the room
   number? Monday and Wednesday   11:00   M305

Grammar Summary

▶ 1. *There is/ There are:* Statements

There	is	a	student computer desk	in the classroom.
	are	a few several a lot of	students computers desks	

▶ 2. Affirmative / Negative

Affirmative	Negative
There **is a** computer in the room.	There **isn't a** computer in the room.
	There **is no** computer in the room.
There **are some** computers in the room.	There **aren't any** computers in the room.
	There **are no** computers in the room.

▶ 3. *How many* questions

How many students are there in the classroom?   There are 20.
How many clocks are there in the classroom?   There is one.
How many computers are there in the classroom?   There aren't any.

Looking at Forms: Registration Form

A. Answer these questions about Adam's registration form.

Give students two minutes to study the registration form. Invite them to ask about anything they don't understand. Then, ask the three questions below the form and call on volunteers to answer.

Grammar Summary

• Review the summary with the class. Invite students to make up alternate sentences for each example in the chart. For example, in place of *There is **a student in the classroom,*** a student might say *There is **a security guard in the security booth.***

• See the Grammar Summary Expansion on page 236 for a more complete explanation of these grammar points.

Unit 9
At Work

Discuss the unit title art. Ask: *What is the person doing?* (He is flying around with a pair of pliers in his hands. Maybe he is fixing something.)

☀ Dictionary:
Occupations

📢 **A. Listen and repeat.**
(CD2, Track 1)

• Before having students listen and repeat, invite them to name objects in the pictures and describe actions they see people doing. Ask:

What is he holding?
What is she doing?
What is he cutting?

Repeat correct responses.

• Ask students to look at the words as they listen to and repeat the names of the occupations.

B. Label the jobs.

Have students label the pictures and check their answers with a partner. Review the answers with the whole class. Encourage students to add comments about each occupation. For example:

Construction workers work hard.
My sister is a cook in a restaurant.

9 At Work

☀ Dictionary: Occupations

📢 **A. Listen and repeat.**

assembler	custodian	machine operator
cable installer	electrician	nurse's aide
construction worker	high-lo driver	packer
cook	landscaper / gardener	painter

B. Label the jobs.

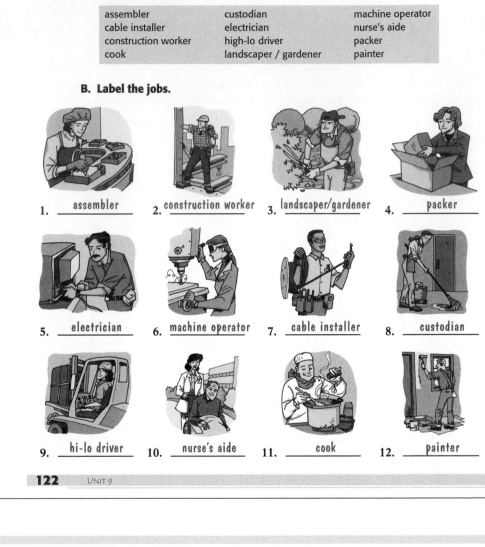

1. assembler
2. construction worker
3. landscaper/gardener
4. packer
5. electrician
6. machine operator
7. cable installer
8. custodian
9. hi-lo driver
10. nurse's aide
11. cook
12. painter

C. Listen and repeat.

apron	flashlight	hammer	leaf blower	mower	shovel
boots	forklift	hard hat	mask	paintbrush	tape
earplugs	gloves	I.D. badge	mixer	safety glasses	tool belt
earphones	hairnet	name tag	mop	screwdriver	work boots

D. Match each tool with the correct picture.

_e_ **1.** flashlight

_a_ **2.** forklift

_f_ **3.** hammer

_j_ **4.** tape

_b_ **5.** mixer

_g_ **6.** mop

_l_ **7.** mower

_c_ **8.** shovel

_k_ **9.** leaf blower

_h_ **10.** tool belt

_d_ **11.** hairnet

_i_ **12.** name tag / I.D. badge

a.

b.

c.

d.

e.

f.

g.

h.

i. Jennifer Brown

j.

k.

l.

At Work   **123**

C. Listen and repeat.
(CD2, Track 2)

Play the audio and have students listen and repeat. Then, ask some questions that can be answered in one word, such as *Which tool does a carpenter use?* and *Who uses a leaf blower?*

D. Match each tool with the correct picture.

Students match answers on their own and compare them in small groups.

Suggestions

• After you finish reviewing the answers with the class, have students take turns pantomiming the use of a tool while the rest of the class guesses which one it is.

• As a variation, you can make the game into a contest. Divide the class into two teams. Team members take turns identifying a pantomime by another member of the same team. A team member gets one point for saying the name of the tool correctly, and a second point for naming the occupation that uses that tool. Have the guessing team close their books to make the game challenging.

A. Match the equipment with the job.

Ask students to complete the matching activity on their own. Review the answers by calling on different students to say the matching number and letter and then use a simple sentence to tell who uses each tool. For example:

1.–d. A gardener uses a shovel.
5.–a. A packer uses tape.

B. Complete about the equipment.

Have students complete the activity in pairs. Review the correct answers by calling on different students to read a completed sentence to the class.

☀ Active Grammar: Present Continuous

A. Match the equipment with the job. You can use a tool more than once.
(Answers may vary. Suggested answers below.)

1. gardener (d.)
2. cable installer (g.)
4. machine operator (e.)
5. packer (a.)
6. construction worker (c.)
7. custodian (h.)
8. painter (f.)
9. nurse's aide (b.)
10. electrician (i.)

a. tape
b. latex gloves
c. work boots
d. shovel
e. safety glasses
f. paintbrush
g. screwdriver
h. mop
i. flashlight

B. Complete about the equipment.

clothes	ears	eyes	feet	hands	head	lungs

1. An apron protects your ____clothes____.

2. Boots protect your ____feet____.

3. Earplugs and earphones protect your ____ears____.

4. A hard hat protects your ____head____.

5. A mask protects your ____lungs____.

6. Safety glasses protect your ____eyes____.

7. Gloves protect your ____hands____.

124 UNIT 9

C. *Who* questions. Ask and answer.

assembler
cable installer
cook
construction worker
custodian
electrician
high-lo driver
landscaper
machine operator
nurse's aide
packer
painter

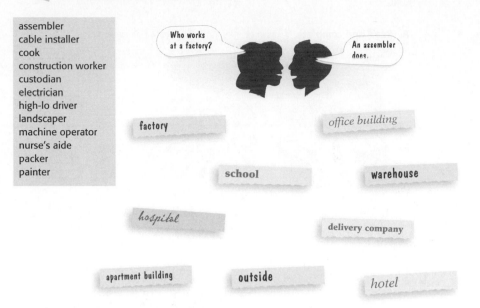

factory

office building

school

warehouse

hospital

delivery company

apartment building

outside

hotel

D. Complete with a partner. (Answers will vary. Sample answers below.)

1. An electrician uses a _screwdriver_.

2. A construction worker uses a _hard hat_.

3. A landscaper uses a _leaf blower_.

4. A(n) _machine operator_ uses earplugs.

5. A(n) _construction worker_ uses a hammer.

6. A(n) _painter_ wears work boots.

7. A(n) _cook_ wears an apron.

8. At my job, I use _____ and _____.

9. At my job, I wear _____ and _____.

C. *Who* questions.

- Read aloud the sample *Who* question and short answer. Ask students to explain why the answer uses *does* instead of *do*. (*Does* is used with words that can take the place of *he, she,* and *it*.)
- Have pairs of students complete the exercise together. Tell them they can look back at page 122 if necessary.
- Review the exercise by calling on one student to ask a *who* question and another student to answer. There is more than one correct answer for some questions. For example, the answer to the question *Who works in a hospital?* could be *a nurse's aide, cook,* or *custodian.* Elicit as many answers as possible for each question.

D. Complete with a partner.

Have students complete the exercise with a partner and then compare answers with another pair of students.

Suggestion

Write two headings on the board: *Jobs* and *Tools.* Invite students whose occupations haven't been mentioned so far to come to the board and add information about their jobs. Then, help them make statements about their jobs. For example: *telephone, telemarketer. A telemarketer uses a telephone to sell things.*

A. Read and complete.

• Point out the list of verbs at the top of the page. Say each one aloud and ask students to repeat. Review the sample answers. Ask what verb ending is used (-*ing*). Then, have students complete the sentences on their own.

• Review the answers to items 1–9 with the class. Explain words and paraphrase sentences if necessary. For example: *He is taking a break.* could be restated as *He is stopping work for a few minutes.*

• Point out that some answers could be either *reading* and *looking at.* For example: *He is reading a magazine.* and *He is looking at a magazine* are both correct.

Actions

A. Read and complete. (Answers may vary. Suggested answers below.)

| drink | eat | go | listen to | look at | read | sit | take |

1. He is ___taking___ a break.
2. He is ___drinking___ a soda.
3. He is ___eating___ some chips.

4. He is ___listening___ to music.
5. He is ___reading___ a magazine.
6. He is ___sitting___ on the couch.

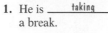

7. She is ___going___ to work.
8. She is ___looking at___ her schedule.
9. She is ___reading___ a newspaper.

(Answers may vary. Suggested answers below.)

greet	install	load	open	pack	talk	wash	wear

10. She is _talking_ to co-workers.

11. She is _greeting_ her co-workers.

12. She is _wearing_ a uniform.

13. They are _talking_ .

14. They are _installing_ cables.

15. They are _washing_ the truck.

16. They are _opening_ boxes.

17. They are _packing_ boxes.

18. They are _loading_ the boxes onto the truck.

A. Read and complete.
(continued)

• Ask students to look at the list of verbs at the top of the page and raise their hands if there are any they aren't sure of. Explain these verbs and use them in sentences. For example: Install *means put something where it belongs. A phone company worker installs phones in people's houses.*

• Have students complete the sentences on their own. Review the correct answers with the class.

Suggestions

• Choose verbs from the top of pages 126 and 127 and ask volunteers to make up original sentences using them. For example: *He is loading suitcases into a taxi.* Call out five verbs and choose five students to write sentences using these verbs on the board. Review the sentences with the class.

• Have students copy into their notebooks any sentences that are particularly useful to them. Help students make up similar sentences about their own occupations. Supply vocabulary as needed.

B. Read and complete.

• Review the present continuous chart and verb box with the class. Then, have two students read aloud the questions and answers in items 1 and 2 under the heading "Picture 1."

• Have students complete the rest of the items on their own.

B. Read and complete. (Answers may vary.)

Present Continuous		
I	am	
You We They	are	
		working.
He She It	is	

clean   drive   cut   pack

Picture 1

1. What's she doing?

   She __is__ __cleaning__ the floor.

2. What's she wearing?

   She __is__ __wearing__ a uniform.

Picture 2

1. What's he doing?

   He __is__ __cutting__ a tree.

2. What's he wearing?

   He __is__ __wearing__ a hat

   and __a tool belt__.

Picture 3

1. What's she doing?

   She __is__ __driving__ a high-lo.

2. What's she wearing?

   She __is__ __wearing__ a hard hat.

Picture 4

1. What are they doing?

   They __are__ __packing__ boxes.

2. What are they wearing?

   They __are wearing hats and uniforms__

   _____.

A. Look at the picture. It's break time. What are the employees doing? Talk about the picture.

| buy | eat | get | read | sit | stand | talk | walk | watch |

B. Complete the sentences. (Answers may vary.)

1. Luis and Gloria __are sitting__ on the couch.
2. They __are watching__ TV.
3. Victor __is getting__ a cup of water.
4. Vladimir __is buying__ some candy.
5. Marie __is talking__ to Mei-Lin.
6. They __are eating__ lunch.
7. Joseph __is sitting__ in the break room.
8. He __is reading__ a newspaper.
9. Anna and Louise __are walking__ around the parking lot.
10. They __are talking__ about babies.

At Work **129**

☀️ In the Break Room

A. Look at the picture.

• Invite students to comment on the picture. Have them point to a person in the picture as they talk about him or her. Rephrase any incomplete or incorrect responses and expand on them using the target vocabulary words in the box. For example:

S1: *He has a candy bar.*
T: *That's right. He's _buying_ a candy bar.*
S2: *They're outside.*
T: *Yes. The two women are _walking_ outside the break room.*

• Review what all nine people are doing. Ask *What is Luis doing?* and call on a student to answer. Correct responses as necessary and have the class repeat.

B. Complete the sentences.

Ask students to complete the sentences on their own. Review the correct answers orally.

Suggestion

Call out a number and a student name. Have the student pantomime an action that is commonly done during break at work or at school. For example: *Number 1. José.* (José pantomimes an action for the class.) The rest of the students write the number followed by the name of the action they see. Review the answers with the whole class and make a list of any new verbs they may mention. Have students repeat the action for a review as a class or with partners.

Negatives

A. Circle the verbs that are true for you.

Review the chart showing present continuous negative forms. Then, ask students to circle the answers that are true for them.

Read your sentences to a partner.

As students read their sentences have them correct each other's errors.

B. Pronunciation: *I'm working.* (CD2, Track 3)

• The first time through, play the audio as students just listen. The second time through, have them repeat. Focus on the *m* in *I'm*, which students sometimes drop. Do the activity several times if necessary.

C. I'm busy. (CD2, Track 4)

• Read through the conversation with students and explain anything they don't understand. Then, have the class repeat each line after you.

• Ask students to find partners and practice the conversation using their own names. Suggest that they switch roles so that both people have a chance to practice both parts.

Suggestion

Invite students to add two or more lines to the conversation in Exercise C. For example, students might change the ending to the following:

A: *Hi, Roger. I can't talk to you now. I'm busy.*
B: *What are you doing?*
A: *I'm painting the kitchen.*
B: *OK. I'll talk to you later.*

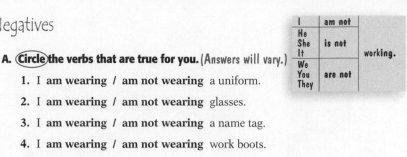

Negatives

I	am not	
He She It	is not	working.
We You They	are not	

A. Circle the verbs that are true for you. (Answers will vary.)

1. I **am wearing** / **am not wearing** a uniform.
2. I **am wearing** / **am not wearing** glasses.
3. I **am wearing** / **am not wearing** a name tag.
4. I **am wearing** / **am not wearing** work boots.
5. I **am using** / **am not using** a pencil.
6. I **am using** / **am not using** a computer.
7. I **am drinking** / **am not drinking** a cup of tea.

Read your sentences to a partner.

B. Pronunciation: *I'm working.* Listen and repeat.

1. I'm working.
2. I'm driving.
3. I'm talking to my boss.
4. I'm sitting in class.
5. I'm eating dinner.

C. I'm busy. Listen to the conversation. Then, practice the conversation with a partner. Use the excuses in Exercise B.

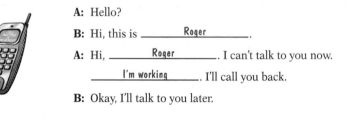

A: Hello?
B: Hi, this is _____Roger_____.
A: Hi, _____Roger_____. I can't talk to you now. _____I'm working_____. I'll call you back.
B: Okay, I'll talk to you later.

A. What's wrong with this picture? Look at the pictures. Something is wrong with each picture. Talk about the pictures with a partner.

| carry | clean | sit | wear | push | pull |

Fred   Miguel   Michelle   Iris and Martha   Mr. Tanaka

EMPLOYEE CAFETERIA

PUSH

> Fred isn't wearing a hard hat and shoes.
> He is wearing a straw hat and slippers.

B. Interview. Talk to a person who works in your school. Ask the person, *"What's your name?"*, *"What's your occupation?"*, and *"When do you work?"* Ask, *"Can I observe you?"* Then, observe the person for 5 to 10 minutes.

C. Complete the sentences about the person that you are observing.

1. _____ **is / isn't** speaking on the telephone.

2. _____ **is / isn't** standing.   (Answers will vary.)

3. **He / She   is / isn't** working behind a counter.

4. **He / She   is / isn't** working at a desk.

5. **He / She   is / isn't** wearing a uniform.

6. **He / She   is / isn't** using a computer.

7. **He / She   is / isn't** answering the telephone.

8. **He / She   is / isn't** handling money.

D. Write five more sentences about your observation.

Working Together

A. What's wrong with this picture?

- Before discussing the pictures with the whole class, ask pairs of students to talk about them. Read the example aloud to provide model language. As they work, move around the room, helping as needed.
- Review all the answers with the class. For example:

Miguel: *He isn't wearing a uniform. He isn't wearing an apron. He's wearing a tuxedo.*
Michelle: *She isn't pushing the door. She's pulling the door.*
Iris and Martha: *They aren't sitting on chairs. They're sitting on boxes.*
Mr. Tanaka: *He isn't wearing a chef's hat. He's wearing a hard hat.*

B. Interview.

- Help students think of a variety of people they might talk to at their school. List them on the board. Discuss where each person can be found.
- You can also brainstorm some other questions students might ask. For example: *What do you call that?* (to find out the names of tools or equipment)
- If possible, have students do the assignment during class. Some students might go in pairs or groups. If this isn't possible, they can do it as homework.

C. Complete the sentences about the person that you are observing.

Review the completed sentences with the whole class.

D. Write five more sentences about your observation.

Ask different students to read their sentences aloud to the class.

The Big Picture: Inspection at the Factory

A. Look at the picture.

Read the title and discuss the picture with the class. You might also ask:

What is he/she doing?
Is she wearing safety glasses?
What do the signs say?

B. Listen and write the names of the employees. (CD2, Track 5)

The first time you play the audio, have students just listen. Then, play the audio again and ask students to write the names next to the employees. Have students check their answers with a partner.

C. Circle the answers.

Students answer the questions on their own. Review the correct answers with the class. *(Exercise C continues on page 133.)*

The Big Picture: Inspection at the Factory

A. Look at the picture. Talk about the employees. What's happening at the factory?

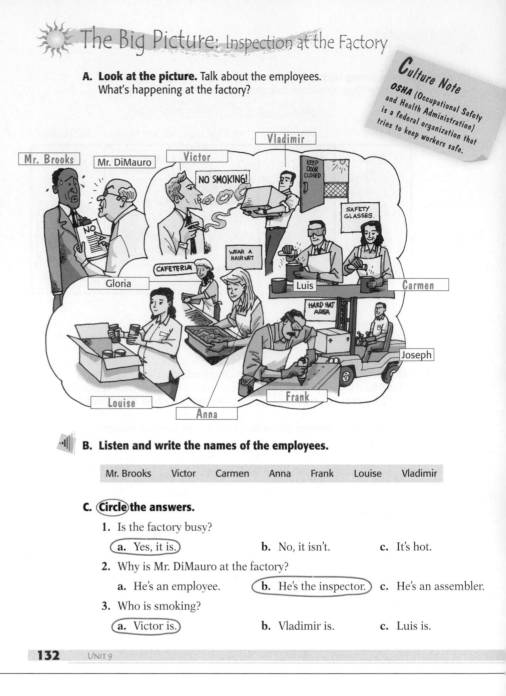

B. Listen and write the names of the employees.

| Mr. Brooks | Victor | Carmen | Anna | Frank | Louise | Vladimir |

C. Circle the answers.

1. Is the factory busy?
   - **a. Yes, it is.**
   - b. No, it isn't.
   - c. It's hot.
2. Why is Mr. DiMauro at the factory?
   - a. He's an employee.
   - **b. He's the inspector.**
   - c. He's an assembler.
3. Who is smoking?
   - **a. Victor is.**
   - b. Vladimir is.
   - c. Luis is.

132   UNIT 9

Audio Script

B. Listen and write the names of the employees. (CD2, Track 5)

It's a very hot summer day. The factory is very busy. Today is a bad day for the factory and for the manager. The manager, Mr. Brooks, is listening to the inspector, Mr. DiMauro. There are many problems in the factory. Mr. DiMauro has a long list of safety violations. Victor is smoking in a non-smoking area. Vladimir is carrying a heavy box. He isn't wearing work boots. He's wearing sandals. Gloria and Anna are working in the cafeteria. Gloria is wearing a hairnet, but Anna isn't. Anna is wearing gloves, but Gloria isn't. Joseph and Frank are in the hard-hat area, but they aren't following factory safety rules. They aren't wearing their hard hats. Louise is six months pregnant, and she is still standing up. She's tired. She needs to sit down. Luis and Carmen are working together. Luis is wearing safety glasses, but Carmen isn't. Finally, the fire door is open. Mr. Brooks looks very upset. He will have to pay a big fine.

4. Who is wearing a hairnet?

   a. Carmen is.   (**b.** Gloria is.)   **c.** Anna is.

5. Is Vladimir wearing work boots?

   a. Yes, he is.   (**b.** No, he isn't.)   **c.** No, she isn't.

6. Who isn't wearing safety glasses?

   a. Luis.   (**b.** Carmen.)   **c.** Joseph.

7. Who isn't wearing a hard hat?

   a. Joseph.   **b.** Victor.   (**c.** Frank and Joseph.)

8. Who is very tired?

   a. Gloria is.   **b.** Joseph is.   (**c.** Louise is.)

D. Complete. Some of the sentences are negative.

   1. Victor _____is smoking_____.

   2. Gloria _____is wearing_____ a hairnet.

   3. Carmen _____isn't wearing_____ safety glasses.

   4. Frank and Joseph _____aren't wearing_____ their hard hats.

   5. Vladimir _____is wearing_____ sandals.

   6. Louise _____is standing_____. She's very tired.

   7. Gloria _____isn't wearing_____ gloves.

   8. Joseph _____is driving_____ the high-lo without his hard hat.

> drive
> ✓ smoke
> stand
> wear
> drive

E. Ask and answer the questions with a partner.

   1. What is Vladimir wearing? He is wearing sandals.

   2. What is he carrying? He's carrying a heavy box.

   3. What is Luis wearing for safety? He is wearing safety glasses.

   4. Who isn't wearing a hairnet? Anna isn't wearing a hairnet.

   5. What is Joseph driving? He is driving a hi-lo.

   6. What aren't Frank and Joseph wearing? They aren't wearing hard hats.

   7. What is Louise doing? She's standing up and packing a box.

   8. Is she sitting? No, she isn't.

   9. Is Mr. Brooks worried? Yes, he is.

D. Complete.

Ask different students to pantomime and explain the meaning of the verbs in the box. Next, call on students to complete each sentence orally. Then, have them complete the sentences in their books.

E. Ask and answer the questions with a partner.

Suggest that students look back at the picture on page 132 as they work with their partner. Set a time limit (perhaps five minutes) for the pairwork. Then, call on different pairs to present one question and answer each to the class.

Suggestion

Extend the practice by asking students to think of other questions about things that are happening in the picture. A student asks his or her question and calls on another student to answer.

Reading: Holiday Deliveries

A. Before You Read.

• Invite students to answer the questions above the passage. Encourage them to add information. For example: *My uncle works for UPS. He says they're really busy on Fridays.*

• Ask students to read the article to themselves. When they finish, invite them to ask about anything they don't understand. Also encourage them to add their own comments about the reading.

Suggestion

Discuss the ad for part-time package handlers. Ask different students to explain in their own words the meaning of *handlers, individual medical benefits,* and *paid vacation.*

B. Read and circle.

Review and discuss the correct answers with the whole class.

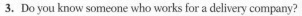

Reading: Holiday Deliveries

A. Before You Read.

1. What season is the busiest season for delivery companies?
2. How many delivery companies can you name?
3. Do you know someone who works for a delivery company?

It's fall, and delivery companies are busy. They are getting ready for the busy holiday season. Every year, in the fall, many delivery companies advertise for part-time positions. The companies need more employees for holiday deliveries. The companies are looking for more package handlers. Package handlers sort and load the many packages that customers want to send.

> **Package handlers**
> Part-time $8.50–$9.50
> 3 ½ – 5 hours per day
> No weekends
> 3 Shifts: 1:00/4:00/5:30
> Individual medical benefits
> Paid vacation

The largest delivery companies deliver packages in more than 200 countries and deliver more than 13.5 million packages a day. They deliver packages by air or on the ground by truck. The truck drivers wear uniforms that change according to the season. In the hot summer, the drivers may wear shorts.

Over a million people work for delivery companies, and there are many jobs available. Would you like to work for a delivery company?

B. Read and circle.

1. Delivery companies need more employees
   a. in the summer.   b. in the winter.   c. in the fall.   d. in the spring.

2. Delivery companies need people to
   a. handle packages.   b. sell packages.   c. help salesmen.   d. fly planes.

3. Delivery companies deliver packages
   a. by air.   b. by sea.   c. by land.   d. both a and c.

4. This classified ad is looking for people who can
   a. work in the morning.   c. work eight-hour shifts.
   b. work weekends.   d. work part time.

5. What benefits will the package handlers receive? (Circle two answers.)
   a. medical benefits   c. prescription plan
   b. paid vacation   d. paid sick days

Writing Our Stories: Home Improvements

A. Look at the picture. Write a story about the people in the picture. What are their occupations? What are they wearing? What are they doing at the house?

build
deliver
fix
install
mow
paint
plant
repair
deck
garage
roof
tree

B. Write your story.

(Answers will vary.)

_____

_____

_____

_____

_____

_____

_____

_____

Writing Note

Give your story a title. Put the title in the center of the top line. The words in the title begin with capital letters.

Writing Our Stories: Home Improvements

A. Look at the picture.

• Help students identify the objects in the picture and the actions the people are doing. You might want to list them on the board as students mention them. Ask:

> *What's this?*
> *What is he/she wearing?*
> *What is he/she using?*
> *What is he/she doing?*

• Ask students to point out actions and objects they don't know how to describe. Provide sample sentences as needed.

• Review the words in the box on the right. Ask students to use each one in a sentence. For any words they don't understand, provide a simple explanation and a sample sentence.

B. Write your story.

Suggest that students begin by writing a sentence telling what the people are doing at the house. Then have them write about at least five of the people in the picture.

Writing Note

Read the Writing Note to the class. Ask for suggestions for a title for students' stories. Write the suggestions on the board. Ask students to give their stories a title.

Suggestion

Invite students to write on the board one sentence each from their stories. Have the rest of the class review the sentences and point out anything they think is an error. When a student finds an error, have him or her make the correction on the board. Ask students to copy any particularly useful sentences in their notebooks.

Practicing on Your Own

A. Look at the picture.

- Invite students to comment on the picture. Ask questions such as:

  What does this sign say?
  What (are they) wearing?
  What (are they) doing?

- Have students complete the sentences on their own and check their answers with a partner.

In your notebook, write four more sentences about the picture.

Ask students to write some of their sentences on the board. Discuss the sentences with the class. Have them locate and correct any errors in content or grammar.

Practicing on Your Own

A. Look at the picture. Read and complete. Some of the sentences are negative.

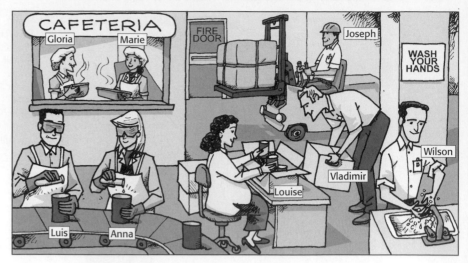

The safety inspector is back at the factory. He is very happy with the changes.

1. Gloria and Marie __are wearing__ hairnets.

2. Gloria and Marie __are cooking__ lunch for the employees.

3. Vladimir __isn't wearing__ sandals. He __is wearing__ work boots.

4. Luis and Anna __are wearing__ safety glasses.

5. Louise __is sitting__ in a chair. She __isn't__ standing.

6. Wilson __is washing__ his hands.

7. Joseph __is wearing__ a hard hat.

8. Joseph __is driving__ a high-lo.

9. All of the employees __are following__ safety rules.

cook
drive
follow
sit
wash
wear

In your notebook, write four more sentences about the picture.

Grammar Summary

1. Present continuous tense   Use the present continuous to talk about what's happening now.

2. Some present continuous time expressions

now	right now	at the present time	at the moment

3. Statements

I	**am** **am not**	
He She It	**is** **is not / isn't**	**packing** boxes. **taking** a break. **wearing** a uniform.
We You They	**are** **are not / aren't**	

4. Spelling

Verb ending	**Spelling**
• Most verbs drink read study	Add **-ing.** drinking reading studying
• Verbs that end with **e** write take	Drop the **e** and add **-ing.** writing taking
• One-syllable verbs that end with a consonant, vowel, consonant sit mop	Double the final vowel and add **-ing.** sitting mopping
• Verbs that end with **x, y,** or **z** fix buy	Do not double **x, y,** or **z.** fixing buying

---

Grammar Summary

• Review the summary with the class. Invite students to make up alternate sentences for each example in the chart. For example, in place of *She **isn't taking** a break,* a student might say, *She **isn't driving** to work.*

• See the Grammar Summary Expansion on page 237 for a more complete explanation of these grammar points.

Unit 10
Fast Food

Discuss the unit title art. Ask: *What do you see?* (A man pulling giant french fries out of a cardboard, fast-food container.)

☀Dictionary:
Working at a Restaurant

📻 A. Listen and repeat.
   (CD2, Track 6)

   • Invite students to comment on the people and things in the pictures. Ask:

   What's this?
   What do you call this person?
   What is he/she doing?

   • Draw students' attention to the words in the box. Have them listen the first time you play the audio. The second time through, have them repeat the words.
   • Repeat the second activity until students feel comfortable pronouncing the words. Then, say each word and ask students to point to where it is illustrated in one of the pictures.

B. Complete.

   Read the sample answer for item 1. Ask students what the verb tense is. (present continuous) Students complete the sentences with present continuous forms of the verbs in the box. Check for correct answers by having students put one sentence each on the board.

Teacher Note

Follow the directions for *Simon Says* on page 139. This activity provides a good review of the new verbs.

---

10 🖐 Fast Food

Dictionary: Working at a Restaurant

📻 **A. Listen and repeat.**

carry	eat	make	pay	serve	wear
cook	greet	order	pour	talk to	wipe

B. Complete.

1. The manager __is__ __greeting__ customers.

2. He __is wiping__ the table.

3. He __is talking to__ the employees.

4. They __are making__ coffee.

5. They __are serving__ customers.

6. They __are wearing__ uniforms.

7. He __is ordering__ a sandwich.

8. He __is paying__ the cashier.

9. He __is eating__ a hamburger.

10. She __is pouring__ some coffee.

11. She __is cooking__ eggs.

12. She __is carrying__ her food.

C. Look at the pictures. Complete the sentences.

mop	prepare	wash	wipe

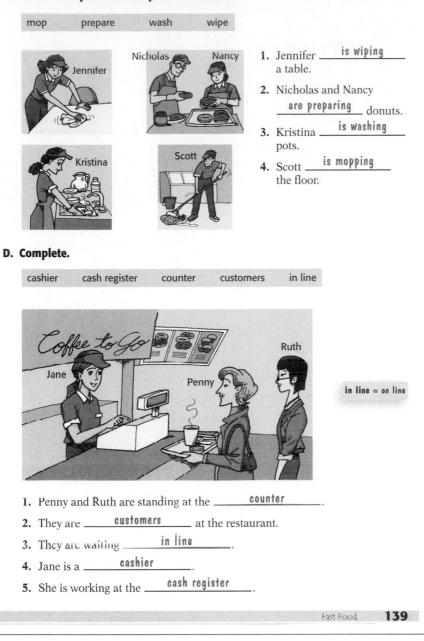

1. Jennifer ___is wiping___ a table.

2. Nicholas and Nancy ___are preparing___ donuts.

3. Kristina ___is washing___ pots.

4. Scott ___is mopping___ the floor.

D. Complete.

cashier	cash register	counter	customers	in line

in line = on line

1. Penny and Ruth are standing at the ___counter___.

2. They are ___customers___ at the restaurant.

3. They are waiting ___in line___.

4. Jane is a ___cashier___.

5. She is working at the ___cash register___.

Fast Food **139**

Have students repeat the words in the box. Explain any they don't understand. Then, have them look at the pictures and fill in the blanks with the present continuous form of the verbs on their own. Review together.

D. Complete.

Review vocabulary words in the box. Have students complete the answers and then share their answers with the class.

Suggestion

Play *Simon Says* with the verbs students are studying in this lesson. Have everyone stand. Explain that every time you say the words *Simon says* followed by a sentence using a new verb, students should pantomime the sentence. For example:

T: *Simon says, "Mop the floor."*
SS: (Students pantomime mopping.)

Every time you leave off the words *Simon says*, students should not do the pantomime. Whoever does the action must sit down. For example:

T: *Wipe the table.*
SS: (Students don't move.)

Gradually increase the speed at which you say the sentences. Continue the game until only a few students are left standing.

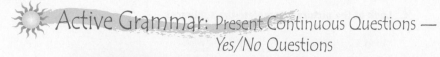

Active Grammar: Present Continuous Questions– Yes/No Questions

A. Read and answer.

- Discuss the picture with students. Ask questions such as:

  Who's this?
  What's she doing?
  What's he saying?
  What's he wearing?

- Point out the short answers. Have students look at the picture and use these short answers to answer the questions. Review the correct answers by reading a question and calling on a student to answer.

B. Write five more questions about the picture.

Set a time limits for each part of this exercise. For example, you might allow five minutes for students to write their questions and five minutes for the pairs to ask and answer the questions. Call on different pairs to present their questions and answers to the class.

Suggestion

When you finish reviewing Exercise B, ask three students at a time to come to the board. Ask each student to write on the board one of the new questions about the picture they heard. Have the three students sit down. Then ask other students to go to the board and make any necessary corrections to the sentences. Finally, read each question and call on a student to respond.

A. Read and answer.

Nicholas — Next! — Coffee Go — Jane

A medium black coffee!

MENU

Mr. Lopez Vince George Pamela

Yes, she is. No, she isn't.   Yes, he is. No, he isn't.   Yes, they are. No, they aren't.

1. **Is** Jane **working** today? ___Yes, she is.___
2. **Is** she **making** sandwiches? ___No, she isn't.___
3. **Is** Mr. Lopez **ordering** coffee? ___Yes, he is.___
4. **Is** he **ordering** a large coffee? ___No, he isn't.___
5. **Is** Nicholas **wiping** the counter? ___No, he isn't.___
6. **Are** customers **waiting** in line? ___Yes, they are.___
7. **Are** the customers **talking** to each other? ___No, they aren't.___
8. **Are** customers **eating** donuts? ___No, they aren't.___

B. Write five more questions about the picture. Ask and answer questions with a partner. (Answers will vary. Sample answers below.)

1. Is Nicholas ___talking to the customers___?
2. Is Mr. Lopez ___ordering a donut___?
3. Are Jane and Nicholas ___waiting in line___?
4. _____?
5. _____?

☀ Wh- Questions

⬛ **A. Listen and complete with the question words.**

decaf — decaffeinated coffee
Decaffeinated coffee does not have caffeine.

Mary

Vera

Patricia

1. __What__ are they eating?   They're eating breakfast.
2. __What__ is Mary eating?   She's eating eggs and a bagel.
3. __Where__ are they having breakfast?   They're having breakfast at Coffee to Go.
4. __What__ is Vera drinking?   She's drinking orange juice.
5. __How many__ donuts is Vera eating?   She's eating two donuts.
6. __Who__ is drinking coffee?   Patricia is.
7. __What kind of__ coffee is Patricia drinking?   She's drinking decaf coffee.
8. __Why__ are they smiling?   Because they're enjoying breakfast.

B. Match each question with the correct answer.

1. Who is Mary eating with? (n.)   a. She's eating two donuts.
2. What is Scott doing? (g.)   b. Patricia is.
3. Who is eating a bagel? (b.)   c. She's eating with her friends.
4. Where are they working? (f.)   d. Because it is dirty.
5. Why is she wiping the table? (d.)   e. A sesame bagel.
6. How many donuts is Vera eating? (a.)   f. At Coffee to Go.
7. What kind of bagel is she eating? (e.)   g. He's mopping the floor.

☀ Wh- Questions

⬛ A. **Listen and complete with the question words.** (CD2, Track 7)

- Invite students to comment on the picture. Ask:
  Where are the three women? What are they doing?

- Read through the answers to the questions in the right-hand column and clarify the meaning of any new words. Then, have students work independently as they fill in the question words as they listen to the audio. Review the correct answers with the whole class.

B. **Match each question with the correct answer.**

Have students complete the matching activity asking and answering the questions with a partner.

Suggestion

Recycle Exercise A by asking students to cover the questions in the first column. See if they can ask an appropriate question with no cues.

Audio Script

A. **Listen and complete with the question words.** (CD2, Track 7)

1. What are they eating?
2. What is Mary eating?
3. Where are they eating breakfast?
4. What is Vera drinking?
5. How many donuts is Vera eating?
6. Who is drinking coffee?
7. What kind of coffee is Patricia drinking?
8. Why are they smiling?

C. *Yes/No* questions.

• Discuss the picture with students. Model new vocabulary as needed and ask students to repeat. Ask questions such as:

Who's this?
What's (he) doing?
What else do you see?

• Review the verbs in the box by saying each one aloud and calling on a student to explain in his or her own words what it means. Then, call on a second student to use the word in a sentence.

• As students complete the sentences, move around the room, helping as needed. Then have students take turns asking and answering the questions with partners.

D. *Wh-* questions.

Have students write the words in each item in the correct order. Review the correct answers by calling on students to read aloud one question each.

Ask and answer the questions with a partner.

Students take turns asking and answering the questions with a partner. Review the answers with the class, eliciting from students several different answers to some questions. For example:

T: *What are you doing?*
S1: *I'm studying English.*
S2: *I'm talking to Erik.*
S3: *I'm looking at my book.*

C. *Yes/No* questions. Look at the picture. Complete the questions. Then, answer the questions with a partner. **(Answers may vary.)**

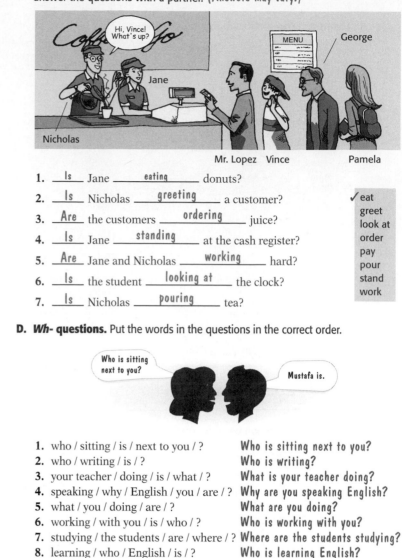

1. __Is__ Jane ____eating____ donuts?
2. __Is__ Nicholas ____greeting____ a customer?
3. __Are__ the customers ____ordering____ juice?
4. __Is__ Jane ____standing____ at the cash register?
5. __Are__ Jane and Nicholas ____working____ hard?
6. __Is__ the student ____looking at____ the clock?
7. __Is__ Nicholas ____pouring____ tea?

✓ eat
greet
look at
order
pay
pour
stand
work

D. *Wh-* questions. Put the words in the questions in the correct order.

1. who / sitting / is / next to you / ?   Who is sitting next to you?
2. who / writing / is / ?   Who is writing?
3. your teacher / doing / is / what / ?   What is your teacher doing?
4. speaking / why / English / you / are / ?   Why are you speaking English?
5. what / you / doing / are / ?   What are you doing?
6. working / with you / is / who / ?   Who is working with you?
7. studying / the students / are / where / ?   Where are the students studying?
8. learning / who / English / is / ?   Who is learning English?

Ask and answer the questions with a partner.

Stating Prices

A. Pronunciation: Prices. Listen and repeat.

a.	$1.29	a dollar twenty-nine	*or* one dollar and twenty-nine cents
b.	$3.50	three fifty	*or* three dollars and fifty cents
c.	$4.16	four sixteen	*or* four dollars and sixteen cents
d.	$6.99	six ninety-nine	*or* six dollars and ninety-nine cents
e.	$10.25	ten twenty-five	*or* ten dollars and twenty-five cents
f.	$12.05	twelve oh five	*or* twelve dollars and five cents
g.	$14.30	fourteen thirty	*or* fourteen dollars and thirty cents

Practice saying these prices with a partner.

a. $3.10	**c.** $5.50	**e.** $2.15	**g.** $17.47	**i.** $15.30
b. $11.05	**d.** $13.87	**f.** $6.75	**h.** $9.25	

Working Together: Student to Student

A. STUDENT A: Turn to page 144. Look at the menu.

STUDENT B: You both have menus with different prices missing. Ask and answer questions about the missing prices and fill in the menu.

How much is a hamburger?

A dollar forty-nine.

Hamburger	$1.49	French fries	small	.99
Cheeseburger	1.79		large	1.39
Super Burger	2.99	Soft drink	small	.89
Chicken Sandwich	3.59		medium	1.09
Fish Sandwich	2.99		large	1.39
Chicken Pieces	2.89	Coffee		.79
Salad bar	3.50	Apple pie		1.29

Fast Food **143**

Stating Prices

A. Pronunciation: Prices.

(CD2, Track 8)

Play the audio of the written-out versions of each dollar amount. Pause after each dollar amount and ask students to point out the differences in wording and pronunciation between the two versions. Then, play the audio again and have students listen and repeat.

Practice saying these prices with a partner.

Ask students to practice saying the dollar amounts both ways, using the short form first and the long form next. Move around the room as they work, helping as needed.

Working Together: Student to Student

A. Student A.

• Explain that both Student A and Student B will look at similar menus, but that both menus are incomplete. The difference is that the information missing from Student A's menu is included on Student B's menu and vice versa.

• Read the instructions and model the first question and answer with a student. Then, have student pairs complete the activity on their own. Have them check each other's answers when they finish.

☀Working Together: Student to Student

B. Student B.

See the instructions for Exercise A on page 143.

☀Ordering Lunch

👥 C. Read and practice.

- Read the dialogue to the class. Answer any questions students may have.
- Have students practice the dialogue in pairs.

👥 D. With a partner, write a new conversation.

- Ask students to talk about foods they would actually order for lunch. Then, have them work together to write both sides of the conversation. They should use the conversation in Exercise C as a model if they wish.
- Have students practice their conversations with partners. Invite some pairs to perform their conversations for the class.

Suggestion

Bring copies of a take-out menu to class and ask students to study it and ask questions about anything they don't understand. Then, have pairs use the food items on the menu to role-play the conversation in Exercise D again. Invite groups to present their new conversations to the class.

☀Working Together: Student to Student

B. STUDENT A: You both have menus with different prices missing. Ask and answer questions about the missing prices and fill in the menus.

How much is a hamburger?

A dollar forty-nine.

Hamburger	$1.49	French fries	small	.99
Cheeseburger	1.79		large	1.39
Super Burger	2.99	Soft drink	small	.89
Chicken Sandwich	3.59		medium	1.09
Fish Sandwich	2.99		large	1.39
Chicken Pieces	2.89	Coffee		.79
Salad bar	3.50	Apple pie		1.29

☀Ordering Lunch

👥 C. Read and practice.

Employee: Can I help you?

Customer: Sure. I'd like a chicken sandwich and a soda.

Employee: What size soda—small, medium, or large?

Customer: Medium.

Employee: Anything else?

Customer: Ummm. An order of large fries.

Employee: Is that it?

Customer: Yes.

Employee: For here or to go?

Customer: To go.

Employee: That's a chicken sandwich, a medium soda, and large fries. That's $6.37.

👥 D. With a partner, write a new conversation. Order lunch from the menu above.

E. Group discussion. Sit in a group of three to four students. Talk about fast-food restaurants in your neighborhoods. Write the answers and report your information to the class. (Answers will vary.)

Questions	Our Answers
1. Which fast-food restaurants are in your neighborhood?	
2. What is your favorite fast-food restaurant? Why?	
3. Which restaurant is cheap?	
4. Which restaurant is expensive?	
5. Which fast foods are good for you?	
6. Which fast-food restaurants are in your countries?	

F. Looking at fast-food facts. Guess the correct answer.

1. What is the most popular dessert in the U.S.?

_____ cake _____ pie _____ ice cream _✓_ cookies _____ fruit

What is *your* favorite dessert? _(Answer will vary.)_

2. Put the ice cream flavors in the correct order of popularity from 1 to 4.

_4_ strawberry _2_ chocolate _3_ butter pecan _1_ vanilla

What is *your* favorite ice cream flavor? _(Answer will vary.)_

3. What is the favorite ice cream topping?

_____ pineapple   _____ strawberries

_✓_ chocolate syrup   _____ whipped cream

What is *your* favorite topping? _(Answer will vary.)_

4. How many hamburgers do Americans eat in a week?

(a.) one   b. two   c. three   d. four

5. Which country sells the most soda?

a. Brazil   b. Mexico   (c.) the United States   d. China

What's the most popular soda in *your* native country? _(Answer will vary.)_

(Source: Beverage Marketing Corporation; International Ice Cream Association; T.G.I. Friday's/Harris Interactive/Yankelovich Partners)

Answers: 1. cookies 2. 1-vanilla; 2-chocolate; 3-butter pecan; 4-strawberry 3. chocolate syrup 4. a. one 5. c. the United States

E. Group discussion.

Ask each group to choose a reporter to take notes and report back to the whole class. As the various groups report their answers, write any new vocabulary words on the board and discuss them with the class. Some students may wish to copy some of these words into their notebooks.

F. Looking at fast-food facts.

Ask students to cover the answers at the bottom of the page with a sheet of paper and to answer the questions without looking at them. Then, have them "correct" their own work. Ask which answers surprised them.

Suggestion

Create simple charts or graphs on the board to show how the class as a whole ranks the various foods. You might write the names of the five desserts in a column and then have students raise their hands for the one they like best. Write the numbers after the name of each dessert. You can do the same thing for ice cream flavors and ice cream toppings.

☼ The Big Picture: Coffee to Go

A. Talk about the picture.

Ask students to explain what they see in the picture. Ask questions to elicit key information about all the people in the picture. For example:

What's this?
Who's this?
Where is he/she?
What is he/she doing?
What is he/she saying?

B. Listen and label the people in the picture. (CD2, Track 9)

Play the audio and have students write each person's name on the picture. You may wish to play the audio several times, pausing after the group of sentences that describes each person. Then, play the audio all the way through once so that students can check their work.

☼ The Big Picture: Coffee to Go

A. Talk about the picture.

B. Listen and label the people in the picture.

Jess	Harry	Mr. Lopez	Pete	Sherri
Kate	Mary	Patricia	Scott	Vera

Audio Script

B. Listen and label the people in the picture. (CD2, Track 9)

It's early in the morning at Coffee to Go. Kate is working behind the counter. She's at the cash register. She's taking another order. She's tired because she's working overtime again. Sherri is standing in front of the counter. She is taking her coffee. She is on her way to work. Pete's another employee behind the counter. He's pouring a large coffee for a customer. Jess is standing behind

Sherri. He always orders the same thing–a large coffee and two donuts. He is giving his order to Kate, but Pete is already pouring Jess a large coffee. Jess comes to Coffee to Go every weekday morning. His office is across the street.

Standing at the table is Mr. Lopez. He's putting sugar in his coffee. He likes his coffee dark and sweet. Sitting at a table are three regular customers: Mary, Vera, and Patricia. They're senior citizens, and they visit Coffee to Go three times a week after they take a walk in the park. They like to

have breakfast together after their walk. Mary is drinking a cup of tea and eating eggs and a bagel. Vera is eating two donuts and drinking some orange juice. Patricia is eating a donut and is drinking a cup of decaf coffee. They're talking and smiling. It's a good morning for them. But, it's not a good morning for Scott. He's a good worker, but he was late again. Harry, his manager, is talking to him. Scott is wiping a table and listening to Harry. Harry is angry. He is telling Scott that he must not be late again. Harry is telling Scott to stay late today.

C. Fill in the question words. Then, complete the answers.

1. __Who__ is working behind the counter?   Pete and Kate __are__.
2. __What__ is Kate doing?   She __is working__ at the register.
3. __Where__ are Mary, Vera, and Patricia?   They __are__ at Coffee to Go.
4. __What__ are they doing?   They __are sitting and eating__.
5. __What__ is Mary drinking?   She __is drinking__ tea.
6. __Who__ is wiping tables?   Scott __is__.
7. __Why__ is Harry talking to Scott?   Because Scott was late for work.
8. __Who__ is working?   Kate, Pete, and Scott __are__.

D. Read and answer the questions.

| Yes, she is. | Yes, he is. | Yes, she does. | Yes, he does. |
| No, she isn't. | No, he isn't. | No, she doesn't. | No, he doesn't. |

1. Is Kate working overtime?   __Yes, she is.__
2. Is she tired?   __Yes, she is.__
3. Does Pete work at the donut shop?   __Yes, he does.__
4. Is Sherri taking a donut?   __No, she isn't.__
5. Does Jess come to the donut shop every day?   __Yes, he does.__
6. Does Jess always order the same thing?   __Yes, he does.__
7. Is Mary drinking coffee?   __No, she isn't.__
8. Is Scott mopping the floor?   __No, he isn't.__
9. Does Scott often come to work late?   __Yes, he does.__
10. Is Scott listening to his boss?   __Yes, he is.__

E. Write a story about the Coffee to Go donut shop.

Fast Food **147**

C. Fill in the question words.

Have students complete the questions and answers on their own. Then, call on one student to read each completed question and another to read the related answer.

D. Read and answer the questions.

• Point out the short answers at the top of the exercise that students will use to answer the questions. Then, ask students to read the questions silently and to ask about any they don't understand.
• Play the audio from Exercise B again **(CD2, Track 9)** and have students fill in the short answers in the blanks at the right. Review the correct answers with the class.

E. Write a story about the Coffee to Go donut shop.

Tell students they can use the information in Exercises B and C as they write their stories.

Suggestion

Encourage students to write about themselves, their family members, their classmates, and their friends. Some people can be working in the donut shop and others can be customers. Invite students to read their completed stories to the class.

Reading: Regional Favorites

A. Before You Read.

- Invite several students to answer the questions above the two passages. Encourage them to add information. For example: *People in my country love to drink coconut milk. Restaurants in the United States don't serve coconut milk.*
- Read the passages aloud as students follow along in their books. Emphasize that it isn't important for them to understand every word; they should try to get the main ideas from each passage.
- Read the passages a second time and ask students to raise their hands when they don't understand a sentence. Read it again and then restate the ideas in the sentence in simple English.

B. Read and circle.

Have students complete the activity on their own. Suggest that they look back at the stories to find the answer to each question.

C. Make a list of five different countries and a popular food from each country.

When the partners finish their lists, have them compare lists with another pair of students.

Reading: Regional Favorites

A. Before You Read.

1. Does your native country or city have a famous food?
2. What city or state should you visit if you want to eat the best food?
3. Can you name a famous food from your city or state?

Pizza: New York City vs. Chicago

If you live in New York City, you probably eat New York style pizza. It has a thin crust, a thin layer of tomato sauce, and a layer of mozzarella cheese. Maybe you like to have sausage or pepperoni on your pizza, too. New York style pizza is not a heavy dish. It's so thin that you can fold it in half and eat it with one hand.

Chicago pizza is different. It is like a pie. It has a thick layer of cheese and other ingredients such as mushrooms, onions, and sausage. The fresh tomato sauce is on top, not on the bottom. Which is better? It depends. Are you from Chicago or from New York?

Chili: Cincinnati vs. Texas

Do you order your chili one-way, two-way, or maybe five-way? Then, you must be from Cincinnati, Ohio. In Cincinnati, chili is a combination of ground beef, tomato paste, onions, beans, and spices such as cinnamon and ginger. There are five different combinations. Here are two of them: "two-way" is chili on top of spaghetti; "three-way" is a two-way chili with cheese on top.

Do you put beans in chili? Not if you are from Texas. Typical Texas chili uses pieces of beef and spices for flavor. The spices and peppers are typical of dishes in Mexico.

B. Read and circle.

1. New York style pizza has a (thin) / thick crust.
2. Chicago style pizza has a thin / (thick) crust.
3. Which pizza is a heavy dish?   a. New York style   (b.) Chicago style
4. Which chili is served on spaghetti?   (a.) Cincinnati style   b. Texas style
5. Which chili has Mexican spices?   a. Cincinnati style   (b.) Texas style
6. Which chili is served five different ways?   (a.) Cincinnati style   b. Texas style

C. Make a list of five different countries and a popular food from each country.

Japan — sushi

A. Look at the pictures. Write a story. What is happening at the diner today? Is the restaurant busy? What are the employees doing? What are the customers doing?

(Answers will vary. Sample answer below.)

The customers are eating lunch at the diner today. Some people are making a salad at the buffet. Jane and Marie ordered drinks from a waitress. Jane is pouring her soda into a glass. Now they are looking at the menu. They are deciding what to eat. The waitress is waiting for their order.

Writing Our Stories: The Diner

A. Look at the pictures.

• Have students look at the three pictures for 60 seconds. Then, ask them to close their books and say what they can remember about the pictures. Repeat each statement and ask other students if they agree. For example:

*One woman is reading the menu.
The other woman is pouring a soda.
They're having lunch.*

• Have students open their books again. Ask them to make other statements about the pictures now that they can see them again.

• Call on different students to answer the questions following the direction line. Then ask the students to complete their stories on their own.

Suggestion

Collect the stories and make corrections. Type up some of the stories and post them on the classroom wall. Encourage students to look at each other's work before or after class.

☀ Practicing on Your Own

A. Contrast.

• Have students read the sentence to themselves and circle their answers.

• After reviewing the correct answers with the class, ask students to name the verb tense that is used with the time expression *now* (present continuous) and the one used with the time expression *every day* (simple present).

B. Read the story.

Ask students to read the story and write the answers on their own. Tell them not to worry if they don't understand every single word. Encourage them to focus only on completing the eight questions.

Suggestion

Go back over the story later and allow students to ask about anything they don't understand. Restate problematic phrases or sentences using different words.

☀ Practicing on Your Own

A. Contrast. Read and circle.

1.	Are they preparing lunch?	(Now)	Every day
2.	Who opens the store in the morning?	Now	(Every day)
3.	Who's working at the counter?	(Now)	Every day
4.	What do you do?	Now	(Every day)
5.	What kind of sandwich are you eating?	(Now)	Every day
6.	Do you wear a uniform at work?	Now	(Every day)
7.	What are you studying?	(Now)	Every day
8.	Is she reading a book?	(Now)	Every day
9.	Who's teaching your class?	(Now)	Every day

B. Read the story. Then, write the questions.

Teresa is a counter clerk at Mr. Burger. This is her first day at the cash register, and she's very nervous. She's working slowly because she doesn't want to make a mistake. The restaurant is getting busy. Now there are six customers waiting in line. One man is getting impatient, and he's making Teresa more nervous. Patty is at the register, and Teresa is taking her order. Patty is ordering a fish sandwich meal and a drink. Patty's order is $4.50, and she's giving Teresa a $10 bill. Teresa is giving Patty $6.50 in change. Oops!

1. Who _is a counter clerk at Mr. Burger_ ?   Teresa is.
2. How many customers _are there_ ?   Six.
3. Is _Teresa working quickly_ ?   No, she's working slowly.
4. Who _is getting impatient_ ?   One man is.
5. What _is Patty ordering_ ?   A fish sandwich meal.
6. How much _is Patty's order_ ? $4.50.
7. How much _is she giving Teresa_ ? $10.00.
8. Is _Teresa giving Patty the correct change_ ?   No, she isn't.

Looking at Numbers: Figuring out a Bill

A. Look at the menu on page 143. Figure out the total for each order.

1. Boris is ordering dinner. He wants a super burger, large French fries, and a large soda. How much is his order? $5.77
2. Tazuko is at Mr. Burger. She is ordering chicken pieces, the salad bar, and a small drink. How much is her order? $7.28
3. Joseph is ordering lunch for his children. He's ordering one order of chicken pieces, one cheeseburger, two orders of small fries, and two small drinks. How much is his order? $8.44

Grammar Summary

1. Present continuous

a. The present continuous describes an action that is happening now.

b. Time expressions such as *now, right now, at this moment,* and *today* are often used with the present continuous.

2. *Yes/No* questions

Am I work**ing?**	Yes, you are.	No, you aren't.	No, you're not.
Are you order**ing?**	Yes, I am.		No, I'm not.
Is he drink**ing** a soda?	Yes, he is.	No, he isn't.	No, he's not.
Is she eat**ing** a salad?	Yes, she is.	No, she isn't.	No, she's not.
Is it work**ing?**	Yes, it is.	No, it isn't.	No, it's not.
Are we pay**ing?**	Yes, we are.	No, we aren't.	No, we're not.
Are they cook**ing?**	Yes, they are.	No, they aren't.	No, they're not.

3. *Wh-* questions

Where **am I** work**ing today?**	You're working in the kitchen.
Where **are you** work**ing?**	I'm working at the counter.
What **is he** order**ing?**	A muffin and coffee.
Why **is she** talk**ing** to the manager?	Because the employees are working slowly.
Where **are we** eat**ing** lunch?	At a fast-food restaurant.
What **are they** cook**ing?**	Eggs and bacon.

4. *Who* questions **Who** takes a singular verb form.

Who is working at the counter?	Teresa is.
Who is eating at the restaurant?	Mary, Patricia, and Vera are.

Looking at Numbers: Figuring out a Bill

A. Look at the menu on page 143.

Have students work in pairs. Ask one pair to do the math on the board for each question and show the rest of the class how they arrived at the answer.

Grammar Summary

- Review the summary with the class. Invite students to make up alternate sentences for each example in the chart. For example, in place of *What is he* ***ordering?,*** a student might say *What is he* ***drinking?*** In place of *A muffin and coffee,* a student might say *Hot tea.*
- See the Grammar Summary Expansion on page 238 for a more complete explanation of these grammar points.

Unit 11
Food Shopping

Discuss the unit title art. Ask: *What do you see?* (A woman pushing a shopping cart.)

☀ Dictionary: Food

📻 A. Listen and repeat.
(CD2, Track 10)

• Before playing the audio, ask students to identify as many of the food items in the pictures on pages 152 and 153 as they can.
• Play the audio several times and have students first listen and then repeat the names of the various foods shown. Introduce each group of foods by reading the name of the group aloud and asking students to explain in their own words what it means. For example: *Produce is fresh fruit and vegetables.*
• Ask students to match each food item with the correct number on the picture.

Suggestion

Ask students to look for cognates among the words. For example, Spanish speakers may discover pairs such as *tomate/tomato* and *patata/potato*.

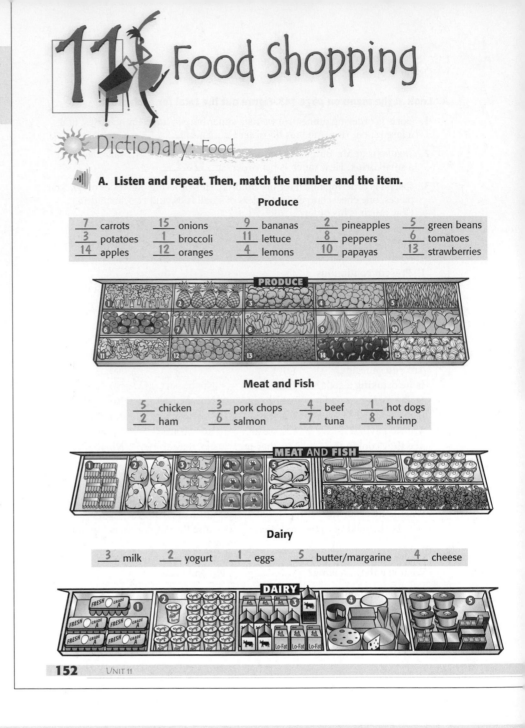

11 Food Shopping

☀ Dictionary: Food

📻 A. Listen and repeat. Then, match the number and the item.

Produce

7 carrots	15 onions	9 bananas	2 pineapples	5 green beans
3 potatoes	1 broccoli	11 lettuce	8 peppers	6 tomatoes
14 apples	12 oranges	4 lemons	10 papayas	13 strawberries

Meat and Fish

5 chicken	3 pork chops	4 beef	1 hot dogs
2 ham	6 salmon	7 tuna	8 shrimp

Dairy

3 milk   2 yogurt   1 eggs   5 butter/margarine   4 cheese

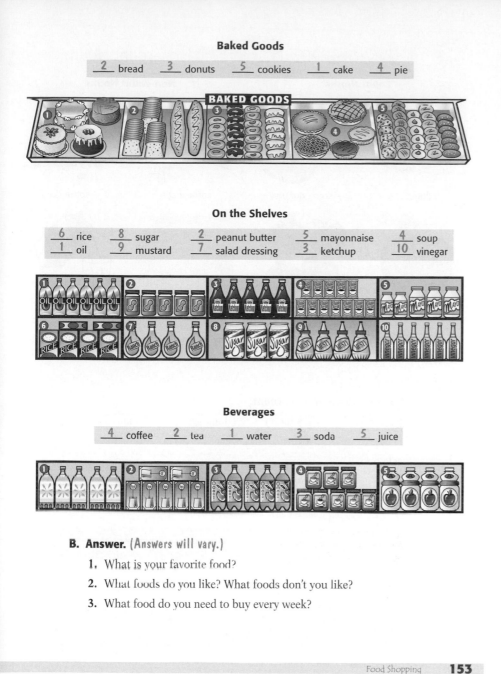

Baked Goods

_2_ bread _3_ donuts _5_ cookies _1_ cake _4_ pie

On the Shelves

_6_ rice _8_ sugar _2_ peanut butter _5_ mayonnaise _4_ soup
_1_ oil _9_ mustard _7_ salad dressing _3_ ketchup _10_ vinegar

Beverages

_4_ coffee _2_ tea _1_ water _3_ soda _5_ juice

B. Answer. (Answers will vary.)

1. What is your favorite food?

2. What foods do you like? What foods don't you like?

3. What food do you need to buy every week?

Food Shopping **153**

B. Answer.

Read the questions together. Ask several students to answer each question. Repeat the answers, correcting any errors in grammar or pronunciation and re-stating any sentence fragments as full sentences. Ask students to repeat. For example:

S1: _My favorite food is the peanut butter._

T: _Oh, your favorite food is peanut butter. Repeat. My favorite food is peanut butter._

SS: _My favorite food is peanut butter._

T: _What's your favorite food, Hilmi?_

S2: _Hamburgers._

T: _So, you like hamburgers best. Repeat. My favorite food is hamburgers._

SS: _My favorite food is hamburgers._

Active Grammar: Count and Non-count Nouns

Suggestion

Discuss with the class the definitions of count and non-count nouns. Write *Count* and *Non-count* on the board. Look back at the food items on pages 152 and 153. Ask students to name some food to list under each category.

A. Circle the items you can count.

Ask students to complete the activity on their own and compare their answers with a partner.

B. Look at the food items.

As students complete the activity, walk around the room offering help as needed. Review the completed lists with the whole class.

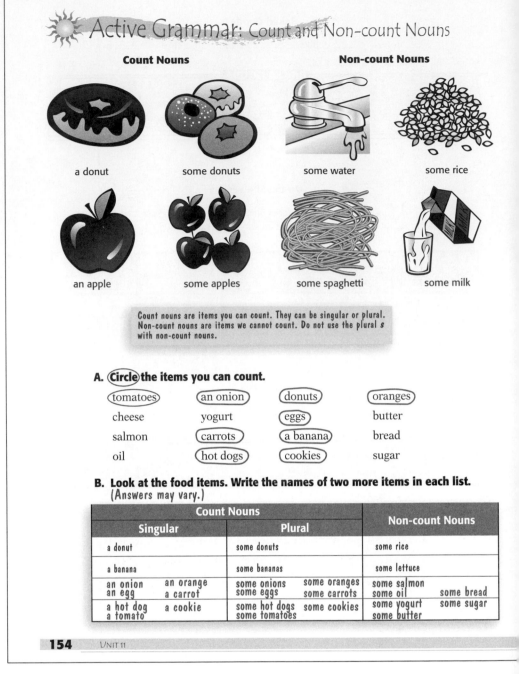

Active Grammar: Count and Non-count Nouns

Count Nouns		Non-count Nouns	
a donut	some donuts	some water	some rice
an apple	some apples	some spaghetti	some milk

Count nouns are items you can count. They can be singular or plural. Non-count nouns are items we cannot count. Do not use the plural *s* with non-count nouns.

A. Circle the items you can count.

(tomatoes)　(an onion)　(donuts)　(oranges)
cheese　　 yogurt　　(eggs)　　butter
salmon　　(carrots)　(a banana)　bread
oil　　　(hot dogs)　(cookies)　sugar

B. Look at the food items. Write the names of two more items in each list.
(Answers may vary.)

Count Nouns				Non-count Nouns	
Singular		**Plural**			
a donut		some donuts		some rice	
a banana		some bananas		some lettuce	
an onion	an orange	some onions	some oranges	some salmon	
an egg	a carrot	some eggs	some carrots	some oil	some bread
a hot dog	a cookie	some hot dogs	some cookies	some yogurt	some sugar
a tomato		some tomatoes		some butter	

☀ Making a Shopping List

📶 **A. Listen to this couple make a shopping list. Check (✓) the items they need.**

		We need	We don't need
1.	milk		✓
2.	hot dogs	✓	
3.	cheese	✓	
4.	lettuce	✓	
5.	a tomato	✓	
6.	a cucumber	✓	
7.	mayonnaise		✓
8.	eggs		✓
9.	an apple pie	✓	
10.	cookies		✓

👥 **B. Talk about each item on the list above.**

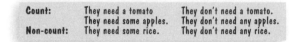

Count:	They need a tomato.	They don't need a tomato.
	They need some apples.	They don't need any apples.
Non-count:	They need some rice.	They don't need any rice.

C. Complete.

1. Do we need any lettuce?

   Yes, we need __some__ lettuce. And please buy __a__ cucumber, too.

2. Do we need any mayonnaise?

   No, we don't need __any__ mayonnaise. But please get __some__ cheese.

3. Do we have hot dogs?

   We need __some__ hot dogs. And we don't have __any__ mustard.

4. How about dessert?

   Let's have __an__ apple pie tonight. We don't need __any__ cookies.

Food Shopping **155**

☀ Making a Shopping List

📶 **A. Listen to this couple make a shopping list.**
(CD2, Track 11)

- Invite students to point to and identify the items in the refrigerator.
- Play the audio once and have students just listen. Then, read through the list of ten items on the page with the class. Check that they understand what each item is. Then, play the audio again several times as students check their answers.
- Review the correct answers with the class.

Suggestion

You may wish to pause (the audio or your reading of the audio script) after each two-line exchange to give students time to record their answers.

👥 **B. Talk about each item on the list above.**

Practice the affirmative and negative statements with the class. Then, have students talk about the items in Exercise A in pairs. Move around the room as they work offering help as needed.

C. Complete.

Have students complete the exercise on their own. Check the correct answers with the whole class.

Audio Script

A. Listen to this couple make a shopping list. Check the items they need.
(CD2, Track 11)

1. A: Do we need any milk?
   B: No, we don't need any milk.
2. A: Do we need hot dogs?
   B: Yes, we need some hot dogs.
3. A: Do we need any cheese?
   B: Yes, we need some cheese.
4. A: How about lettuce? Do we need any lettuce for the salad?
   B: Yes, we do. I don't see any in here. And please get a tomato and a cucumber.

5. A: Do we have any mayonnaise?
   B: Yes, we have some. We don't need any.
6. A: Do we need eggs?
   B: No, we have six, seven, eight eggs. We don't need any.
7. A: Do we have any dessert?
   B: Yes. Let's have an apple pie tonight. But, we don't need any cookies. We have a lot of cookies.

Teacher's Guide, Unit 11 **155**

D. Read.

• Ask students to follow along in their books as you read the dialogue. Then, read each line and ask students to repeat. Have pairs of students read the dialogue to the class.
• Answer any questions students may have.

E. Complete with *some* or *any*.

• Have students do the exercise on their own. Suggest that they look back at the words *a lot of, some,* and *any* in Exercise A as they complete the sentences.
• Review the correct answers with the class.

F. Make a list of the items you need for each recipe.

• Ask students to work in pairs to complete the two lists. Walk around the room providing vocabulary words as needed.
• On the board, write any new words students need help with. Point out this list to the class and invite them to make use of it if they wish.

G. Write a dialogue.

Remind students to use the dialogues in Exercises D and E as models. Invite several (or all) student pairs to read their dialogues to the class.

D. Read.

A: Let's make banana splits. We have a lot of ice cream.

B: Great idea. But we don't have any bananas.

A: We have some nuts. And we have some chocolate sauce.

B: But we don't have any whipped cream.

A: And we don't have any cherries for the top.

E. Complete with *some* or *any*.

A: Let's make an apple pie. We have ___some___ apples.

B: We don't have a pie crust. Let's buy a frozen one.

A: We don't have ___any___ sugar. We need ___some___ sugar and ___some___ butter.

B: And we don't have ___any___ vanilla ice cream for the top. Let's buy ___some___.

F. Make a list of items you need for each recipe. (Answers will vary. Sample answers below.)

Pizza	Fruit salad
a pizza crust	a pineapple
some tomato sauce	an apple
some tomatoes	an orange
some cheese	some strawberries
some pepperoni	a banana
an onion	
a pepper	

G. Write a dialogue. Talk about what you have and what you need to make one of the recipes in Exercise F.

A. Match the food below and the container. Add one more item to each list.
(Answers will vary.)

box	bottle	can	bag	jar
cookies	soda	soup	potatoes	jelly
cereal	oil	tomato sauce	onions	mayonnaise
spaghetti	soy sauce	(oil)	potato chips	coffee
	(tomato sauce)	(coffee)	(coffee)	

onions	mayonnaise	potato chips
tomato sauce	coffee	cereal
oil	soy sauce	spaghetti

B. Pronunciation: *of.* Listen and repeat.

1. a can of coffee
2. a jar of mustard
3. a bottle of ketchup
4. a box of cereal
5. a bag of cookies
6. a box of rice

Practice saying these food items with a partner.

1. a can of tuna fish
2. a jar of mayonnaise
3. a bottle of salad dressing
4. a box of crackers
5. a bag of onions
6. a box of macaroni

C. Complete. There are many kinds of containers. Can you complete these?

a gallon of orange juice   a six-pack of soda   (Answers will vary.)

a quart of milk   a package of tacos

a container of yogurt   a slice of pizza

☀ Identifying Containers

A. Match the food below and the container.

• Ask students to complete the exercise individually and compare answers with a partner. Point out that there may be more than one correct place to write some words. For example, some people may buy uncooked spaghetti in a bag, whereas others may buy prepared spaghetti in a can or a jar.

• Review the completed lists with the class. Write the names of the containers on the board and, under each, list some of the additional items students suggest.

B. Pronunciation: *of.*
(CD2, Track 12)

Ask students to listen as you point to each item and play the audio. Point out that *of* sounds like *ah*. Link the *ah* sound with the word before. Then have students repeat each item several times.

Practice saying these food items with a partner.

Model the pronunciation of the food items and ask students to repeat. Students then practice saying the phrases to a partner. Move around the room monitoring the pair work and correcting pronunciation as needed.

C. Complete.

Do this exercise with the whole class. Write the names of the containers on the board. Under each, add some of the words suggested by students.

A. Complete these questions and answers about prices.

• Read the instructions and discuss the meaning of the term *reasonable price*. (A price that isn't too high.)
• Work through the exercise with the whole class, calling on different students to suggest prices for each item. Encourage discussion of what a reasonable price for each item is.
• When the questions and answers are filled in, call on different pairs of students to read each exchange to the class.

B. Ask and answer questions about these items, using *How much.*

• Ask a student to name all of the food items shown. Then, ask pairs of students to begin by deciding on a reasonable price for each item in the picture and writing that price next to the food item.
• As the pairs ask and answer each other's questions, move around the room helping as needed.

A. Complete these questions and answers about prices. What is a reasonable price? (Answers to questions will vary.)

| How much is the lettuce? It's $1.29 a pound. | How much are the onions? They're 59¢ a pound. |

1. How much __are__ the apples?   They're 69¢ _____ a pound.
2. How much __is__ the coffee?   It's $4.99 _____ a pound.
3. How much __are__ the green beans?   They're 80¢ _____ a pound.
4. How much __is__ the soup?   It's $3.50 _____ a quart.
5. How much __are__ the carrots?   They're 65¢ _____ a pound.
6. How much __is__ the butter?   It's $3.00 _____ a pound.
7. How much __is__ the soda?   It's 75¢ _____ a bottle.
8. How much __are__ the pears?   They're 90¢ _____ a pound.
9. How much __is__ the milk?   It's $1.75 _____ a quart.
10. How much __are__ the donuts?   They're $4.00 _____ a dozen.

B. Ask and answer questions about these items, using *How much*. Decide on the prices together. (Answers will vary.)

Save $2.00

$5.99 Each

Culture Note

Americans use coupons to save money at the supermarket. You can find coupons in the newspaper and on the Internet. Give the coupons to the cashier at the cash register. Stores sometimes offer double coupons. How do you save money on food?

Suggestion

If possible, bring coupon pages from a newspaper as well as some coupons you have printed out from the Internet. Pass the coupons around and invite students to comment on them and ask questions about anything they don't understand. Point out that there are limitations on most coupons. For example, they must be used before a certain date, or they are only good if you buy several cans of a certain item.

Working Together: Student to Student

A. Two supermarkets. Complete the chart about these two supermarkets.

> **STUDENT A: Ask Student B about prices at Shop and Save. Give prices for Food King.**
>
> **STUDENT B: Turn to page 160.**

How much are eggs at Shop and Save?

	Food King	Shop and Save
Eggs	79¢ a dozen	$1.19 a dozen
Butter	$2.19 a pound	$2.59 a pound
Chicken	$1.99 a pound	$2.39 a pound
Shrimp	$10.99 a pound	$7.99 a pound
Apples	69¢ a pound	49¢ a pound
Cola	$1.69 a bottle	$1.39 a bottle
Bananas	49¢ a pound	69¢ a pound

Food Shopping **159**

Working Together: Student to Student

A. Two supermarkets.

- Explain that the food items on Student A's list and Student B's list are the same. Point out that Student A has only the prices for Food King and Student B has only the prices for Shop and Save.
- Read the instructions and model the first question and answer with a student. Then, have student pairs complete the activity on their own. Have them check each other's answers when they finish.

B. Two supermarkets.

See the instructions for Exercise A on page 159.

C. Use the information in your chart.

Ask students to circle the correct word and complete the sentences on their own. Check for accuracy by having different students read their answers aloud to the class.

D. Food brands.

• Ask students to work alone as they fill in as many brand names as they can. Then, have them form small groups.
• As students work in groups, move around the room offering help with the spelling and pronunciation of brand names as needed.
• Have students explain to each other why they like a particular brand of each item. As you listen in on groups and discover words and phrases they wish to use, supply the correct wording and pronunciation and write them on the board for other groups to use. For example: *It tastes better. It's less expensive. It's more delicious.*

B. Two supermarkets. Complete the chart about these two supermarkets.

STUDENT B: Ask Student A about prices at Food King. Give prices for Shop and Save.

> How much are eggs at Food King?

	Food King	Shop and Save
Eggs	79¢ a dozen	$1.19 a dozen
Butter	$2.19 a pound	$2.59 a pound
Chicken	$1.99 a pound	$2.39 a pound
Shrimp	$10.99 a pound	$7.99 a pound
Apples	69¢ a pound	49¢ a pound
Cola	$1.69 a bottle	$1.39 a bottle
Bananas	49¢ a pound	69¢ a pound

C. Use the information in your chart. Circle more or less.

1. Eggs are **more** / less expensive at Shop and Save.
2. Butter is **more** / less expensive at Shop and Save.
3. Chicken is **more** / less expensive at Shop and Save.
4. Shrimp is more / **less** expensive at Shop and Save.
5. Apples are more / **less** expensive at Shop and Save.
6. A bottle of cola is less expensive at Shop and Save.
7. Bananas are more expensive at Shop and Save.

D. Food brands. Complete this list with your favorite brands of these products. Compare your list with a small group. Explain why you prefer this brand. (Answers will vary.)

coffee _____   tuna fish _____

yogurt _____   rice _____

mayonnaise _____   peanut butter _____

tomato sauce _____   soup _____

What is she buying? What is Mrs. Gibson buying? Write 10 sentences about her order. (Answers may vary.)

1. She's buying two boxes of rice.
2. She's buying one bag of potatoes.
3. She's buying a turkey.
4. She's buying one lemon.
5. She's buying a box of tea bags.
6. She's buying a bottle of soda pop.
7. She's buying a jar of peanut butter.
8. She's buying a bag of apples.
9. She's buying two boxes of spaghetti.
10. She's buying a can of coffee.

E. What is she buying?

• First, ask students to discuss the picture in a small group. They can identify the various foods using the name of the container or the quantity of food, as well as the name of the food. Point out the example: *She's buying two boxes of rice.*

• Ask students to work together to say and write sentences about what Mrs. Gibson is buying. Have them check each other's work as they go along.

• Review the answers by calling out the names of foods shown and having different students write one sentence each on the board.

Suggestion

Ask students to take turns naming multiple containers of food items that they have purchased recently. For example: *three quarts of milk, two jars of peanut butter, six pounds of hamburger.*

☀ The Big Picture:
The Shopping List

A. Answer these questions about the picture.

Discuss the questions with the whole class. Accept any reasonable answers, even if they don't agree with the audio students are going to hear. Encourage students to give reasons for their answers. For example:

T: *Why do you think they are married?*

S1: *They're in the kitchen together.*

T: *Gina, do you think they're married?*

S2: *No, I think they're brother and sister. They look alike.*

B. Listen. (CD2, Track 13)

The first time through, have students just listen as you play the audio. The second time, have students circle and cross out items on the list in the book. You may wish to pause the audio from time to time to give students a chance to mark their answers. Review the correct answers with the whole class.

☀ The Big Picture: The Shopping List

A. Answer these questions about the picture. (Answers may vary.)

1. Where are this man and woman?
   They are in the kitchen.
2. What is their relationship?
   They are married *or* They are friends.
3. What are they doing?
   They are making a shopping list.
4. Who is going to do the shopping?
   They are going to do the shopping.
5. Who is making the list?
   The man is making the list.
6. What is the woman looking at?
   She's looking at food in the refrigerator.

B. Listen. This couple needs some food at the supermarket. Circle the items they need. Cross out the items they don't need.

apples	orange juice	toilet paper	spaghetti
bananas	apple juice	tissues	coffee
oranges	chicken	paper towels	peanut butter
pineapple	pork chops	cereal	vegetables
milk	beef	rice	ice cream

Audio Script

B. Listen. This couple needs some food at the supermarket. Circle the items they need. Cross out the items they don't need. (CD2, Track 13)

M: What do we need at the store?

W: Not too much. I went to the store a few days ago. We need fruit–apples, bananas, but we don't need any oranges. There are four in the refrigerator. And we have a pineapple, too.

M: How about milk and juice?

W: Milk, yes. We always need milk. But we have orange juice and apple juice.

M: What about meat?

W: Get some chicken and some pork chops. We don't need any beef.

M: OK.

W: There's a sale on paper products. Get about four rolls of toilet paper and two boxes of tissues. But we don't need any paper towels.

M: Any cereal?

W: Let's see. There are three boxes in the cabinet. But we need a large box of rice and some spaghetti.

M: Are there any good coupons in the paper today?

W: I cut out some coupons. There are coupons for coffee and peanut butter.

M: OK. Anything else?

W: Yes, some fresh vegetables, any kind you like. And pick up some ice cream for the kids.

M: I never forget the ice cream.

C. **Complete with *a*, *some*, or *any*.**

1. We need ___some___ fruit.

2. We have ___some___ oranges, but we don't have ___any___ apples.

3. We need ___some___ milk, but we don't need ___any___ orange juice.

4. Please get ___a___ can of coffee.

5. We have ___some___ beef, so we don't need ___any___.

6. We need ___some___ toilet paper, but we don't need ___any___ paper towels.

7. Please buy ___a___ jar of peanut butter and ___a___ box of spaghetti.

8. We don't need ___any___ cereal.

D. **Coupons.** Complete these sentences. Use your imagination for the new price. (Answers will vary. Sample answers below.)

1. Apples are 59¢ a pound. With the coupon, _they are 49¢ a pound._

2. A can of tuna fish is $1.19. With the coupon, _it is 69¢ a can_.

3. Milk is $1.19 a quart. With the coupon, _it is 99¢ a quart_.

4. Donuts are $3.29 a dozen. With the coupon, _they are $2.29 a dozen_.

5. Ice cream is $3.79 a gallon. With the coupon, _it is $3.00 a gallon_.

6. Pork chops are $4.29 a pound. With the coupon, _they are $3.29 a pound_.

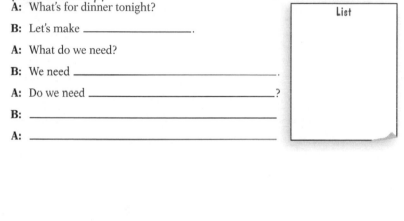

E. **Complete this conversation.** You and your partner are roommates. What are you going to have for dinner? Make a list and complete the conversation. (Answers will vary.)

A: What's for dinner tonight?

B: Let's make _____.

A: What do we need?

B: We need _____.

A: Do we need _____?

B: _____

A: _____

List

C. Complete with *a, some,* or *any.*

Students complete the activity on their own and then review their answers with a partner.

D. Coupons.

Remind students that some answers will begin with *it* and some with *they.* Ask students to complete the activity individually and compare answers with a partner. Then, call on different students to read their answers to the class.

E. Complete this conversation.

Have students complete the activity orally with a partner before writing the answers in their books. Encourage them to choose foods that haven't already been discussed in this unit. Move around the room helping as needed.

Suggestion

Have several pairs of students act out their conversations for the class.

☀ Reading: How to Make an Omelet

A. Vocabulary.

Read aloud the list of cooking utensils in the pictures. Ask students to repeat each one.

B. Label the ingredients.

• Point to the various ingredients and call on different students to name each one. Repeat any words that are new to some students and ask the whole class to repeat them. Have students write the name of each ingredient next to its picture.

C. Look at the recipe.

• Point out that there are 14 steps in this recipe on pages 164 and 165. First, read it once all the way through using the word *something* each time you come to a blank line.

• Go through the recipe with the class, reading one instruction at a time and asking them to fill in the missing word. Explain the meaning of any of the new food preparation words such as *break, beat,* and *chop* etc. Ask students to pantomime as many of these words as possible as you say them aloud.

• Have students read the completed recipe to themselves. Answer any remaining questions.

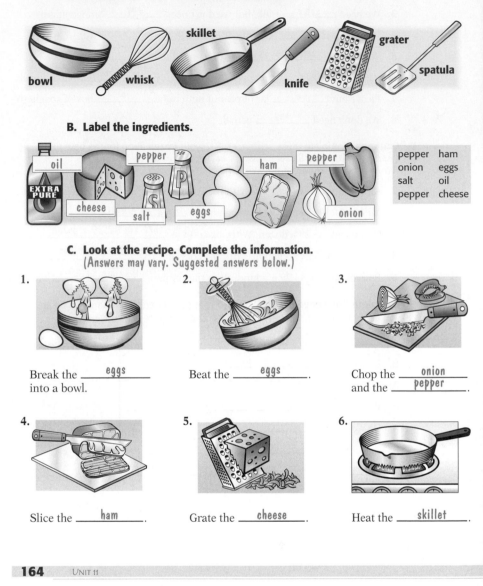

☀ Reading: How to Make an Omelette

A. Vocabulary. You will need the following.

bowl   whisk   skillet   knife   grater   spatula

B. Label the ingredients.

oil   cheese   pepper   salt   eggs   ham   pepper   onion

pepper	ham
onion	eggs
salt	oil
pepper	cheese

C. Look at the recipe. Complete the information.
(Answers may vary. Suggested answers below.)

1. Break the _____eggs_____ into a bowl.

2. Beat the _____eggs_____.

3. Chop the _____onion_____ and the _____pepper_____.

4. Slice the _____ham_____.

5. Grate the _____cheese_____.

6. Heat the _____skillet_____.

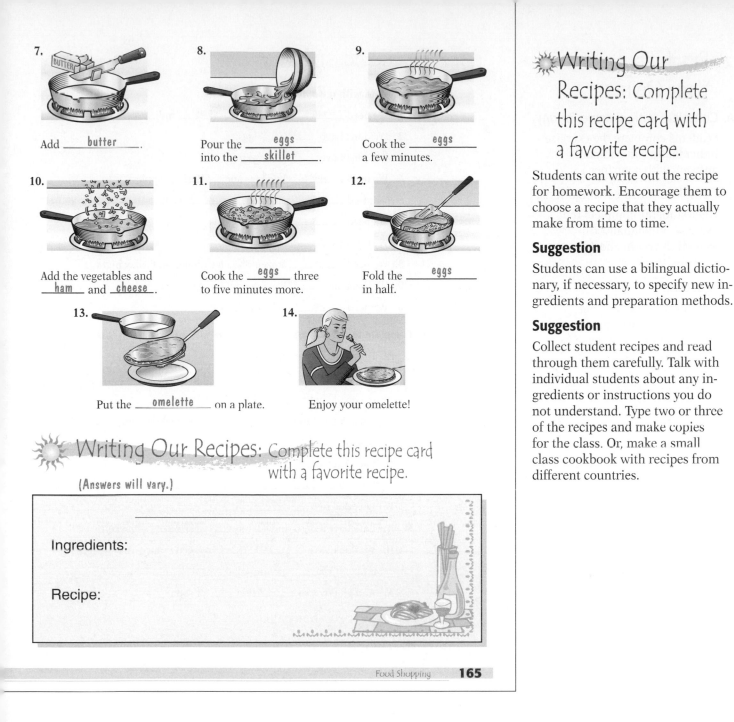

7. Add ___butter___ .

8. Pour the ___eggs___ into the ___skillet___ .

9. Cook the ___eggs___ a few minutes.

10. Add the vegetables and ___ham___ and ___cheese___ .

11. Cook the ___eggs___ three to five minutes more.

12. Fold the ___eggs___ in half.

13. Put the ___omelette___ on a plate.

14. Enjoy your omelette!

☀ Writing Our Recipes: Complete this recipe card with a favorite recipe.

(Answers will vary.)

_____

Ingredients:

Recipe:

☀ Writing Our Recipes: Complete this recipe card with a favorite recipe.

Students can write out the recipe for homework. Encourage them to choose a recipe that they actually make from time to time.

Suggestion

Students can use a bilingual dictionary, if necessary, to specify new ingredients and preparation methods.

Suggestion

Collect student recipes and read through them carefully. Talk with individual students about any ingredients or instructions you do not understand. Type two or three of the recipes and make copies for the class. Or, make a small class cookbook with recipes from different countries.

Practicing on Your Own

A. Complete with *a, some,* or *any.*

Students complete the exercise individually and compare answers with a partner.

B. Complete these conversations.

Have students complete the exercise individually. Go around the room checking students' work.

Suggestion

Ask students to find partners. Have them take turns practicing the conversations completed by both partners.

Practicing on Your Own

A. Complete with *a, some,* or *any.*

1. We need ___some___ cereal and ___some___ milk.
2. We don't have ___any___ eggs.
3. We don't have ___any___ soup.
4. We need ___some___ bananas and ___some___ apples.
5. We need ___some___ rice and ___some___ beans.
6. We need ___a___ six-pack of soda.
7. We don't have ___any___ oranges.
8. We need ___a___ frozen pizza for dinner on Friday night.
9. We don't have ___any___ peanut butter.
10. We need ___a___ cake for dessert.

B. Complete these conversations. (Answers will vary. Sample answers below.)

1. **A:** Do we need anything at the store?

   B: Yes, we need a ___jar___ of mayonnaise, a ___box___ of cereal, and a ___bag___ of sugar.

2. **A:** I'm going to buy a ___box___ of crackers and a ___jar___ of jelly.

   B: Please get a ___jar___ of peanut butter.

3. **A:** Shrimp is on sale. ___Shrimp___ ___is___ only $5.99 a pound.

   B: Let's buy two ___pounds___.

4. **A:** Let's have a barbecue. I'll buy ___some___ chicken.

   B: We don't have ___any___ barbecue sauce. And we'll need ___some___ potato salad.

   A: And I'll buy two ___cans___ of soda.

Looking at Graphs: Favorite Vegetables

A. Americans list these five vegetables as their favorites. What vegetables do you like?
(Answers will vary.)

1. I like _____.

2. I don't like _____.

3. My favorite vegetable is _____.

4. Survey your class and find the five most popular vegetables.

Adults' Favorite Vegetables
1. Broccoli
2. Corn
3. Beans
4. Carrots
5. Potatoes

Grammar Summary

---

1. Count and non-count nouns

a. Count nouns are things we can count. Count nouns can be singular or plural.

a donut   one donut   two donuts   three donuts   some donuts

b. Non-count nouns are things we can't count. We do not use the plural **s** with non-count nouns.

rice   some rice   oil   some oil   milk   some milk

c. We can put food in containers and count the containers.

a box of donuts   two boxes of donuts   a bag of rice   two bottles of oil

---

2. Count nouns

There is a donut in the box.

There are two donuts in the box.

There are some donuts in the box.

There aren't any donuts in the box.

Do we need any apples?

Apples are on sale. How much are they? They're 59¢ a pound.

---

3. Non-count nouns

There is some water in the cup.

There isn't any water in the cup.

Do we need any soda?

Soda is on sale. How much is it? It's 99¢ a bottle.

Looking at Graphs: Favorite Vegetables

A. Americans list these five vegetables as their favorites.

- Review the list of favorite vegetables. Next, call on several students to complete the first three sentences orally. Then, have them write their answers to items 1–3 in their books.

- Ask different students to write the name of their favorite vegetable on the board until every student's favorite is listed. Then, read the name of each vegetable and note how many students say it is their favorite. When you finish, circle the names of the five most popular vegetables.

Grammar Summary

- Review the summary with the class. Invite students to make up alternate sentences for each example in the chart. For example, in place of *There are some **donuts** in the **box**,* a student might say *There are some **apples** in the **refrigerator**.* In place of *Do we need any **soda**,* a student might say *Do we need any **orange juice**?*

- See the Grammar Summary Expansion on page 239 for a more complete explanation of these grammar points.

Unit 12
Last Weekend

Discuss what the person in the unit title art is doing. Ask: *What is the man doing?* (He's doing three different things: listening to music on headphones, reading a book, and exercising with free weights.)

☀️Dictionary:
Last Saturday

🎧 **A. Listen and repeat.**
(CD2, Track 14)

Play the audio and ask students to listen and repeat. Correct pronunciation errors such as making *called* into a two-syllable word, or pronouncing *washed* with an /əd/ sound at the end instead of a /t/ sound.

Suggestion

Ask students to study the words at home. During the next class, have students give each other spelling tests on the words. Students take turns saying the words as their partners write them down.

B. Maria was busy last Saturday.

- Point to the pictures one at a time and invite students to comment on the things and people they see. Encourage comments such as: *She's cleaning the floor. Her car is red. Her friend is young.*
- Call on different students to complete each sentence orally with a word from the box in Exercise A. Have students write the words in their books. After they have filled in the blanks, call on students to read the sentences aloud. Correct pronunciation as needed.

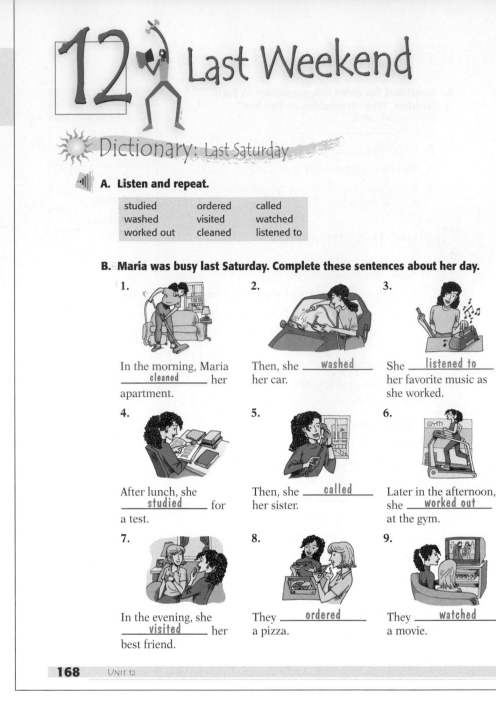

12 🔊 Last Weekend

☀️ Dictionary: Last Saturday

🎧 **A. Listen and repeat.**

studied	ordered	called
washed	visited	watched
worked out	cleaned	listened to

B. Maria was busy last Saturday. Complete these sentences about her day.

1. In the morning, Maria _____cleaned_____ her apartment.

2. Then, she __washed__ her car.

3. She __listened to__ her favorite music as she worked.

4. After lunch, she __studied__ for a test.

5. Then, she __called__ her sister.

6. Later in the afternoon, she __worked out__ at the gym.

7. In the evening, she __visited__ her best friend.

8. They __ordered__ a pizza.

9. They __watched__ a movie.

168 UNIT 12

C. Past time expressions. Study these past time expressions. Then, complete the sentences. (Answers will vary.)

last	ago	yesterday
last night	10 minutes ago	yesterday
last Sunday	an hour ago	yesterday morning
last weekend	three days ago	yesterday afternoon
last week	a week ago	yesterday evening
last month	a month ago	the day before yesterday
last year	a year ago	

1. Today is _____.

2. Yesterday was _____.

3. The day before yesterday was _____.

4. The year is _____.

5. Last year was _____.

6. Today's date is _____.

7. One week ago today was _____.

D. Last weekend. What did you do last weekend? Check the sentences that are true for you. (Answers will vary.)

1. ☐ I cleaned my house.
2. ☐ I washed my clothes.
3. ☐ I worked.
4. ☐ I watched TV.
5. ☐ I called my family.

6. ☐ I visited friends.
7. ☐ I walked in the park.
8. ☐ I washed my car.
9. ☐ I studied.
10. ☐ I played _____.

E. Ask and answer questions about last weekend.

> What did you do last weekend?

> I cleaned my house.

C. Past time expressions.

• Ask students to read through the list of past time expressions and circle any they aren't familiar with. Write these expressions on the board and explain each one.

• Have students fill in the blanks with the correct day. Review answers together.

Suggestion

Ask students to compare these past time expressions with similar ones in their native language. Are any the English expressions word-for-word translations of the corresponding native language expressions? How are corresponding pairs of expressions similar? How are they different?

D. Last weekend.

Ask students to complete the activity individually. Walk around the room answering questions as needed.

E. Ask and answer questions about last weekend.

Ask a pair of students to role-play the sample dialogue. Then, have student pairs take turns asking and answering questions about what they did last weekend.

Active Grammar: Past Tense of Regular Verbs

A. Listen: Ali's morning.
(CD2, Track 15)

• Point out the buildings on the map and the write-on lines where students will write their answers. Ask students to name each building.

• Have students just listen as you play the audio the first time. Then, play the audio again as many times as needed for students to record their answers and check their work. Go over the correct answers with the whole class.

B. Put Ali's morning in order.

Have students read through the sentences and circle any they don't understand. Explain the meaning of any new words or phrases as needed. After students have completed the exercise, have one student write the correct sequence of numbers on the board. Call on other students to read the answers in the order indicated. Correct any mistakes in ordering as you go along.

Describe Ali's morning.

Call on different students to say one sentence each, using one of the sequence words (*first, after that, then, next,* and *finally*) at the beginning of the sentence. Point out that the sequence words *then, after that,* and *next* are often interchangeable.

Active Grammar: Past Tense of Regular Verbs

A Busy Morning

Main Street

A. Listen: Ali's morning. Ali went downtown on Saturday morning. Where did he go first, second, third, etc.? Number the locations from 1 to 8 on the map above.

B. Put Ali's morning in order.

__4__ He picked up a prescription at the drugstore.

__7__ Ali enjoyed a cup of coffee.

__2__ He tried on some sneakers.

__5__ He dropped off some film at the camera store.

__1__ Ali deposited his paycheck.

__8__ He applied for a library card.

__6__ He rented a movie.

__3__ He mailed a letter to his brother.

Describe Ali's morning. Use *first, after that, then, next,* and *finally*.

170   UNIT 12

Audio Script

A. Listen: Ali's morning. Ali went downtown on Saturday morning. Where did he go first, second, third, etc.? Number the locations from 1 to 8 on the map above. **(CD2, Track 15)**

I always go downtown on Saturday morning. It's the only day I have free all week. So, last Saturday I walked downtown as usual. First, I went to the bank and deposited my paycheck. Then, I walked across the street to the shoe store. I tried on two or three pairs of sneakers, but I didn't see anything that I liked. Next, I stopped at the post office and mailed a letter to my brother. Then, I walked to the drugstore and picked up a prescription for my wife. Next door at the camera store, I dropped off some film and I picked up the pictures from my son's birthday party. After that, I rented a movie at the video store for Saturday night. My family always watches a movie on Saturday night. I was a little hungry, so I stopped at the coffee shop and ordered juice, a cup of coffee, and a donut. Then, I walked over to the library. They have a lot of newspapers and I looked at the Arabic language paper from my country. Also, I finally applied for a library card. That was my last stop and I walked back home.

170   ENGLISH IN ACTION 2

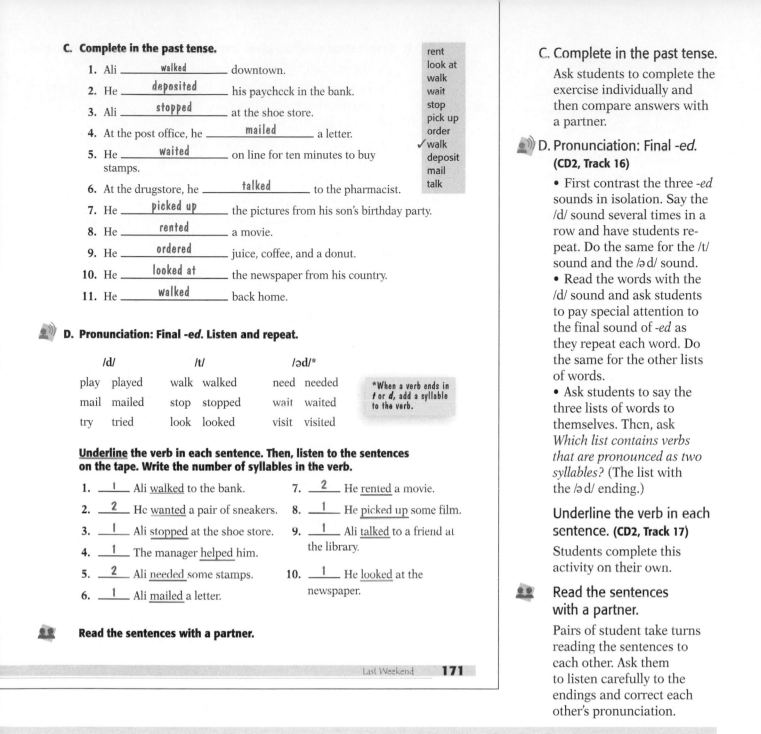

C. Complete in the past tense.

rent
look at
walk
wait
stop
pick up
order
✓ walk
deposit
mail
talk

1. Ali ___walked___ downtown.

2. He ___deposited___ his paycheck in the bank.

3. Ali ___stopped___ at the shoe store.

4. At the post office, he ___mailed___ a letter.

5. He ___waited___ on line for ten minutes to buy stamps.

6. At the drugstore, he ___talked___ to the pharmacist.

7. He ___picked up___ the pictures from his son's birthday party.

8. He ___rented___ a movie.

9. He ___ordered___ juice, coffee, and a donut.

10. He ___looked at___ the newspaper from his country.

11. He ___walked___ back home.

D. Pronunciation: Final -ed. Listen and repeat.

/d/		/t/		/əd/*	
play	played	walk	walked	need	needed
mail	mailed	stop	stopped	wait	waited
try	tried	look	looked	visit	visited

*When a verb ends in **t** or **d**, add a syllable to the verb.

Underline the verb in each sentence. Then, listen to the sentences on the tape. Write the number of syllables in the verb.

1. __1__ Ali walked to the bank.

2. __2__ He wanted a pair of sneakers.

3. __1__ Ali stopped at the shoe store.

4. __1__ The manager helped him.

5. __2__ Ali needed some stamps.

6. __1__ Ali mailed a letter.

7. __2__ He rented a movie.

8. __1__ He picked up some film.

9. __1__ Ali talked to a friend at the library.

10. __1__ He looked at the newspaper.

Read the sentences with a partner.

Last Weekend **171**

C. Complete in the past tense.

Ask students to complete the exercise individually and then compare answers with a partner.

D. Pronunciation: Final -ed. (CD2, Track 16)

• First contrast the three -ed sounds in isolation. Say the /d/ sound several times in a row and have students repeat. Do the same for the /t/ sound and the /əd/ sound.

• Read the words with the /d/ sound and ask students to pay special attention to the final sound of -ed as they repeat each word. Do the same for the other lists of words.

• Ask students to say the three lists of words to themselves. Then, ask *Which list contains verbs that are pronounced as two syllables?* (The list with the /əd/ ending.)

Underline the verb in each sentence. (CD2, Track 17)

Students complete this activity on their own.

Read the sentences with a partner.

Pairs of student take turns reading the sentences to each other. Ask them to listen carefully to the endings and correct each other's pronunciation.

E. Answer these questions about last weekend.

Ask students to work with a partner and ask one another these questions. Walk around the class, assisting students with their answers and with pronunciation.

F. Spelling: Past Tense.

Go through the spelling rules one at a time with the whole class. Encourage students to suggest additional verbs that follow each of the four spelling patterns. Write these new verbs with their past tense endings on the board.

Write the past tense.

Students complete this exercise on their own and check their answers with a partner.

Suggestion

Play an active game using the past tense endings. Divide the class into three groups and assign one of the three endings (/d/, /t/, and /əd/) to each group. Then, say sentences with each type of ending in random order and ask each group to stand up when they hear the past tense sound assigned to them. Later you can continue the game and have individual students take turns saying sentences to their classmates.

E. Answer these questions about last weekend. Practice your pronunciation.
(Answers will vary.)

1. Did you study? Where did you study?
2. How long did you study?
3. Did you take a walk? Where did you walk?
4. Who did you visit?
5. Did you watch TV? What TV program did you watch?
6. What kind of music did you listen to?
7. Who did you call?
8. Did you work? Which days did you work?
9. Did you use a computer? What did you do? Did you play a game? Did you e-mail anyone?
10. Did you help anyone? What did you do?
11. Did you clean your house? What did you do?
12. What did you cook for dinner? Did you order any take-out food?

> Did you study?
> Yes, I did.
> No, I didn't.

F. Spelling: Past Tense

1. Most verbs: Add **-ed.**

open	open**ed**
mail	mail**ed**
walk	walk**ed**

2. Verbs that end with **e**: Add **-d.**

like	like**d**
close	close**d**
use	use**d**

3. Verbs that end in consonant + **y:** Change the **y** to **i**, add **-ed.**

study	stud**ied**
cry	cr**ied**
apply	appl**ied**

4. Verbs that end with a consonant, vowel, consonant: Double the final consonant.

stop	stop**ped**
shop	shop**ped**

*Do not double final **w, x,** or **y.**
fix   fix**ed**   play   play**ed**

Write the past tense.

clean	cleaned		study	studied
prepare	prepared		arrive	arrived
rent	rented		stop	stopped
apply	applied		visit	visited
live	lived		try	tried
watch	watched		want	wanted

A. Listen and repeat.

be	was, were	fly	flew	say	said
begin	began	forget	forgot	see	saw
break	broke	get	got	send	sent
buy	bought	go	went	sit	sat
come	came	have	had	sleep	slept
do	did	know	knew	speak	spoke
drink	drank	leave	left	spend	spent
drive	drove	lose	lost	take	took
eat	ate	make	made	tell	told
fall	fell	pay	paid	think	thought
feel	felt	put	put	wear	wore
find	found	read	read	write	wrote

B. Answer. (Answers will vary.)

1. What time did you get up today?
2. How did you feel when you got up?
3. What did you eat for breakfast?
4. What did you drink for breakfast?
5. What time did you leave your house?
6. How did you get to school? Did you take the bus?
7. What did you bring to school?
8. What did you forget?
9. What time did this class begin?
10. Who did you speak to before class?
11. How much did you pay for your pen?
12. What did you read yesterday?
13. Where did you go last night?
14. How many hours did you sleep last night?
15. What did you wear to school yesterday?

Active Grammar: Past Tense of Irregular Verbs

A. Listen and repeat.
(CD2, Track 18)

• Point out the word *irregular* and ask a student to explain what it means (*different from all the others*). Then, have students look at the verbs in the list and circle any they don't understand. Explain the meaning of these verbs and use the past tense form of each one in a sentence, or call on a volunteer to use the past tense form in a sentence.
• Ask students to listen carefully as you play the audio.

Suggestion

Have students study the list in groups for about ten minutes. Then, have a contest. All students stand. You say a simple present tense sentence using one of the verbs (*Class begins at 9:00.*) and call on a student to say a similar sentence using the correct past tense form. (*Class began at 9:00.*) When a student answers correctly, he or she continues standing. When a student answers incorrectly, he or she sits down. See how many students remain standing after 10 minutes.

B. Answer.

Ask one or two students to answer each question orally in class. Focus any corrections on the pronunciation of the past tense irregular verb in each response. Then, ask students to work with a partner and ask each other the questions.

C. Talk about each picture.

• Discuss the pictures. Encourage students to use their imaginations. Ask questions in the present and past tense, such as these:

Picture 1
Who's this?
Where was she?
What did she buy?

Picture 2
What is he wearing?
What did he win?
Why did he receive a trophy?

• Have pairs of students take turns telling each other about the pictures. Check their answers by calling on different students to describe each picture to the class.

D. Negatives.

• Ask students to comment on the man in the picture. Ask:

Who is this man?
Where was he?
What was wrong with him?
What's this?

• Read the story aloud to the class. Answer any questions students may have. Ask students to underline all the past tense verbs in the story.

Use the phrases below.

• Discuss the meaning of *negative*. Point out that the negative uses the words *did* and *not* plus the simple form of the verb (except for the verb *be*). Then, ask different students to read aloud the sentences in the sample language box.

• Do this activity with the whole class. Call on various students to use each phrase to make up an affirmative or a negative sentence about Bill.

C. Talk about each picture. Use the past tense.

1. 2. 3.

4. 5. 6.

D. Negatives.

Sick in bed

Bill didn't feel well on Thursday, but he went to work. By 12:00, he knew he was sick. He felt tired and hot. He had a bad headache. He spoke to his boss and asked to go home. When he got home, he took his temperature. It was 102°. Bill was in bed for the next three days.

Use the phrases below. What did Bill do this weekend? What didn't he do?

> **Past Tense: Negatives**
> Use **didn't** and the simple form of the verb.
> He **didn't go** to work.
> He **didn't visit** his friends.
> He **didn't wash** the car.

work out at the gym

get a haircut

do his laundry

go to school   watch TV   take aspirin   drink juice

go to work   clean the house   do his homework   cook

call the doctor   drink tea   take a walk   sleep

☀ How was your weekend?

A. Read and complete these complaints about air travel. Suggested answers below.

(Answers may vary.

sick	broken	cold	late	uncomfortable
crowded	hot	terrible	dirty	

1. The plane was ___crowded___ .

2. The plane was ___late___ .

3. The seats were ___uncomfortable___ .

4. The cabin was too ___hot___ .

5. The woman in the next seat was ___sick___ .

6. The food was ___cold___ .

7. The weather was ___terrible___ .

8. My headset for the movie was ___broken___ .

9. The bathrooms were ___dirty___ .

B. Practice this conversation using different complaints from above.

A: Where were you on Friday? You weren't at work.

B: I took a day off. My son was in a soccer championship in Florida.

A: In Florida! Did you fly?

B: Yes. And the flight was terrible.

A: How come?

B: Well, _____ .

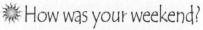

☀ How was your weekend?

A. Read and complete these complaints about air travel.

Point out the nine words in the box and work with the whole class to match each word with one of the pictures. As students make matches, call on a student to say the sentence aloud. Elicit other sentences using each key word. For example:

S1: *The seats were uncomfortable.*

T: *That's right. They were not comfortable. What else was uncomfortable?*

S2: *The cabin was uncomfortable.*

B. Practice this conversation using different complaints from above.

Encourage each student to give different explanations for why the flight was terrible. Have two students read the conversation. Point out that the last response can use any complaint from Exercise A. Ask students to work in pairs and practice the conversation.

C. Complete the conversation.

Ask students to complete the conversation individually and then check their answers with a partner. Check for correct answers by having a pair of students read the completed dialogue to the class.

D. Complain about each situation.

• Ask students to read through the exercise silently and circle any words they don't know. Elicit these words and write them on the board. Explain what each one means in simple English.
• Have students complete the fill-ins on their own. Check the answers with the whole class.

E. Complain about each of these situations or people.

Do this exercise in class. Invite several different students to respond to each question.

C. Complete the conversation.

They were great!	He was terrific!
It was exciting.	We were in the first row.

A: How was the game?
B: It was exciting_____.

A: How were your seats?
B: They were great!_____. We were in the first row_____.

A: How was your son?
B: He was terrific!_____. He scored a goal. His team won!

D. Complain about each situation. Use *was* or *were*.

1. How was the restaurant?

   The food ___was___ too spicy.

   The service ___was___ too slow.

   The waiters ___were___ unfriendly.

2. How was the motel?

   The room ___was___ dirty and noisy.

   The beds ___were___ uncomfortable.

3. How was the weather?

   It ___was___ cloudy. It ___was___ cold and windy.

E. Complain about each of these situations or people. Use your imagination!
(Answers will vary.)

1. How was the traffic on your way to school today?

2. How was your last job? How was your last boss?

3. How was your last boyfriend / girlfriend?

4. How was your last test?

5. How was your weekend? Why?

Working Together: Student to Student

A. Irregular past quiz. Give your book to your partner. Your partner will look at page 173 in your book and say the simple form of the verb. You will say the past form. With a light pencil, your partner will circle the verbs you need to study.

B. My weekend. Check the places you went last weekend. Then, tell your partner about each place and what you did there. (Answers will vary.)

☐ the bank   ☐ work   ☐ a restaurant
☐ the post office   ☐ the mall   ☐ the supermarket
☐ the library   ☐ the gym   ☐ a friend's house
☐ the park   ☐ the drugstore   ☐ _____
☐ the travel agency   ☐ school   ☐ _____
☐ the laundromat   ☐ the barber shop   ☐ _____
☐ church   ☐ the beauty parlor

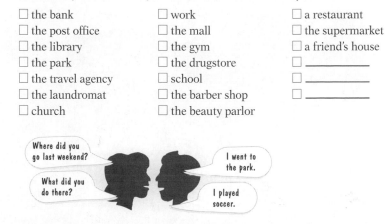

Where did you go last weekend?
What did you do there?

I went to the park.
I played soccer.

Write five sentences about <u>your partner's</u> weekend.

Example: <u>Carlos went to the park and played soccer.</u>

1. (Answers will vary.) _____
2. _____
3. _____
4. _____
5. _____

Working Together: Student to Student

A. Irregular past quiz.

Read the instructions and ask a student to repeat them in his or her own words. Then, have pairs of students complete the activity.

Suggestion

Do a quick survey of the five verbs that were missed by the most students. Write the simple form of each one on the board and review the past forms. Then, point to the verbs in random order and have the class call out the past tense form in unison.

B. My weekend.

• Have students complete the activity in pairs. Encourage each student to come up with at least one original activity and note it in the last column.
• Invite volunteer pairs to present their conversations to the class.

Write five sentences about your partner's weekend.

• Have pairs of students sit next to one another as they write the sentences about each other. They can talk to their partner if they don't remember all of the information about last weekend's activities.
• Invite volunteers to read the sentences about their partner to the class.

The Big Picture: The Wrong Directions

A. Answer.

- Discuss the picture with the class. Ask:

  What is the man's job?
  What is he looking at?
  Where is the woman?
  *What is she asking
    the officer?*

- Call on several different students to answer the three questions above the picture about what happened when they got lost.

B. Listen to the story about Paula. (CD2, Track 19)

Point to the woman in the picture and tell students that they are going to hear a story about what happened to her when she got lost. Ask students to listen for the main ideas the first time you play the audio. Present the story a second time and then discuss the answers to the questions.

The Big Picture: The Wrong Directions

A. Answer. (Answers will vary.)

1. Did you ever get lost?
2. Where were you going?
3. Who gave you directions?

B. Listen to the story about Paula. Then, answer the questions.

1. Where was the party? **The party was at a friend's house.**
2. What did Paula's friend give her? **Her friend gave her directions.**
3. What exit did she take? **She took Exit 14.**
4. Where did she leave her cell phone? **She left it at home on the kitchen table.**
5. Who finally gave her directions? **A police officer gave her directions.**
6. What exit did she really want? **She wanted Exit 15.**
7. Did she have a good time at the party? **Yes, she did.**

Audio Script

B. Listen to the story about Paula. Then, answer the questions. (CD2, Track 19)

Paula was very excited. She was going to a birthday party. The party was at the house of a friend from work.

Paula's friend carefully wrote the directions to the party. Paula didn't know the town where her friend lived, so she left her house early. For twenty minutes, she followed the directions carefully and got off at Exit 14. Then, she began to have problems. She couldn't find the street. She drove around and around, and soon she was lost.

She stopped and asked people for directions, but no one knew that street. Paula didn't have her cell phone with her; she left it at home on the kitchen table. Finally, she saw a police officer. She stopped and asked for directions. The officer looked at the directions and smiled. "You wanted Exit 15, not Exit 14." He showed Paula how to get back on the highway. She got off at Exit 15 and easily found the house. She was very late! When she walked in, everyone was singing "Happy Birthday" to her friend. After a few minutes, Paula relaxed and began to enjoy the party.

C. Match.

1. Paula tried to follow the directions, **(d.)**
2. Paula spoke to several people, **(a.)**
3. Paula wanted to call, **(g.)**
4. She tried to find a pay phone, **(f.)**
5. Paula took Exit 14, **(b.)**
6. Paula wanted to arrive on time, **(e.)**
7. At first she was upset, **(c.)**

   a. but they couldn't give her the directions.
   b. but she really wanted Exit 15.
   c. but she started to relax and enjoy the party.
   d. but she got lost.
   e. but she arrived two hours late.
   f. but she didn't see one.
   g. but she left her cell phone at home.

D. Complete in the past tense. Some of the sentences are negative.

1. A friend from work ___invited___ Paula to a birthday party.
2. Her friend ___didn't give___ her the correct directions.
3. Paula ___left___ her house early.
4. She ___followed___ the directions carefully.
5. She ___began___ to have problems.
6. She ___asked___ several people for directions.
7. She ___took___ the wrong exit.
8. Paula ___didn't have___ her cell phone with her.
9. She ___didn't see___ a pay telephone.
10. A police officer ___gave___ her the right directions.

see
begin
ask
take
✓ give
have
leave
✓ invite
follow
give

E. Paula and her friend are talking. Put their conversation in order. Practice with another student.

___5___ I'm really sorry! How did you find the street?

___2___ I got lost.

___1___ Paula, you're here! What happened?

___4___ I did. But you wrote Exit 14. You meant Exit 15.

___6___ I finally found a police officer and asked him.

___3___ Did you follow the directions?

C. Match.

Have students complete the matches individually and then check their answers with a partner. Discuss any answers that students aren't sure of.

Suggestion

Ask students to work in small groups to make up some other problems like those in Exercise C. Then, have them present their problems to the class. Write some of the most useful ones on the board. For example:

I wanted to use my cell phone, but the battery was dead.
I took the bus, but I got to school late anyway.

D. Complete in the past tense.

Point out the list of the simple forms of verbs at the right. Complete the activity orally with the whole class. Then ask students to write in the answers on their own.

E. Paula and her friend are talking.

Read the six sentences aloud. Then, ask students to work with partners as they figure out the proper sequence. When they have finished numbering, have the pairs practice the conversation together. Call on one pair to present the conversation to the class.

☼ Reading:
The Iowa State Fair

A. Before You Read.

• Ask students to locate Iowa on a map of the United States. (See the map on page 246.) Then, take a few minutes to orient students to the map of the Iowa Sate Fair. Ask questions such as:

What is a state fair?
What are some of the names of the buildings?
What kind of animals do you see?
Who attends a state fair?

• Have students circle on the map the locations listed in the box. Then, read the list of locations and ask students to raise their hands when you read one they don't understand. (In some classes, almost all items may need explanation.) Explain and discuss what each location involves, using the pictures on the map to clarify your explanations whenever possible.

☼ Reading: The Iowa State Fair

A. Before You Read. Look at the map. Circle these locations at the Iowa State Fair.

Heritage Village	Ferris Wheel	Sky Glider	Sheep Barn
Race Track	Agriculture Building	Poultry Building	Grandfather's Farm
Midway	Horse Barn	Machinery Grounds	Riley Stage

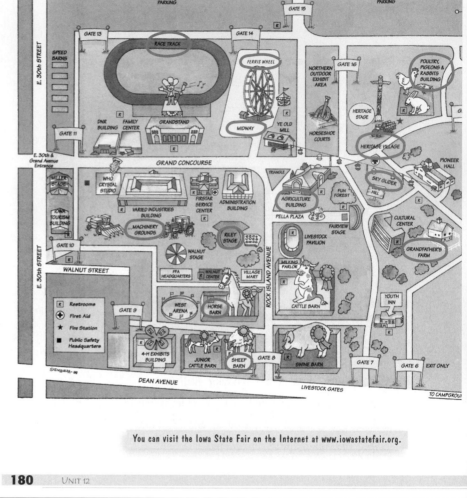

You can visit the Iowa State Fair on the Internet at www.iowastatefair.org.

B. These are some activities at a state fair. Can you explain each?

shows	car races	rides	fair
exhibits	competitions	fireworks	contests

The Iowa State Fair

"I couldn't believe my eyes!", said Pablo Ospina. "I expected a small fair with rides and animals. I loved it! I went to the fair with a friend on Friday night. Then, I drove back with my family on Saturday and again on Sunday."

Pablo is talking about the Iowa State Fair, one of the largest state fairs in the United States. This year the Fair was 10 days long and almost one million visitors attended. The first Iowa State Fair was in 1854, on a small farm. Farmers came together and talked about farming, animals, and new ideas. Today the Fair is the size of a small town. It's not only for farmers. City and country people enjoy the many entertainment shows, the car and horse races, many rides, hundreds of exhibits and competitions, and the fireworks at night.

Pablo enjoyed the contests. He watched the Pie Eating Contest. The winner ate two pies in ten minutes. He laughed at the Mother and Daughter Look-a-Like Contest. He listened to the Guitar-Playing Contest.

Pablo's wife, Nancy, is a gardener. In the Agriculture Building, she looked at the largest tomato and the biggest peppers. She saw beautiful vegetables, apples, cheese, popcorn, ham, and other farm products. She watched the competition for the most beautiful roses.

Pablo's two boys wanted to see Heritage Village. Grandfather's Farm showed farm life in early times. They went into the old-fashioned general store, the country schoolhouse and the barber shop. The boys also liked all the animals, so they stopped at the Horse Barn and the Sheep Barn. They watched how to milk a cow and how to make butter. Of course, the boys went on many rides at the Midway, such as the Ferris Wheel and the Sky Glider.

Everyone was hungry and thirsty all day. They stopped every hour and tried different food. The most popular kind of food at the fair was food-on-a-stick. They tried chicken-on-a-stick, pork chop-on-a-stick, and fried candy-bar-on-a-stick. Later in the afternoon, the family walked to the race track and watched car races. They stayed for the fireworks in the evening. Everyone had a great time. Pablo is already planning to return for next year's fair.

C. Underline each place this family visited at the state fair.

Writing Our Stories:
A Special Weekend

Write about a special weekend that you enjoyed with friends or family. Where did you go? What did you do? Give many examples.

Writing Note
Edit your story.
Underline each verb.
Did you use the past tense?

B. These are some activities at a state fair.

• Point out the eight activities in the box and discuss each one. Ask students to watch for information about them in the article. Then, read the article aloud to the class. (You might ask students to circle the eight activities as they encounter them in the reading.)
• Reread the article, a sentence at a time, pausing to answer any questions students may have. When you finish, refer back to the eight activities in the box and ask a different student to explain each one.

C. Underline each place this family visited at the fair.

Ask students to complete the activity individually and then check their answers with a partner. Go over the correct answers with the whole class.

Writing Our Stories:
A Special Weekend

• Ask students to name a place they visited and enjoyed with friends or family. Make a list of 5 to 10 places on the board, such as the beach, the country park, the zoo, and so on.
• Have students write the name of the place they want to write about. Then, ask students to quickly jot down ideas that they may want to include in their stories. Tell them not to worry about writing complete sentences or putting their ideas in the correct order. Emphasize that the purpose of this part of the exercise is just to get a lot of ideas down on paper.
• Ask students to use these ideas, and any others that come to them, to write about their special weekend. Read the Writing Note and remind students to edit their stories after they finish writing them.

Practicing on Your Own

A. Past tense.

Have students complete the activity individually and check their answers with a partner.

B. Negatives.

Read the instructions and point out that the answers in Exercise B are related to the facts presented in Exercise A. When students finish, go over the correct answers with the whole class.

Practicing on Your Own

A. Past tense. Complete this story with the past tense of the verbs.

My wife and I go out almost every Saturday. Sometimes we go to a restaurant, a movie, or to a party. We think it's good to relax after a hard week's work.

Last Saturday, we _____did_____ (do) our chores in the morning. We ____cleaned____ (clean) our house and _____went_____ (go) food shopping. After that, we ____visited____ (visit) my wife's parents. We _____got_____ (get) home by 5:00, so we ____decided____ (decide) to go out for dinner. We _____ate_____ (eat) at Faroles Restaurant and we _____had_____ (have) Spanish food.

It _____was_____ (be) a little uncomfortable for us in the restaurant because we _____had_____ (have) our daughter with us. Lizzie is only 20 months old and is sometimes very noisy. She _____said_____ (say) "Hi!" to everyone. Thankfully, she _____sat_____ (sit) quietly under our table most of the time!

After we ____finished____ (finish) dinner, we _____drove_____ (drive) to the park. We _____put_____ (put) Lizzie in her stroller and we _____walked_____ (walk) around the lake. It _____was_____ (be) so beautiful and quiet. My daughter _____fell_____ (fall) asleep in her stroller.

B. Negatives. Complete these sentences about the story in Exercise A. Write the verbs in the negative.

They ____didn't go____ out on Friday night; they went out on Saturday night.

They ____didn't visit____ his wife's sister; they visited his wife's parents.

They ____didn't eat____ in an Indian restaurant; they ate at a Spanish restaurant.

Their daughter ____didn't sit____ in a chair; she sat under the table.

They ____didn't go____ to a movie; they went to the park.

Their daughter ____didn't fall____ asleep in the car; she fell asleep in her stroller.

They ____didn't get____ home late; they got home early.

Looking at Graphs: State Fair Attendance

A. Look at the chart and talk about fair attendance in 2000. (Answers will vary.)

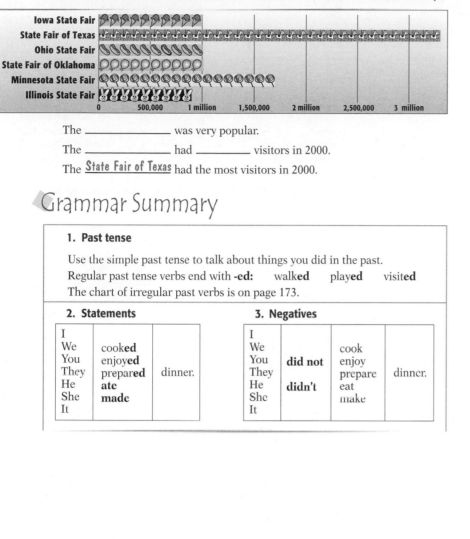

Iowa State Fair	
State Fair of Texas	
Ohio State Fair	
State Fair of Oklahoma	
Minnesota State Fair	
Illinois State Fair	

0 500,000 1 million 1,500,000 2 million 2,500,000 3 million

The _____ was very popular.

The _____ had _____ visitors in 2000.

The <u>State Fair of Texas</u> had the most visitors in 2000.

Grammar Summary

1. Past tense

Use the simple past tense to talk about things you did in the past.

Regular past tense verbs end with **-ed:**   walk**ed**   play**ed**   visit**ed**

The chart of irregular past verbs is on page 173.

2. Statements

I We You They He She It	cook**ed** enjoy**ed** prepar**ed** **ate** **made**	dinner.

3. Negatives

I We You They He She It	**did not** **didn't**	cook enjoy prepare eat make	dinner.

Looking at Graphs: State Fair Attendance

A. Look at the chart and talk about fair attendance in 2000.

• Go over the information on the chart with the class. Ask different students to tell about how many people attended each state fair in 2000. Then, have students choose one of the state fairs and fill in the blanks using information about that fair.

Grammar Summary

• Review the summary with the class. Point out the regular and irregular past tenses in Section 2. Invite students to make up alternate sentences for regular and irregular past tense verbs. For example, in place of *They prepared dinner,* a student might say *I cooked breakfast.* In place of *She made dinner,* a student might say *I bought ice cream.*

• See the Grammar Summary Expansion on page 240 for a more complete explanation of these grammar points.

Discuss what the person in the unit title art is doing. Ask: *What is the man doing?* (He's carrying a big birthday cake with one candle on it.)

☀ Dictionary:
Important Events

ıl A. Listen and repeat the regular past tense verbs and verb phrases.
(CD2, Track 20)

• First, play the audio once all the way through as students just listen. Then, pause the audio and ask students to repeat it.
• Discuss the meaning of each phrase. Ask students to explain the meaning of each one in their own words. For example:

> **T:** *What does* celebrate a birthday *mean?*
> **S1:** *To celebrate a birthday you have a party and give the person gifts.*
> **T:** *What else do we celebrate?*
> **S2:** *We celebrate weddings and new jobs.*

B. Write a past tense verb phrase in Exercise A under the correct picture.

• Work with the whole class as you ask students to match each of the phrases with one of the pictures.
• Point out that there is no picture for the verbs *die* and *change jobs.*

Suggestion

Ask volunteers to describe their own lives using these verb phrases. Encourage them to add relevant information. For example:

> *I celebrated my birthday last week.*
> *I changed jobs in December.*
> *I returned to my home country for two weeks last summer.*

---

13 🎂🎈 Growing Up

☀ Dictionary: Important Events

ıl A. Listen and repeat the regular past tense verbs and verb phrases.

celebrate a birthday	**celebrated** a birthday	move to another state	**moved** to another state
change jobs	**changed** jobs	retire from my job	**retired** from my job
die	**died**	return to my country	**returned** to my country
graduate from high school	**graduated** from high school	study English	**studied** English

B. Write a past tense verb phrase in Exercise A under the correct picture.

1. returned to my country

2. graduated from high school

3. moved to another state

4. studied English

5. celebrated a birthday

6. retired from my job

C. Irregular verbs. Listen and repeat the irregular verbs.

began	fell	got	had	met
came	found	✓grew up	made	went

D. Look at the pictures. Then, write the correct verbs.

1. Laura ___grew up___ in Lima, Peru.

2. She ___went/came___ to the U.S. in August 1999.

3. She ___got___ a job at the Tropicana Restaurant.

4. She ___had/went to___ English classes at the local college.

5. Laura ___met___ her future husband, Luca, in her class.

6. After one month, they ___fell___ in love.

7. Laura ___got___ engaged to Luca on February 14, 2000.

8. Luca ___began___ the local soccer team.

9. Laura and Luca ___got___ married December 31, 2000.

10. Laura and Luca ___went___ on a honeymoon to Peru.

C. Irregular verbs.
(CD2, Track 21)

Play the audio once while students listen. Play it again and ask students to repeat the irregular past tense verbs aloud.

Suggestion

List the present tense form of each verb on the board. Have students close their books. Point to a present tense form and call on a student to say the present tense form followed by the past tense form. Write the past tense form next to the present tense verb as each student says it.

D. Look at the pictures.

Work through the exercise with the whole class. After a student suggests a correct verb for each sentence, read the sentence aloud and ask the class to repeat. Answer any questions students may have.

Active Grammar:
Past Tense Yes/No Questions

A. Read and circle.

Have students complete the answers individually. (Each student's answers will be different.) Check the answers by having one student read the questions aloud and calling on several different students to give their answers.

B. Pair practice.

• Ask a pair of students to read the sample dialogue aloud to the class twice. Give each student the opportunity to respond with both answers.
• Review the meaning of the expressions in the list in the box. Then, have students work in pairs. They can take turns asking and answering questions using the phrases at the bottom of the page. Ask them to give answers that are true about their lives. Move around the room as they work offering help as needed.
• Finish the exercise by inviting several pairs of students to ask questions using the phrases at the bottom of the page and to answer them truthfully.

Active Grammar: Past Tense Yes/No Questions

Yes/No Questions – *Did*	
Did you	take a vacation?
	get married?
	get your license?

A. Read and circle. (Answers will vary.)

1. Did you take a vacation last year?   Yes, I did.   No, I didn't.

2. Did you move to a new apartment last month?   Yes, I did.   No, I didn't.

3. Did you get married last year?   Yes, I did.   No, I didn't.

4. Did you begin English classes last week?   Yes, I did.   No, I didn't.

5. Did you get married two years ago?   Yes, I did.   No, I didn't.

6. Did you have a baby five years ago?   Yes, I did.   No, I didn't.

7. Did you go back to your country last winter?   Yes, I did.   No, I didn't.

8. Did you get a driver's license last year?   Yes, I did.   No, I didn't.

B. Pair practice. Ask and answer the questions with a partner.

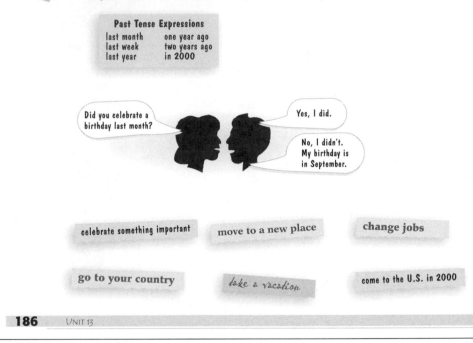

Past Tense Expressions
last month	one year ago
last week	two years ago
last year	in 2000

Did you celebrate a birthday last month?

Yes, I did.

No, I didn't. My birthday is in September.

celebrate something important   move to a new place   change jobs

go to your country   take a vacation   come to the U.S. in 2000

C. Look at the pictures. Talk about these important events in Alex's life.

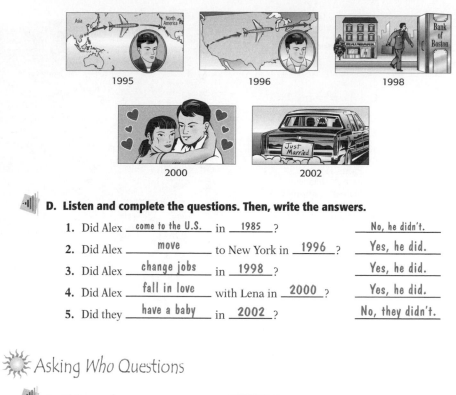

1995   1996   1998

2000   2002

D. Listen and complete the questions. Then, write the answers.

1. Did Alex ___come to the U.S.___ in ___1985___ ?   No, he didn't.
2. Did Alex ___move___ to New York in ___1996___ ?   Yes, he did.
3. Did Alex ___change jobs___ in ___1998___ ?   Yes, he did.
4. Did Alex ___fall in love___ with Lena in ___2000___ ?   Yes, he did.
5. Did they ___have a baby___ in ___2002___ ?   No, they didn't.

Asking *Who* Questions

A. Listen and answer.

Answers
Paul did.
Marta did.

Paul

Marta

1. Who grew up in El Salvador?
   Marta did.
2. Who went to nursing school?
   Marta did.
3. Who got a job at a bank?
   Paul did.
4. Who worked at a hospital?
   Marta did.
5. Who worked in New York City?
   Paul did.
6. Who changed jobs?
   Paul did.

Growing Up **187**

C. Look at the pictures.

• Ask students to identify the people and places in the pictures. Ask:

Who is this?
What year is it?
Where was Alex in 1995?
What did he do?

• Ask different students to describe the events in each picture. Repeat correct sentences and ask the class to repeat.

D. Listen and complete the questions. (CD2, Track 22)

Review the sample answer. Then, play the audio and have students fill in the rest of the answers.

Asking *Who* Questions

A. Listen and answer.
(CD2, Track 23)

Play the audio several times. Then, ask the questions and call on different students to answer.

Audio Script

D. Listen and complete the questions. Then, write the answers. (CD2, Track 22)

1. Did Alex come to the U.S. in 1985?
2. Did Alex move to New York in 1996?
3. Did Alex change jobs in 1998?
4. Did Alex fall in love with Lena in 2000?
5. Did they have a baby in 2002?

A. Listen and answer. (CD2, Track 23)

Paul:
Hi, I'm Paul. I grew up in New Jersey. After college, I got a job at a bank in New York City. I didn't like my job, so I changed jobs. I found a job at a computer company.

Marta:
Hi, I'm Marta. I grew up in El Salvador. I went to nursing school there, and then, last year, I moved to the United States. I got a job at a hospital in New Jersey.

B. Look at the pictures.

- Help students identify the people in the pictures. Ask questions such as:

  Who is this?
  Where is this man from?
  What sport does this woman play?
  Is this person still living?

- Review the sample dialogues with the class. Then, have students complete the activity in pairs. Review the correct answers by calling on different pairs to ask and answer the questions for the class.

☀ Asking Wh- questions

C. Read.

- Read the conversation aloud to the class. Answer any questions students may have.
- Read each line of the conversation and ask students to repeat. Divide long sentences into two or more parts.

D. Practice the dialogue above.

- Ask pairs to take turns doing each of the roles exactly as they are in the book so that they get practice both asking and answering the questions.
- Have students work out the answers about their own lives. Next, ask them to take turns interviewing each other. Have them practice the conversation more than once.
- Invite volunteer pairs to present their conversations to the class.

Suggestion

Some students may wish to make notes or write down the words they are going to say so that they can be sure they are forming the answers correctly. Encourage them to try doing the conversation without their notes after they have practiced it once or twice.

B. Look at the pictures. Ask and answer the questions with a partner.

> Who grew up in the U.S.?
> Janet Jackson did.
>
> Who played tennis?
> Steffi Graf did.

1. Who performed with her brothers? (Janet Jackson)
2. Who lived in Spain? (Pablo Picasso)
3. Who was born in Hong Kong? (Jackie Chan)
4. Who sold many CDs? (Janet Jackson)
5. Who won many tennis matches? (Steffi Graf)
6. Who painted famous art works? (Pablo Picasso)
7. Who studied Kung Fu? (Jackie Chan)
8. Who grew up in Germany? (Steffi Graf)

Janet Jackson

Pablo Picasso

Jackie Chan

Steffi Graf

☀ Asking Wh- questions

C. Read.

A: Where were you born?
B: **I was born in Russia.**
A: When did you come to this country?
B: **I came here in 1998.**
A: Who came with you?
B: **My husband and my children did.**
A: Did you understand English?
B: **No, I didn't.**
A: How did you learn English?
B: **I went to an English class, and I watched TV programs in English.**

D. Practice the dialogue above. Talk about your life.

E. Complete the questions. Ask and answer the questions with a partner.

did	were	born	come
live	find	grow up	learn

1. Where ___were___ you ___born___?
2. Where ___did___ you ___grow up___?
3. When ___did___ you ___come___ to this country?
4. Why ___did___ you ___come___ to this country?
5. How ___did___ you ___come___ to this country?
6. How ___did___ you ___learn___ English?
7. When ___did___ you ___find___ a job?
8. Where ___did___ you ___live___ after you came here?

F. My teacher. Complete these past tense questions. Ask your teacher about his/her life. (Answers will vary.)

1. Where ___were___ you born?
2. Where ___did___ you _____?
3. What _____ you _____?
4. What university _____ you _____?
5. When _____ you _____?
6. How _____ you _____?
7. Why _____ you _____?

Write three more questions for your teacher. (Answers will vary.)

8. _____?
9. _____?
10. _____?

E. Complete the questions.

Have students fill in the blanks individually. Review the correct answers with the class. Then, ask students to work in pairs, taking turns asking and answering the questions.

F. My teacher.

Again, have students fill in the blanks on their own. Then, have different students ask you the questions. If the questions are incorrectly phrased, restate the question before you answer.

Write three more questions for your teacher.

Students can write their questions on their own or work in pairs. Remind them to ask questions about the past using question words such as *when, where, what, how,* and *why.*

☀ Talking About a Party

A. Read and put the sentences in order from 1–10.

- Read the sentences aloud and ask students to repeat. Focus on the pronunciation of the past tense verb forms.
- Have students number the sentences to show the order in which the events happened.

B. Look at the pictures and tell the story.

- Work with the whole class. Point out the sequence words in the box and ask students to include one in each sentence.
- Call on different students to say a sentence for each picture. Repeat each correct sentence and ask the class to repeat it after you.
- When a different sequence word is possible at the beginning of a sentence, ask another student to say the sentence a different way.

S1: *Then, the man told his parents.*
T: *Can someone say this sentence a different way?*
S2: *Next, the man told his parents.*
T: *That's right. You can use* Then *or* Next *at the beginning of this sentence.*

C. In your notebook, write a story about the pictures in Exercise B.

- Have students write the story in class. Go around the room helping as necessary. Ask different students to write one sentence each on the board and go over the complete story with the class.
- Review the Writing Note and have students check their writing for this comma placement.

☀ Talking About a Party

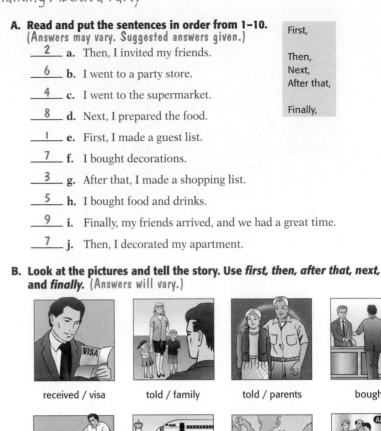

A. Read and put the sentences in order from 1–10.
(Answers may vary. Suggested answers given.)

__2__	**a.**	Then, I invited my friends.
__6__	**b.**	I went to a party store.
__4__	**c.**	I went to the supermarket.
__8__	**d.**	Next, I prepared the food.
__1__	**e.**	First, I made a guest list.
__7__	**f.**	I bought decorations.
__3__	**g.**	After that, I made a shopping list.
__5__	**h.**	I bought food and drinks.
__9__	**i.**	Finally, my friends arrived, and we had a great time.
__7__	**j.**	Then, I decorated my apartment.

First,

Then,
Next,
After that,

Finally,

B. Look at the pictures and tell the story. Use *first, then, after that, next,* and *finally.* (Answers will vary.)

received / visa	told / family	told / parents	bought

packed	went	flew	met

C. In your notebook, write a story about the pictures in Exercise B.

Writing Note

Put a comma after *First,* and *Next,* at the beginning of a sentence.

D. Pronunciation: *Did you* and *Did he.* Listen and repeat.

Did you = Did_you   Did he = Did_he

1. Did you change jobs?
2. Did you get married?
3. Did you find a job?
4. When did you find a job?
5. What did you do yesterday?

6. Did he study English?
7. Did he get divorced?
8. Did he go back to his country?
9. How did he get there?
10. Why did he go back?

Practice asking these questions with a partner.

Working Together: Student to Student

A. STUDENT A: Listen to Student B. Write questions 1 to 3. Then, read questions 4 to 6.

STUDENT B: Turn to page 192. Read questions 1 to 3.

1. When did they get married?   On July 8th.
2. Where did they get married?   At a church.
3. What time did the ceremony begin?   At 3.00.
4. Where did they have the reception?
5. How many people did they invite?
6. How much did the wedding cost?

D. Pronunciation: *Did you* and *Did he.* (CD2, Track 24)

• Point out the two pronunciation keys at the top. Play the audio several times and ask students to repeat each time.

• Repeat the process with the sample sentences. Run through the sentences several times if you wish. Then, call on individuals to say one sentence each using the shortened forms.

Practice asking these questions with a partner.

Have students practice the question pronunciation in pairs. Tell them to make up any answer that makes sense to them.

Suggestion

Have students work in pairs to create personalized dialogues using the questions and answers in Exercise D as a starting point. They can change *he* to *you* in items 6–10. Invite several pairs to present their dialogues to the class.

Working Together: Student to Student

A. Student A.

• Explain that both Student A and Student B will look at similar lists. One student has the questions and the other student has the answers.

• Talk about the pictures with the class. Ask:

What do you call this person? What are the man and woman doing?

• Read the instructions and model the first question and answer with a student. Then, have student pairs complete the activity on their own. Have them check each other's answers when they finish.

Working Together: Student to Student

B. Student B.

See the instructions for Exercise A on page 191.

C. A timeline.

• Elicit the names of some important personal events and write them on the board (For example: *a wedding, college graduation, retirement*).

• Model this activity for your students. Draw five boxes on the board (as on page 192 in the Student book.) and write a date in each one. For example,

1970	*I was born in Kansas City in 1970.*
1991	*I graduated from the University of Colorado in 1991.*
1994	*I got married in 1994.*
1997	*I had a little boy in 1997.*
2000	*I started to work at this school in 2000.*

• Ask students to complete the timeline on their own. Go around the room offering help as needed.

Tell your partner about your life.

Have students tell each other about key events in their lives using the information they wrote for Exercise C.

Working Together: Student to Student

B. STUDENT B: Read questions 1 to 3. Then, listen to Student A. You will write questions 4 to 6.

1. When did they get married?

2. Where did they get married?

3. What time did the ceremony begin?

4. Where did they have the reception? _____ At a restaurant.

5. How many people did they invite? _____ 175 people.

6. How much did the wedding cost? _____ $6,000.

C. A timeline. Think of five important dates and events in your life. Then, write the dates in the boxes in chronological order. Write one sentence next to each date. (Answers will vary.)

	_____
	_____
	_____
	_____
	_____

Tell your partner about your life.

D. Find someone who . . . Walk around the classroom and ask questions about growing up. (Answers will vary.)

Did you go to high school in the United States?
No, I didn't. (Ask another person.)

Did you go to high school in the United States?
Yes, I did. (Write the name.)

Find someone who . . .	Classmate
1. went to high school in this country.	_____
2. had a pet.	_____
3. spent time with his or her grandparents.	_____
4. wore a uniform to school.	_____
5. won a competition.	_____
6. went to a lot of parties.	_____
7. attended a university in his / her native country.	_____
8. lived in another state.	_____

E. Memories. Bring in a photograph of an important day in your life. Tell a group of classmates about that day. What happened? Your classmates will ask you questions.

How did you break your leg?
Did you stay in the hospital?
How long did you wear a cast?
Did you stay home from school?
Who helped you?

D. Find someone who . . .

• Read through the question cues with the class and answer any questions students may have. Review the instructions and sample exchanges.

• Have students stand up and move around the room as they ask each other the questions.

• Close the exercise by calling on volunteers to tell the class interesting facts they learned about their classmates while doing this exercise.

E. Memories.

• Ask students to describe the picture. Ask questions such as:

Where is this person?
What happened to him?

• Role-play the activity using the picture and the sample questions in the box. Have one student pretend to be the person in the picture and invite other students to ask the questions. As the student answers, confirm correct answers by repeating them. If the student makes any errors, give clues about where the error is and ask him or her to try to say the sentence correctly. For example:

S1: *I breaked my leg playing soccer.*
 T: *What is the past tense of* break?
S2: *Oh, it's* broke. *I broke my leg playing soccer.*
 T: *That's right. Break. Broke.*

• Have students share personal photos in small groups. Move around the room helping students with new vocabulary or question forms.

Suggestion

Invite students to write a short story about the picture they shared with their group. Later, you can post the stories and pictures side by side where students can read them at their leisure.

A. Listen and look at the pictures. (CD2, Track 25)

Before playing the audio or reading the Audio Script, talk about the pictures and introduce the new vocabulary. Have students repeat any new words. Ask questions such as:

Where did the boy come from?
What are these things on his face?
What is he doing in this picture?

B. Listen again. (CD2, Track 25)

After students have heard the story several times, ask different students to make statements about Oscar's life.

C. Listen and circle. (CD2, Track 26)

Play the audio and ask students to circle the correct answer. Pause the audio after each question. Review together.

The Big Picture: Growing Up

A. Listen and look at the pictures.

B. Listen again. Talk about Oscar's life.

C. Listen and circle.

1. **a.** Texas	**b.** El Salvador	**c.** Mexico
2. **a.** He fell out of bed.	**b.** He fell off a bicycle.	**c.** He fell in love.
3. **a.** In second grade	**b.** In seventh grade	**c.** In sixth grade
4. **a.** When he was 10	**b.** When he was 12	**c.** When he was 2
5. **a.** Detroit	**b.** Denver	**c.** Dallas
6. **a.** A little	**b.** A lot	**c.** None
7. **a.** When he was 15	**b.** When he was 16	**c.** When he was 17
8. **a.** His mother did.	**b.** The manager did.	**c.** His father did.

194 UNIT 13

Audio Script

A. Listen and look at the pictures. (CD2, Track 25)

Hi, my name is Oscar Vega. I'm 21 years old, and I'm a student here at the University of Texas. I was born in a small town in Mexico. I started school when I was 6 years old. Let's see, what can I remember? One summer, when I was 7, I fell off my bicycle and broke my arm. When I was in second grade, I got the chicken pox. My brothers and sister got the chicken pox, too. And when I was a kid, I played soccer all the time—before school, after school, and on weekends. I made the school team. When I was 12, our team won a championship and I got a trophy. Then, when I was 14, I moved to the United States with my parents. We moved here, to Dallas, Texas. I started high school here in Dallas, but I didn't like it at first. I didn't know anyone, and I wasn't on the soccer team. But, I knew a little English and I learned it fast. The year I turned 16 was great for me. My father taught me how to drive, and I got my license. When I was 17, I found my first job–it was at a pizza place. After I graduated from high school, I started college. I'm still working at the pizza place, and now I'm the assistant manager. I'm majoring in business and working nights and weekends.

C. Listen and circle. (CD2, Track 26)

1. Where was Oscar born?
2. How did he break his arm?
3. When did he get the chicken pox?
4. When did his team win the soccer championship?
5. Where did Oscar move?
6. How much English did Oscar know?
7. When did he get his first job?
8. Who taught him how to drive?

D. Ask and answer *Yes/No* questions about Oscar and about your life.
(Answers 6-10 will vary.)
1. Did Oscar break his arm?
   Yes, he did.
2. Did Oscar have the measles?
   No, he didn't.

   Yes, he did.
   No, he didn't.

3. Did Oscar move to the United States with his family?
   Yes, he did.
4. Did Oscar play a sport in high school?
   No, he didn't.

   Yes, I did.
   No, I didn't.

5. Did Oscar fall in love in high school?
   No, he didn't.
6. Did you break your arm or leg?

7. Did you work when you were in high school?

8. Did you have chicken pox?

9. Did you play a sport in high school?

10. Did you fall in love in high school?

(Answers may vary.

E. Complete these questions. Then, answer the questions. Suggested answers below.)

Who	What	When	Where	Why	How	Did

1. ___How___ many times a week did he play soccer? (7 days a week.)
2. ___Who___ taught Oscar to drive? (His father)
3. ___Did___ he get his license when he was 16? (Yes, he did.)
4. ___Where___ did he go to school? (He went to school in Mexico and in Dallas.)
5. ___What___ did he win when he was a child? (A championship.)
6. ___When___ did he get his first job? (At the age of 17.)
7. ___Where___ did he get a job? (At a pizza place.)
8. ___Did___ he like high school at first? (No he didn't.)
9. ___What___ did he do after high school? (He started college.)
10. ___How___ old is Oscar? (He's 21 years old.)

D. Ask and answer *Yes/No* questions about Oscar and about your life.

Complete this exercise with the whole class. Pause to explain new vocabulary as necessary.

E. Complete these questions.

Have students fill in the question words on their own. Then, review the answers by calling on different students to read one question each to the class. For additional practice, you can invite other students to answer each question.

Suggestion

Ask five volunteer students to sit at the front of the class. Invite students to ask questions similar to the questions in Exercises D and E.

☀ Reading: Jackie Chan

A. Before You Read.

- Invite students to answer the questions above the reading. Some titles students may have heard of include *Rush Hour; Little Tiger from Canton; Mr. Nice Guy; Police Story I, II, III, and IV; Rumble in the Bronx;* and *Shanghai Noon.*
- Read the passage aloud as students follow along in their books. Emphasize that it isn't important for them to understand every single word. They should try to get the main ideas from each paragraph.
- Read the passage a second time and ask students to raise their hands when they don't understand a sentence. Read it aloud and then restate the ideas in the sentence in simple English.

B. Underline the answers to these questions.

Have students go back to the story and underline the sentence that contains the answer to each question. Review the answers with the whole class.

☀ Reading: Jackie Chan

A. Before You Read.

1. Who is Jackie Chan? What country is he from?

2. Can you name the title of one of Jackie Chan's movies?

① <u>Jackie Chan was born on April 7, 1954, in Hong Kong.</u> His parents left mainland China for Hong Kong a short time before he was born. His parents named him "Chan Kong-sang", which means "born in Hong Kong." They wanted to celebrate a safe trip to Hong Kong.

At first, Jackie's family lived in the French Embassy. ② <u>His father was a cook,</u> and his mother was a housekeeper. When Jackie was seven years old, his family moved to Australia. His father got a job as head chef in the American Embassy. Later, back in Hong Kong, Jackie's father sent Jackie to the ③ <u>China Drama Academy.</u> Jackie studied and worked 19 hours a day. The students practiced Kung Fu and learned how to do many stunts, such as flips and somersaults.

When Jackie was 17, he began to perform dangerous stunts for movies. In the early 1980s, Jackie went to Hollywood, but ④ <u>he wasn't very successful.</u> He continued to make movies in Hong Kong and had great success. Finally, in 1995, Jackie Chan became famous in the United States with his movie, ⑤ <u>"Rumble in the Bronx."</u> Today, Jackie Chan has both Chinese and American fans, and his movies make millions of dollars.

B. <u>Underline</u> the answers to these questions. (See answers above.)

1. Where was Jackie Chan born?

2. What was his father's occupation?

3. Where did Jackie Chan study Kung Fu?

4. Was his first trip to Hollywood successful?

5. What was the name of Jackie Chan's first successful Hollywood movie?

Writing Our Stories: Coming to the United States

A. Read.

I came to the United States from Cuba two years ago. I came here with my two sons. My father was here in Florida, so my sons and I found an apartment in Florida, too.

In Cuba, I studied to be a pharmacist. I worked in a hospital. My family and my friends helped me a lot. I was never alone.

At first, I had a problem with English. I couldn't understand people. I couldn't find a good job and use my education. I had to go to school to learn how to communicate. Also, I wanted to bring my mother here, but I had to find a good job and a place to live.

Now, many things are different. I have a good job in a pharmaceutical company. I study at a college and I can communicate in English. My mother is here now, and my sons speak English very well. It's not easy, but I like my life very much.

Liliana

B. Complete. (Answers will vary.)

1. I came to this country on _____.
   date

2. I arrived **on foot / by air / by boat.**

3. I came **alone / with** _____.

4. I **knew / didn't know** English.

C. In your notebook, write about your move to this country.

Writing Our Stories: Coming to the United States

A. Read.

Ask students to read the story and underline any words or phrases they don't understand. Write these items on the board and discuss them with the class. Then, have them read the story a second time. Ask what kind of information Liliana included in her story. For example, information about:

- Her family
- Her job in Cuba
- Problems in the United States
- Her life now

B. Complete.

Students complete the four sentences on their own. Call on several different students to share their answers with the class.

C. In your notebook, write about your move to this country.

As students write about their moves, encourage them to add information similar to the model story.

Suggestion

Ask students to share their writing in small groups. They can take turns reading their stories and asking each other questions about the events in their lives.

Practicing on Your Own

A. Read.

• Ask students questions about the picture. For example:

Who is this?
What is she doing?
Does she look happy or sad?

• Ask students to read the story on their own. When they finish, ask if there are any words or phrases they need help with. Explain the meaning of these items, using simple pictures on the board or by demonstrating the meaning using objects. For example, you might demonstrate *going straight* and *backing up* by using a blackboard eraser to represent a car and two lines on the board to represent the street.

B. Put the words in the questions in the correct order.

Have students complete the exercise individually and check their answers with a partner. Go over the answers with the whole class.

Practicing on Your Own

A. Read.

When I came to this country three years ago, I didn't know how to drive. Bus service wasn't good, so I needed to drive to get to my job. My brother taught me how to drive. Every weekend, he took me to the high school parking lot. I practiced going straight, backing up, turning, stopping, and parking. After six weeks, I took the driving test at the Department of Motor Vehicles. I made a lot of mistakes. I forgot to signal when I turned, I didn't stop at a stop sign, and I didn't park correctly. I failed the test. After that, I practiced in my neighborhood and downtown. Four weeks later, I passed the test.

B. Put the words in the questions in the correct order. Then, answer the questions.

1. to this country / did / come / when / Julia
   <u>When did Julia come to this country</u>_____?

2. good / the bus service / was
   <u>Was the bus service good</u>_____?

3. Julia / did / need / a driver's license / why
   <u>Why did Julia need a driver's license</u>_____?

4. taught / Julia / who / how to drive
   <u>Who taught Julia how to drive</u>_____?

5. where / Julia / practice / did
   <u>Where did Julia practice</u>_____?

6. pass / the first time / the test / Julia / did
   <u>Did Julia pass the test the first time</u>_____?

Looking at Graphs: A Survey

A. Complete this graph about the students in your class.

Write six countries represented in your class.	Write the number of students.	Complete the graph. Color in one block for each number.
(Answer as a class.)	_____	
_____	_____	
_____	_____	
_____	_____	
_____	_____	
_____	_____	

1 2 3 4 5 6 7 8 9 10

Grammar Summary

▶ **1. Yes/No questions**

| **Did** you **study** English? | Yes, I **did.** |
| **Did** he **come** to the country alone? | No, he **didn't.** |

▶ **2. Who questions**

| Who **came** here with you? | My parents **did.** |
| Who **changed** jobs? | I **did.** |

▶ **3. Wh- questions**

What did you do yesterday?

Where did you live?

How did she find a job?

When did they get married?

Why did he come to this country?

Looking at Graphs: A Survey

A. Complete this graph about the students in your class.

- Write the names of students' countries on the board and ask students to raise their hands as you write the name of their country. Write the number of students next to each country name on the board.
- Demonstrate how to fill in blocks on the graph to represent various numbers of students. Then, have them complete the graph on their own.

Grammar Summary

- Review the summary with the class. Invite students to make up alternate sentences for each example in the chart. For example, in place of *Who **came** here with you?* a student might say *Who **helped** you come here?* In place of When *did they* **get married***?* a student might say When *did they* **come here***?*
- See the Grammar Summary Expansion on page 241 for a more complete explanation of these grammar points.

Unit 14
Weekend Plans

Discuss what the person in the unit title art is doing. Say: *Tell me about the man.* (He's wearing a suit. Maybe he's going to go to a party. And he's holding a soccer ball. Maybe he's going to play soccer.)

☀Dictionary:
Weekend Activities

⏹ **A. Listen and repeat.**
   (CD2, Track 27)

   • See how many of the activities shown in the pictures students can identify. Point and ask:

   What's he doing?
   What's she doing?
   What are they doing?

   Accept one-word answers.

   • Play the audio once all the way through as students just listen. Then, play the audio again, pausing after each verb or verb phrase so that students can repeat it.
   • Call on a student to point out a picture and tell the class which action it represents. Have the student say the phrase followed by a complete sentence. For example: *Do homework. She's doing her homework.* Continue until all twelve actions have been identified.

B. Write the verb or verb phrase under the correct picture.

   Ask students to write the appropriate verb or verb phrase under each picture. Review the correct answers by playing the audio again.

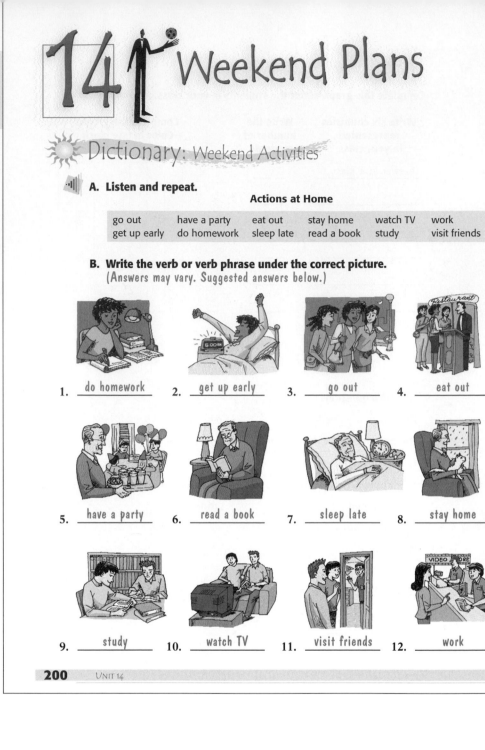

☀ Dictionary: Weekend Activities

⏹ **A. Listen and repeat.**

Actions at Home

go out	have a party	eat out	stay home	watch TV	work
get up early	do homework	sleep late	read a book	study	visit friends

B. Write the verb or verb phrase under the correct picture.
(Answers may vary. Suggested answers below.)

1. do homework
2. get up early
3. go out
4. eat out
5. have a party
6. read a book
7. sleep late
8. stay home
9. study
10. watch TV
11. visit friends
12. work

Suggestion

Have students take turns acting out the various verb phrases while the rest of the class guesses which one the person is pantomiming. Have students guess by saying the appropriate phrase and then using it in a complete sentence. For example: *Sleep late. Lina is sleeping late.*

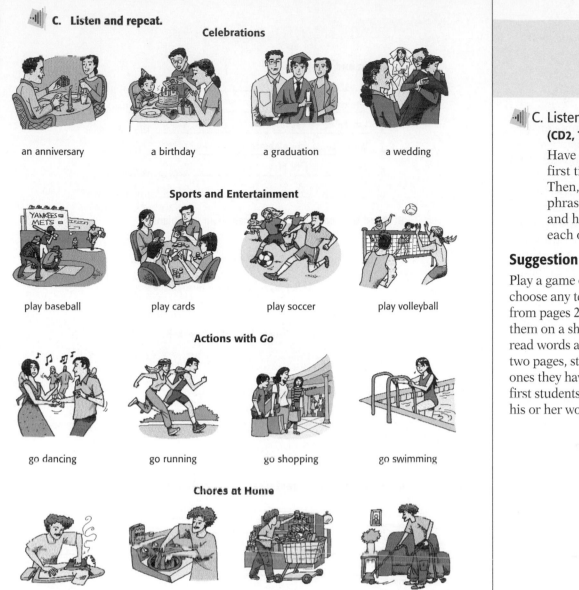

C. Listen and repeat.

Celebrations

an anniversary   a birthday   a graduation   a wedding

Sports and Entertainment

play baseball   play cards   play soccer   play volleyball

Actions with *Go*

go dancing   go running   go shopping   go swimming

Chores at Home

iron my clothes   do the laundry   do the shopping   vacuum the living room

Weekend Plans   **201**

C. Listen and repeat.
(CD2, Track 28)

Have students just listen the first time you play the audio. Then, present the words and phrases several more times and have students repeat each one.

Suggestion

Play a game of word Bingo. Students choose any ten words or phrases from pages 200 and 201 and write them on a sheet of paper. As you read words and phrases from these two pages, students cross off the ones they have on their papers. The first students to cross off all ten of his or her words is the winner.

Active Grammar:
Future Tense

A. Listen and complete.
(CD2, Track 29)

• Discuss the sample answer. Write the words *going to* on the board. Ask students what the words *going to* mean when they are used before the base form of a verb. (They show that something will happen in the future.)

• Play the audio as students write their answers in the book. Present the sentences several times if you wish. Have different students put one answer each on the board.

B. Read the chart.

• Ask different students to read aloud one sentence each from the box above the chart. Point out that all the words in these sentences can be found in the chart.

• Invite students to take turns making truthful statements about things they plan to do. Repeat each response, changing the pronoun as necessary, and ask the class to repeat. For example:

S1: *I'm going to go to work tonight.*

T: *Karlo is going to go to work tonight. Repeat.*

SS: *Karlo is going to go to work tonight.*

C. Write five of your sentences from Exercise B.

Ask students to write five true sentences about their future plans or plans of friends and family.

Active Grammar: Future Tense

A. Listen and complete.

1. He's going to do _____ the laundry.
2. She's going to wash _____ the dishes.
3. I'm going to vacuum _____ the carpet.
4. We're going to celebrate _____ a birthday.
5. They're going to play _____ volleyball.
6. I'm going to do _____ my homework.

B. Read the chart. Make sentences about your plans.

> I am **going to read** a book tonight.
> They are **going to get up** early on Saturday.
> My family and I are **going to watch** TV tonight.
> She is **going to celebrate** her birthday next week.

Future: *be + going to + verb*

I	am		read a book	tomorrow.
You			go out with friends	tonight.
We	are		get up early	this weekend.
They			go dancing	on Saturday.
My family and I		going to	go to bed late	on Sunday
			go to work	next week.
He			watch TV	next month.
She	is		celebrate a birthday	next year.
It			visit friends	in a few minutes.
				in an hour.

C. Write five of your sentences from Exercise B. (Answers will vary.)

1. _____
2. _____
3. _____
4. _____
5. _____

Audio Script

A. Listen and complete. (CD2, Track 29)

1. He's going to do the laundry.
2. She's going to wash the dishes.
3. I'm going to vacuum the carpet.
4. We're going to celebrate a birthday.
5. They're going to play volleyball.
6. I'm going to do my homework.

D. Look at the pictures. With a partner, ask and answer questions about the pictures. (Answers may vary. Possible answers below.)

What is he going to do?

He's going to see the dentist.

What's she going to do?
What's he going to do?
What are they going to do?

call the police	sing "Happy Birthday!"
get a shot	take an exam
go to bed	take a trip
see the dentist	

1. He's going to see the dentist.

2. They're going to sing "Happy Birthday!"

3. They're going to call the police.

4. They're going to take a trip.

5. She's going to get a shot.

6. She's going to go to bed.

7. They're going to take an exam.

Use your imagination with these pictures. (Answers may vary.)

1.

2.

3.

Weekend Plans **203**

D. Look at the pictures.

• Focus on the seven pictures in the middle of the page. Ask students to work in pairs as they try to figure out what all the phrases in the box mean and match them up with the correct picture.
• Point out the three sample questions and have different students read each one aloud. Then, have two students read the sample dialogue aloud. Have students work in pairs, asking and answering questions about the people in each picture.

Use your imagination with these pictures.

Approach this section playfully. Encourage students to give unusual or silly answers to these questions. However, make sure they use the correct verb forms. For example:

S1: *What is she going to do?*
S2: *She's going to quit her job.* OR *She's going to walk home.*

E. Pronunciation: *going to* versus /*gonna*/.

(CD2, Track 30)

• Point out the note about *going to* and *gonna* and discuss it with the class. Then, ask students to listen to the audio. Make a clear distinction between the slow form and the reduced form.

• Repeat the contrasting forms several times. Then, have students repeat the two different forms several times.

Practice saying both forms with a partner.

Students practice the two different forms with a partner. Move around the room, monitoring their work and modeling pronunciation as necessary.

F. Listen and complete.

(CD2, Track 31)

• Have students listen the first time through. Then, play the audio once or twice more while students write their answers.

• Make sure that students don't write *gonna*. Draw their attention to the box next to Exercise E if they do.

Practice saying these sentences with a partner.

Students practice the sentences in pairs. Move around the room, correcting pronunciation as needed.

E. Pronunciation: *going to* versus /*gonna*/. Listen and repeat the slow form, *going to*, and the reduced form /*gonna*/.

1. Tom**'s going to take** a test tomorrow.
2. Ellen**'s going to have** a baby in January.
3. Steven**'s going to study** for a test.
4. Venus **is going to play** a tennis match.
5. You**'re going to buy** a new car.
6. I**'m going to do** the laundry.
7. They **aren't going to get** married next year.
8. We**'re not going to take** a trip next month.
9. She**'s not going to cook** dinner tonight.
10. I**'m not going to eat** dessert this week.

> *Going to* is pronounced [gonna] in natural speech. Do not write **gonna**.

Practice saying both forms with a partner.

F. Listen and complete.

1. I <u>'m going to wash</u> my car tomorrow.
2. The students <u>are going to study</u> after class.
3. Some students <u>aren't going to do</u> homework tonight.
4. Our teacher <u>is going to give a test</u> next week.
5. The school <u>is going to close</u> for the holidays.
6. They <u>aren't going to be</u> late tomorrow morning.
7. The class <u>isn't going to end</u> next month.
8. I <u>'m going to arrive</u> at 11 o'clock.

Practice saying these sentences with a partner.

Audio Script

F. Listen and complete. (CD2, Track 31)

1. I'm going to wash my car tomorrow.
2. The students are going to study after class.
3. Some students aren't going to do homework tonight.
4. Our teacher is going to give a test next week.
5. The school is going to close for the holidays.
6. They aren't going to be late tomorrow morning.
7. The class isn't going to finish next month.
8. I'm going to arrive at 11 o'clock.

G. Listen to Mariana's plans. Circle the activities that she's going to do. Cross out the activities that she's *not* going to do.

H. Complete the sentences about Mariana's weekend. Some of the sentences are negative.

clean	do	✓ get up	sleep
cook	eat	go	study

1. Mariana _____ is going to get up _____ early.
2. She _____ is going to clean _____ her apartment.
3. She _____ is going to do _____ her laundry.
4. She _____ is going to study _____ in her apartment.
5. She _____ isn't going to go _____ to the library.
6. Mariana _____ is going to go _____ to the supermarket.
7. Mariana _____ is going to cook _____ a special meal.
8. Mariana and her boyfriend _____ aren't going to eat _____ at a restaurant.
9. They _____ are going to eat _____ at her apartment.

G. Listen to Mariana's plans.
(CD2, Track 32)

• Have students scan the pictures and name the action in each picture before they listen to the audio. Play the first part of the audio that explains how to mark the pictures. Ask students to listen for the activities that Mariana is going to do and to circle them on the page. Present the sentences several times if you wish.

• Go over the correct answers with the whole class. First, ask different students to point to an activity Mariana is going to do and say the appropriate sentence. Then, ask volunteers to tell what she's not going to do. For example: *She's not going to sleep late.*

H. Complete the sentences about Mariana's weekend.

Ask students to try to answer the questions on their own, but not to worry if they can't answer them all. Go over the answers with the whole class. Have different students write one correct sentence each on the board. Have students correct their own work and copy any missing sentences into their books.

Suggestion

If possible, have students tape record themselves as they read aloud the sentences in Exercise H. Remind them to pronounce *going to* as if it were *gonna*.

Audio Script

G. Listen to Mariana's plans. Circle the activities that she's going to do. Cross out the activities she's *not* going to do.
(CD2, Track 32)

I'm going to be very busy this weekend.
First, I'm going to get up early.
Then, I'm going to do my laundry.
After that, I'm going to study in my apartment.
I'm not going to go to the library.

Then, I'm going to go to the supermarket to shop for dinner.
I'm going to cook a special meal for my boyfriend because it's his birthday.
After dinner, my boyfriend and I are going to rent a movie and watch it in my apartment.

Working Together

A. Find someone who . . .

- Explain that students will be interviewing each other. Ask everyone to stand up and move around the room as they ask one another the questions. They will continue to ask different students each question until they get a "yes" answer.
- Set a time limit for this activity–perhaps 10 minutes. At the end of that time, call on individual students to report their answers. For example: *Ahmed is going to take a vacation this year.*

Suggestion

Use some of the activities in this exercise to make a graph on the board. First, make a grid with 8 rows and 10 to 12 columns. To the left of this grid, at the beginning of each row, write the number and some key words indicating each question in the exercise. Then, survey the class to find out how many people are planning to do each thing and shade in that number of boxes in that row. For example, if three people are going to take a vacation this year, shade in three boxes in the first row.

B. Weekend plans.

Have students complete the survey individually. Then, ask them to find partners and describe their plans to each other. They will use sentences beginning with *I'm going to . . .* or *I'm not going to . . . .*

Working Together

A. Find someone who . . . Ask your classmates questions about their plans. If the answer is "Yes," write the student's name on the blank. If the answer is "No," ask another student. (Answers will vary.)

Question	Classmate
1. Are you going to take a vacation this year?	_____
2. Are you going to celebrate a birthday this month?	_____
3. Are you going to exercise tomorrow?	_____
4. Are you going to clean your house this weekend?	_____
5. Are you going to go dancing on Saturday night?	_____
6. Are you going to get up early on Sunday morning?	_____
7. Are you going to study this weekend?	_____
8. Are you going to visit friends this weekend?	_____

B. Weekend plans. Check (✓) your plans for this weekend. Then, read your sentences to your partner. Check your partner's plans. (Answers will vary.)

Weekend Plans	You		Your partner	
	Yes	No	Yes	No
1. I'm going to get up early this weekend.				
2. I'm going to stay home this weekend.				
3. I'm going to work this weekend.				
4. I'm going to play a sport this weekend.				
5. I'm going to do the shopping this weekend.				

C. **Complete the sentences about you and your partner.** (Answers will vary.)

1. I _____ get up early.

2. My partner _____ get up early.

3. I _____ stay home this weekend.

4. My partner _____ stay home this weekend.

5. My partner and I _____.

D. **What are their plans for the future? Talk about these famous people's plans.**
(Answers may vary. Sample answers below.)

> He's going to make a movie.
> She's going to give a concert.

He's going to sing
at a concert.
Marc Anthony

He's going to win
a prize.
Denzel Washington

She's going to
make a movie.
Julia Roberts

Shaquille O'Neal
He's going to
win a game.

Michelle Kwan
She's going to
skate on tour.

Yo Yo Ma
He's going to play
at a concert.

**C. Complete these sentences
about you and your partner.**

Have students look back at their
charts on page 206 and fill in
their answers on their own. They
can check them with their partner. Call on several students to
read their answers to the class.

**D. What are their plans for
the future?**

• Help students identify the people in the pictures. Ask questions
such as:

> *Who is Marc Anthony?*
> (He's a famous singer.)
> *Do you have any of his CDs?*
> *Who is that?* (Julia Roberts.
> She's a movie actress.)
> *Did you ever see her in a
> movie?*

• Next, discuss what each one
does for a living and what special abilities each one has. Then,
ask students to work in pairs
sharing their ideas about what
plans these people may have for
the future.

• Invite students to share their
ideas with the class. Elicit several
possible plans for each person.

The Big Picture: A Visitor

A. Look at the picture.

Ask students to look at the picture and try to guess what Masa is going to do this weekend.

B. Look at the picture.
(CD2, Track 33)

The first time through, have students look at the pictures and just listen. Then, present the story a second time. Ask students what they remember about Masa's plans.

C. Read and circle.

Ask students to answer the questions individually. Go over the answers with the whole class. You can replay portions of the audio to confirm any answers students have difficulty with.

The Big Picture: A Visitor

A. Look at the picture. Masa Ohtani is looking forward to his mother's visit. Talk about his plans. (Answers will vary.)

B. Look at the picture. Listen to the story.

C. Read and circle.

1. Masa is tired. — True **(False)**
2. Mrs. Ohtani is going to arrive at the airport. — **(True)** False
3. Mrs. Ohtani is going to come from Japan. — **(True)** False
4. Mrs. Ohtani is going to stay at a hotel. — True **(False)**
5. They are going to go to a restaurant. — True **(False)**
6. On Saturday, they are going to sleep late. — **(True)** False
7. Mrs. Ohtani is going to get married next year. — True **(False)**
8. Mrs. Ohtani is going to meet Masa's girlfriend. — **(True)** False

208 UNIT 14

Audio Script

B. Look at the picture. Listen to the story.
(CD2, Track 33)

I'm excited. Tomorrow my mother's going to arrive at the San Francisco Airport. She's coming to visit for two weeks. She's coming from Osaka, Japan. Today I'm going to clean my apartment because she's going to stay with me. Tomorrow, I'm going to pick her up. Then, we're going to drive to my sister's house. We're going to have dinner with all of our friends and family that lives in the Bay Area. On Saturday, we're going to sleep late. After a late breakfast, my sister and I are going to show her the beautiful city of San Francisco. We're going to take a cable car ride. We're going to visit my favorite park. Then, I'm going to take her to my girlfriend's house. We want to get married next year, so I want my mother to meet her. I hope she likes her.

208 ENGLISH IN ACTION 2

D. Read and put the plans in order from 1 to 6.

<u> 6 </u> **a.** Mrs. Ohtani is going to meet his girlfriend.

<u> 2 </u> **b.** Masa is going to meet his mother at the airport.

<u> 3 </u> **c.** They're going to have dinner with his sister.

<u> 4 </u> **d.** They're going to sleep late.

<u> 1 </u> **e.** Masa's going to clean his apartment.

<u> 5 </u> **f.** Masa's going to take his mother around San Francisco.

E. Read each sentence. Correct the sentence. Say the sentence again.

1. Masa's father is going to come for a visit.

> Masa's **father** isn't going to come for a visit.
> Masa's **mother** is going to come for a visit.

2. His mother is going to stay for ~~a month.~~ *two weeks*

3. She's going to arrive at the ~~Oakland~~ *San Francisco* airport.

4. She's going to stay ~~in a hotel.~~ *with Masa*

5. They're going to drive to his ~~brother's~~ *sister's* house.

6. On Saturday, they're going to get up ~~early.~~ *late*

7. They're going to visit ~~the art museum.~~ *Masa's favorite park*

8. Masa's going to get married next ~~month.~~ *year*

F. What are you going to do? A friend from your country is going to visit you next week. What are you going to do? Complete the sentences.

1. I <u>am going to pick him up at the airport.</u>

2. I <u>(Answers will vary.)</u>

3. We _____

4. We _____

5. We _____

D. Read and put the plans in order from 1 to 6.

Ask students to fill in the answers individually. Check the answers by going around the room and asking students to read the sentences in order. Ask for the sentences one by one. For example: *Khalil, what is sentence number 1? Amparo, what is sentence number 2?*

E. Read each sentence.

Read the instructions and sample item aloud. Point out that students will say a negative sentence followed by an affirmative sentence using *going to*. Call on different students to do each item.

F. What are you going to do?

Give students five minutes to think about and write out their responses. Then, ask several students to put one sentence each on the board. With the class, discuss the various plans and check the sentences for grammatical accuracy. Invite other students to add their suggestions orally.

☀️ Reading: Hosting the Olympic Games

A. Before You Read.

• Invite several students to answer the questions above the passage. Use an almanac, if necessary, to find out when various countries hosted the Olympics.

• Ask students to read the story to themselves. When they finish, invite them to ask about anything they don't understand. If students have difficulty with words such as *security, support,* or *facilities,* write them on the board and discuss their meaning with the class.

• Ask different students to paraphrase each of the eight questions. For example, item 1 might be restated as: *Are there enough buses and taxis to get everyone to the Olympic site?*

B. You and your committee want to hold the Olympics in your city.

Read and discuss the instructions. Suggest that the groups use the eight questions to help organize their proposals. Set a time limit–perhaps 15 minutes–for students to prepare. Then, have two or three students role-play the I.O.C. committee asking questions. They can ask the eight questions in the reading. Members of each group take turns answering questions.

☀️ Reading: Hosting the Olympic Games

A. Before You Read.

1. Is your country going to host an Olympics some time in the future?
2. Did your country ever host the Olympics?
3. Do you know someone who is going to participate in the Olympics?

Every two years, the Winter or the Summer Olympic Games take place. It is a great honor for a country to have the Olympics. Many countries want to host the Olympics, so it is very competitive to get the Games.

The International Olympic Committee, or the I.O.C., chooses the city for the Olympics. When a city decides that it wants to host the Olympic Games, it makes a committee of local residents. Then, there are many questions that the I.O.C. asks the committee.

1. Is your city going to have good transportation to the Olympic events?
2. Is the city going to have enough hotels for the visitors?
3. Who's going to be responsible for security?
4. Is the weather going to be good for the events?
5. Is the public going to support the Olympics?
6. Which airport are the visitors going to use?
7. What facilities does the city have now? What facilities is the city going to build?
8. How is the city going to pay for this project?

For many cities, it is very expensive to have the Olympics. For example, if a city has an old stadium, it is probably going to build a big, new stadium. If a city doesn't have enough hotels, it is going to build more hotels.

B. You and your committee want to hold the Olympics in your city. How is your city going to prepare for the Games? With a group of students, prepare a proposal for the Summer or Winter Olympic Games. Each group is going to present its proposal to the "I.O.C." Choose another group of students to be the "I.O.C." They are going to select the winner.

☀ Writing Our Stories: My Weekend Plans

A. Read.

This weekend, I'm going to have a surprise party for my wife. We're going to have a cake, ice cream, and some punch. On Saturday morning, she's going to go to work. She doesn't know anything about the party. I'm going to clean our apartment. Then, I'm going to wrap her present in a special box. It's a pair of airline tickets to our native country. Our children are going to decorate the apartment. They're going to give her presents, too. We're going to have a great party on Saturday night.

B. Write about your weekend plans. (Answers will vary.)

This weekend, I am going to _____ .

_____ On Saturday morning, I _____

_____

In the afternoon, _____

In the evening, _____

On Sunday morning, _____ .

_____ On Sunday evening, I

_____

> **Writing Note**
>
> Use a comma after a time expression at the beginning of a sentence.
>
> **On Saturday evening,** we're going to see a movie.

☀ Writing Our Stories: My Weekend Plans

A. Read.

- Point to people and things in the picture and ask:

  What is this?
  Who is the party for?
  Why are they having the party?

- Ask students to read the story once all the way through. Ask simple comprehension questions, such as:

  What is the man going to do?
  Where is the woman going to go on Saturday?
  What is the man going to give his wife?
  What are the children going to do?

B. Write about your weekend plans.

- The story in Exercise A can serve as a model for this writing.
- Ask several students to read their weekend plans to the class. Encourage other students to ask questions

Suggestion

For the next class, copy some sentences from the students' writing, leaving out the verbs that contain the *going to* future. Have students fill in these missing parts. Then, have different students read the completed sentences aloud.

A. Contrast: future, present, and present continuous.

Students do the activity individually and check their answers with a partner. Go over the answers with the whole class.

B. Contrast: future, present, and present continuous.

Read through the eight sentences with the class. Ask students to point out the time expression in each sentence. Then, have them fill in the answers on their own. Check the answers by calling on different students to read one sentence each.

A. Contrast: future, present, and present continuous. Read and circle.
What time does the sentence describe?

1. The children are watching TV. — (Now) Future Every day
2. He works at an express delivery company. — Now Future (Every day)
3. They're going to buy a new car this year. — Now (Future) Every day
4. She is vacuuming her apartment. — (Now) Future Every day
5. Belinda is going to make a salad for dinner. — Now (Future) Every day
6. I eat cereal and fruit for breakfast. — Now Future (Every day)
7. We're preparing our house for a party. — (Now) Future Every day
8. The students are going to take a test. — Now (Future) Every day

B. Contrast: future, present, and present continuous. Read and complete the sentences about an English class. Pay attention to the time expressions.

arrive	begin	do	end	go
listen	play	take	visit	write

1. Our class _____begins_____ at 9:00 every morning.
2. One student _____arrives_____ late for class every day.
3. The students _____are going to take_____ a test tomorrow.
4. Right now, the teacher _____is playing_____ a tape recorder.
5. The students _____are going to listen_____ to a tape about the news in a few minutes.
6. The students _____go_____ to the computer lab once a week.
7. The students _____are going to do_____ a lot of homework tonight.
8. At the moment, the teacher _____is writing_____ on the chalkboard.
9. Next month, the students _____are going to visit_____ a museum.
10. Our class always _____ends_____ at 12:00.

A. Read the graph. What do people like to do on weekends? Complete the sentences with the correct percentages.

1. __58__ % of Americans like to visit friends or family on the weekends.
2. __55__ % like to go to a park or outdoor place.
3. __35__ % like to watch professional sports.
4. __34__ % like to play sports.
5. __28__ % like to exercise.
6. __19__ % like to watch TV.
7. __15__ % like to use the Internet.

Favorite Weekend Activities

Source: The Shell Poll

B. What is your favorite weekend activity?

Grammar Summary

▶ **1. Future tense statements**

Use **be + going to** to talk about actions in the future.

I **am going to take** a vacation next month.
She **is going to have** a baby in January.
We **are going to buy** a new car tomorrow.
They **are not going to look** for a new apartment this year.
You **are not going to work** overtime on Saturday.

▶ **2. Future time expressions**

Put the time expressions at the beginning or at the end of a sentence.

Tomorrow morning, I'm going to get up early.

She's going to visit her brother **next week.**

tonight	tomorrow	tomorrow night	the day after tomorrow
next week	next month	next year	next Sunday
in a few minutes	in a few hours	in a week	in a month

▶ **3. Pronunciation**

In natural, reduced speech, **going to** is pronounced /gonna/.
Do **not** write *gonna*.

Looking at Graphs: Favorite Weekend Activities

A. Read the graph.

• Point out the percentages across the top of the chart and the activities listed on the bars of the chart. Do the first percentage as a sample answer. Tell students it's OK to give approximate answers if they wish. For example, the answer to number 1 could be *58%* or *about 60%*.

• Ask students to check their answers with a partner. Then, confirm the answers with a whole-class review.

B. What is your favorite weekend activity?

Have a class discussion about students' favorite weekend activities. On the board, write the names of any new activities they suggest.

Grammar Summary

• Review the summary with the class. Invite students to make up alternate sentences for each example in the chart. For example, in place of *We **are going to buy** a new car tomorrow*, a student might say *We **are going to take** a test next week*.

• See the Grammar Summary Expansion on page 242 for a more complete explanation of these grammar points.

Unit 15
Going on Vacation

Discuss the unit title art. Ask: *What is the woman doing?* (She's holding a beach toy and reading a road map. I think she is going to take a vacation.)

☀Dictionary: Vacation Destinations and Plans

Suggestion

Before beginning Exercise A, ask students to identify as many of the items in the pictures as they can. Help them identify the others. Use the phrases in sentences and ask questions to help clarify the meaning of each. For example:

T: *There's an amusement park at Crystal Beach. They have a big roller coaster. Has anyone visited Crystal Beach Amusement Park?*
S1: *Yes, I went there last weekend.*
T: *What did you do?*
S1: *We ate hot dogs and rode on the rides.*

A. Listen and repeat.
(CD2, Track 34)

• Have students just listen as you play the audio the first time. The second time through, pause after each phrase and ask students to repeat.
• Ask students to write the phrases under the correct pictures. Check the answers with the whole class.

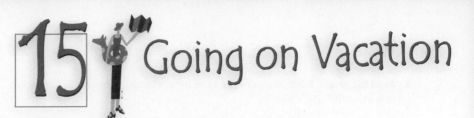

15 Going on Vacation

Dictionary: Vacation Destinations and Plans

A. Listen and repeat. Then, label the pictures.

an amusement park	a beach	a historic site	a play
an art museum	a cabin	a lake	a sporting event
an aquarium	a carnival	a national park	a zoo

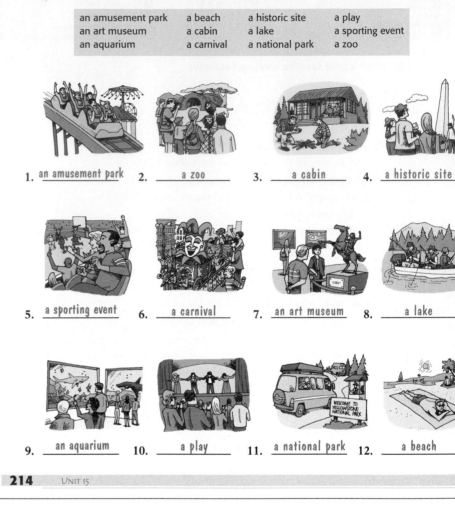

1. an amusement park
2. a zoo
3. a cabin
4. a historic site
5. a sporting event
6. a carnival
7. an art museum
8. a lake
9. an aquarium
10. a play
11. a national park
12. a beach

214 UNIT 15

| rent a car | sunbathe | take a tour |
| rent a house | take pictures | visit a city |

1. take a tour
2. visit a city
3. take pictures
4. rent a car
5. sunbathe
6. rent a house

C. **Verbs with *go*. Listen and repeat. Then, label the pictures.**

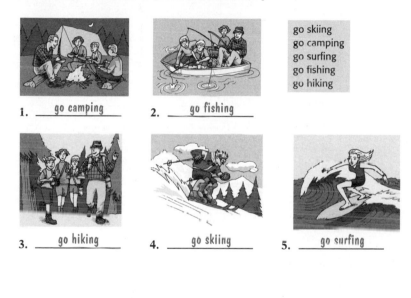

| go skiing |
| go camping |
| go surfing |
| go fishing |
| go hiking |

1. go camping
2. go fishing
3. go hiking
4. go skiing
5. go surfing

Going on Vacation **215**

B. Listen and repeat.
B. Listen and repeat.
(CD2, Track 35)

• Play the audio and ask students to repeat. Then, go through the phrases again and ask them to guess what each one means. Have them explain each one in their own words. For example: *When you rent a car, you pay someone to use the car for a few days.*

• Ask students to write the phrases under the correct pictures. As you review the correct answers, use the vocabulary words to ask questions and talk about the pictures. For example: *Who's taking pictures? That's right, the father is taking pictures.*

C. Verbs with *go*.
(CD2, Track 36)

Have students look at the pictures in the book as you play the audio. Then, present the verbs again and have students repeat each one. Ask students to write the correct phrase under each picture.

Suggestion

Write three headings on the board: *In the city, Not in the city,* and *Both places.* Ask students to take turns coming to the board and writing one of the items on pages 214 and 215 in the correct column. *An art museum* would go under *In the city. Go fishing* would go under *Not in the city. Take pictures* would go under *Both places.*

Active Grammar: Future Tense Questions

A. Read and check.

Ask students to mark their answers individually. Then, discuss these answers with the whole class. Ask students to mention a specific example of each type of vacation place or activity. For example, for *historic site* they might mention an ancient palace or a place where an important battle was fought. For *surfing* they might name a beach that is popular with surfers.

Discuss the checked items with a partner.

Students tell each other about the places and activities they checked on their lists. If possible, pair up students from different countries. If necessary, have students from different parts of the same country work together.

B. What can you do in your state?

Complete this activity with the whole class. Write student suggestions on the board and have students copy them in the appropriate places in their books.

Active Grammar: Future Tense Questions

A. Read and check (✓). Which are popular vacation places and activities in your country? (Answers will vary.)

☐ resorts   ☐ skiing

☐ carnivals   ☐ camping

☐ museums   ☐ dancing

☐ historic sites   ☐ going to sporting events

☐ an aquarium   ☐ visiting cities

☐ an amusement park ☐ surfing

☐ mountains   ☐ fishing

Discuss the checked items (✓) with a partner.

B. What can you do in your state? (Answers will vary.)

My state is _____.
               name of your state

1. I can _____ in / at _____.
          action   place / city / location

2. I can _____ in / at _____.
          action   place / city / location

3. I can _____ in / at _____.
                   place / city / location

4. I can _____ in / at _____.

5. I can _____ in / at _____.

6. In my state, I can't _____.
               action

7. In my state, I can't _____.
               action

8. In my state, I can't _____.

9. In my state, I can't _____.

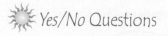
A. Read the chart. Look at the picture.

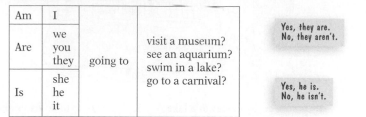

Am	I			
Are	we you they	going to	visit a museum? see an aquarium? swim in a lake? go to a carnival?	Yes, they are. No, they aren't.
Is	she he it			Yes, he is. No, he isn't.

B. Listen and complete.

1. Are Ben and Belinda _____*going to visit*_____ their grandparents?
2. Are they _____*going to go*_____ alone?
3. Are they _____*going to travel*_____ by train?
4. Are they _____*going to stay*_____ in a hotel?
5. Are they _____*going to stay*_____ at the beach?
6. Are they _____*going to go*_____ hiking?
7. _*Is*_ Ben _____*going to go fishing*_____?
8. _*Is*_ Belinda _____*going to go swimming*_____ in the lake?

Practice asking and answering the questions with a partner.

Going on Vacation **217**

Yes/No Questions

A. Read the chart.

• Review the chart with the class. Ask students to take turns making questions using the information shown. For example: *Am I going to see an aquarium?*

• Ask students to comment on what they see in the picture. You can ask questions to get them started. For example:

T: *How old are the boy and girl?*
S1: *I think they're about eight and ten years old.*
T: *What are they going to do?*
S2: *Visit their grandparents.*

B. Listen and complete.
(CD2, Track 37)

Play the audio and ask students to just listen the first time. Then, play it again and have them fill in the blanks. Review the correct question forms by calling on different students to read each one aloud.

Practice asking and answering the questions with a partner.

Pairs of students practice asking and answering the questions in Exercise B. Help students with correct question intonation.

Audio Script

B. Listen and complete. (CD2, Track 37)

1. Are Ben and Linda going to visit their grandparents?
2. Are they going to go alone?
3. Are they going to travel by train?
4. Are they going to stay in a hotel?
5. Are they going to stay at the beach?
6. Are they going to go hiking?
7. Is Ben going to go fishing?
8. Is Belinda going to go swimming in the lake?

C. Look at the picture.

• Ask students to identify objects and comment on what they see in the picture. You might say:

What's this?
What is the man doing?
What is he thinking about?

Repeat correct words and statements and rephrase any incomplete or grammatically incorrect statements as full English sentences. Ask the class to repeat each one.

• Call on different students to answer each question. Refer back to the picture as you discuss the answers to the questions.

D. Look at the picture.

• Discuss the picture with the class. Invite students to say who they think the women are and what they are doing.
• Point out the five verbs in the box and ask them to complete the questions using these verbs. Review the correct question forms orally with the class.

Practice asking and answering the questions with a partner.

Pairs of students practice asking and answering the questions in Exercise D. Help students with correct question intonation.

C. Look at the picture. Read and answer the questions. (Answers may vary.)

Yes, he is.
No, he isn't.

1. Is José going to stay at a lake?
   No, he isn't.
2. Is he going to stay a week?
   No, he isn't.
3. Is he going to travel alone?
   Yes, he is.
4. Is he going to travel by public transportation?
   No, he isn't.
5. Is he going to go fishing?
   No, he isn't.
6. Is he going to stay in a hotel?
   Yes, he is.

D. Look at the picture. Read and complete.

| go | rent | see | stay | visit |

1. __Are__ Donna and Debbie __going to go__ to Boston?
2. __Are__ they __going to stay__ two weeks?
3. __Are__ they __going to stay__ at a hotel?
4. __Are__ they __going to visit/see__ their cousins?
5. __Are__ they __going to rent__ a car?
6. __Are__ they __going to visit/see__ a historic site?

Practice asking and answering the questions with a partner.

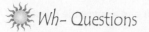
A. Listen and complete.

1. _____Who_____ is going to _____go_____ on a honeymoon?
2. _____Where_____ are _____they_____ going to _____go_____ ?
3. _____How long_____ are _____they_____ going to _____travel_____ ?
4. _____How long_____ are _____they_____ going to _____stay_____ ?
5. _____Where_____ are _____they_____ going to _____stay_____ ?
6. _____Which cities_____ are _____they_____ going to _____visit_____ ?
7. _____What_____ are _____they_____ going to _____do_____

during the day?

8. _____Where_____ are _____they_____ going to _____go_____

in the evening?

B. Ask and answer the questions with a partner.

Wh- Questions

A. Listen and complete.
(CD2, Track 38)

- Invite students to comment on the picture. Ask questions such as:

  Who is this?
  What are they going to do?
  Where are they now?

- Play the audio and have students complete the sentences. Review the completed sentences with the class.

B. Ask and answer the questions with a partner.

Students take turns asking and answering the questions using the picture to guide their responses. Check the exercise by asking volunteer pairs to present one or two exchanges each while the rest of the class listens.

Audio Script

A. Listen and complete. (CD2, Track 38)

1. Who is going to go on a honeymoon?
2. Where are they going to go?
3. How are they going to travel?
4. How long are they going to stay?
5. Where are they going to stay?
6. Which cities are they going to visit?
7. What are they going to do during the day?
8. Where are they going to go in the evening?

C. Look at the information in the chart below.

- Point out the information about the Lee Family in the first column of the chart. Then, role-play with a student the three exchanges in the sample conversation at the top of the page. Answer any questions students may have.
- Ask students to find partners and talk about the other people in the chart. As they work together, move around the room, helping as needed. Review the answers by calling on different pairs to ask and answer several questions each.

D. Answer the questions, using a time expression.

Review the meaning of the time expressions. Students should work in pairs, asking and answering the questions.

C. Look at the information in the chart below. Ask and answer the questions with a partner.

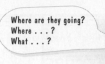

Where are they going?
Where . . . ?
What . . . ?

They're going to Colorado.
They're going to stay at a cabin.
They're going to go hiking and . . .

Who	The Lee Family	Jim and Linda	Makiko
Where	A cabin in the mountains of Colorado	A nice hotel in Hawaii	Her sister's house in Washington, D.C.
What	go hiking go swimming go fishing	go sunbathing go swimming ride a boat	visit the museums see the zoo take a lot of pictures

D. Answer the questions, using a time expression. (Answers will vary.)

tomorrow	next week	later	in (year)
this weekend	next month		in (month)
	next summer		
	next year		

1. When are you going to take a vacation?   I'm going to take a vacation . . .
2. When are you going to visit your country? I'm going to visit my country . . .
3. When is your teacher going to give a test? My teacher's going to give a test . . .
4. When is this class going to finish?   This class is going to finish . . .
5. When are you going to see your family?   I'm going to see them . . .
6. When are you going to see a movie?
7. When are you going to visit a new city?
8. When are you going to have a day off?

Questions with /gonna/

A. Pronunciation: Questions with /gonna/. Listen and repeat.

1. Are you going to leave tomorrow?
2. Is she going to visit her family?
3. Is he going to take the bus?
4. Are they going to stay at a hotel?
5. Is it going to take a long time?
6. How are you going to get there?
7. How much are we going to pay?
8. Who is going to go with you?
9. What are you going to do there?
10. When is she going to return?

Practice the questions with a partner.

Working Together: Student to Student

A. STUDENT A: Turn to page 222.

STUDENT B: Listen to Student A. Answer questions 1 to 4. Then, read questions 5 to 8. Student A will answer.

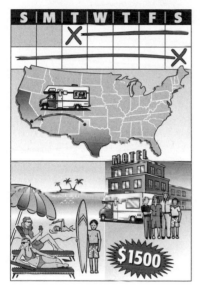

1. a. Yes
   b. No
2. a. Yes
   b. No
3. a. 11 days
   b. Next week
   c. By air
4. a. The grandparents
   b. The Gardner Family
   c. The children
5. Are they going to go to the beach?
6. Are they going to stay at a hotel?
7. How much are they going to spend?
8. When are they going to return?

Going on Vacation **221**

Questions with /gonna/

A. Pronunciation: Questions with /gonna/. (CD2, Track 39)

• Model the pronunciation of *going to*'s short form /gonna/. Then, model the contrast between the long form *going to* and the short form /gonna/. Ask students to repeat. Remind them that the short form is only used when speaking and is never written.
• Play the audio and ask students to listen and repeat.

Suggestion

Ask students to take turns reading one of the questions aloud. Focus on /gonna/, correcting students' pronunciation as necessary and having them repeat the whole sentence after you.

Practice the questions with a partner.

Students practice asking each other the questions in pairs. Have partners raise their hands if they need help with any of the questions. Model the pronunciation of /gonna/ as well as the entire sentence when working with the pairs.

Working Together: Student to Student

A. Student B.

• Discuss the picture. Have students identify the places and items they see and guess who the people are.
• Explain that both Student A and Student B will be asking and answering questions. One student has the questions and the other student has the answers. Then, the roles are reversed.
• Read the instructions and model the first question and answer with a student. Then, pairs complete the activity on their own. Have them check each other's answers when they finish.

Teacher's Guide, Unit 15 **221**

Working Together: Student to Student

B. Student A.

See the instructions for Exercise A on page 221.

C. Read and practice.

- Read the dialogue to the class. Answer any questions students may have. Refer to the picture as necessary.
- Have students practice the dialogue in pairs. As they work together, move around the room checking on pronunciation of *going to*/gonna/.

D. Write a conversation about a vacation you plan to take.

Students can use the conversation in Exercise C as a model. It begins with a question about where the person is going to go, and then goes on to talk about what the person is going to do and where he or she is going to stay.

Suggestion

Collect the completed conversations. Correct any errors and make copies. Distribute some of the conversations during the next class and have pairs of students read someone else's conversation to the class. You might recommend that students rewrite or type the conversation if there are many corrections.

Working Together: Student to Student

B. STUDENT A: Read questions 1 to 4. Student B will answer. Then, listen and answer questions 5 to 8.

1. Are they going to leave on Thursday?
2. Are they going to go to Texas?
3. How long are they going to stay?
4. Who's going to go on vacation?
5. a. Yes
   b. No
6. a. Yes
   b. No
7. a. 12 days
   b. $1,500
   c. By airplane
8. a. Tomorrow
   b. 11 days
   c. Next week

C. Read and practice.

A: Are you going to take a vacation next summer?

B: Yes, I am.

A: Where are you going to go?

B: My family and I are going to the beach.

A: The beach? Where are you going to stay?

B: We're going to rent a house.

A: What are you going to do there?

B: We're going to go swimming, we're going to visit friends, and we're going to barbecue every day.

A: How long are you going to stay?

B: We're going to stay for a week.

A: Have a good trip.

D. Write a conversation about a vacation you plan to take.

E. Travel poster. Make a travel poster of your native country or the city where you live now. Use the travel poster here as an example. You can add a simple map of your country, post cards, or other information to make your poster interesting. Present your poster to the class. **(Answers will vary.)**

Enjoy Beautiful _____ on Your Next Vacation!

Spend time at _____.
_____(park)

Tour _____
_____(historic site)

Relax in the sun on our beautiful beaches in _____ on the
_____.   (city/town)
(body of water)

See the exhibits at _____.
_____(museum)

Enjoy the _____.
_____(carnival)

Relax in your room at the _____.
_____(hotel)

Taste delicious _____ food, such as _____
_____(nationality)

and _____.

At night, dance to _____ music at _____
club.

Come to _____!
_____(country)

E. Travel poster.

• Read and discuss the instructions. Emphasize that the poster doesn't have to look like the one in the book and that students may include any drawing, pictures, postcards, or photographs they wish.

• Display the completed posters in the classroom. Invite each student to present his or her poster to the class and answer questions about it.

Suggestion

Leave the posters on the wall or display them in a public hallway if students are comfortable with that idea. Encourage students to examine each other's posters and ask each other for more information about things to do in their native countries.

☀ The Big Picture:
Vacation Plans

Suggestion

Before doing the exercise, encourage students to talk about the map. Ask questions such as:

Where are we now?
What is the name of this state?

A. Write the names of these cities on the map of the United States.

- Ask students to look at the names of the six cities. Help them find these cities on their maps. You might want to use a large wall map of the United States to confirm their answers.
- Have students write in the names of the cities on the map and check their work with a partner.

B. Listen and fill in the information on the map.
(CD2, Track 40)

Point out the *Who, How,* and *When* spaces near Chicago, Boston, and Denver. Play the audio and have students fill in the answers.

C. Read and circle.

Students complete this activity on their own and check their answers with a partner.

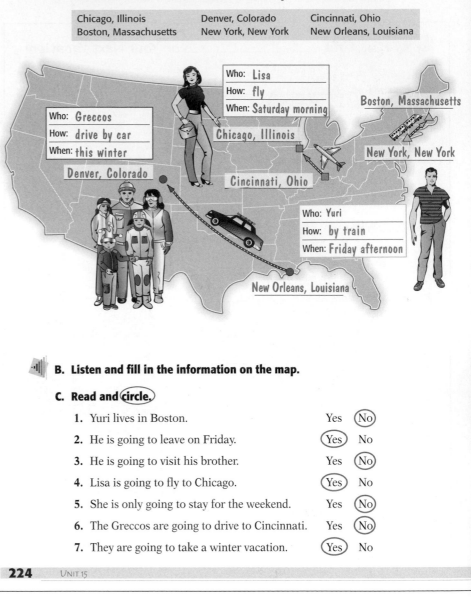

☀ The Big Picture: Vacation Plans

A. Write the names of these cities on the map of the United States.

| Chicago, Illinois | Denver, Colorado | Cincinnati, Ohio |
| Boston, Massachusetts | New York, New York | New Orleans, Louisiana |

Who: Lisa
How: fly
When: Saturday morning

Who: Greccos
How: drive by car
When: this winter

Denver, Colorado

Chicago, Illinois

Cincinnati, Ohio

Boston, Massachusetts

New York, New York

Who: Yuri
How: by train
When: Friday afternoon

New Orleans, Louisiana

B. Listen and fill in the information on the map.

C. Read and circle.

1.	Yuri lives in Boston.	Yes	**No**
2.	He is going to leave on Friday.	**Yes**	No
3.	He is going to visit his brother.	Yes	**No**
4.	Lisa is going to fly to Chicago.	**Yes**	No
5.	She is only going to stay for the weekend.	Yes	**No**
6.	The Greccos are going to drive to Cincinnati.	Yes	**No**
7.	They are going to take a winter vacation.	**Yes**	No

224 UNIT 15

Audio Script

B. Listen and fill in the information on the map. (CD2, Track 40)

Yuri:
Yuri lives in New York and he likes to travel. This weekend, he's going to visit Boston, Massachusetts. He's going to leave Friday afternoon and take the train to Boston. It's a three-hour ride. He's going to stay in a downtown hotel. On Friday night, he's going out to dinner with his sister. On Saturday, he's going to the aquarium. Then, he's going to walk around the historic areas. On Sunday morning, Yuri and his sister are going to

visit the Museum of Fine Arts. After lunch, Yuri's going to take the train back home.

Lisa:
Lisa and her sister, Linda, are very close, but they don't live in the same city. On Saturday morning, Lisa's going to fly from Cincinnati to Chicago to visit her sister. Lisa's going to stay for a week at her sister's apartment. They're going to visit two museums. They're also going to visit the zoo. Next week, Lisa's going to visit the University of Chicago. She's going to a job interview. Next Sunday morning, she's going to fly home.

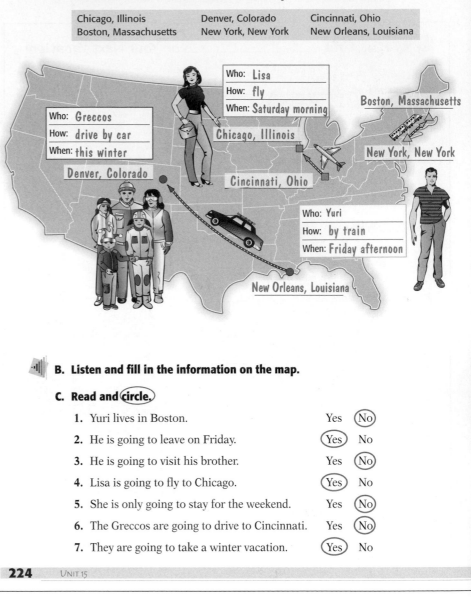
(Continued on page 225.)

D. *Who* questions. Read and check (✓) the answers.

Question	Yuri	Lisa	The Greccos
1. Who's going to travel by train?	✓		
2. Who's going to stay for a week?		✓	
3. Who's going to visit a relative?	✓	✓	
4. Who's going to play a sport?			✓
5. Who's going to go to the mountains?			✓
6. Who's going to visit museums?	✓	✓	
7. Who's going to spend time on the road?			✓

E. Match each question with the correct answer.

1. Where is Lisa going to go? (d.)
2. Is she going to drive? (f.)
3. Where is she going to stay? (a.)
4. What is she going to do ? (g.)
5. Is Yuri going to take the train? (b.)
6. Where is Yuri going to stay? (c.)
7. What is he going to do in Boston? (e.)

a. She's going to stay at her sister's apartment.
b. Yes, he is.
c. He's going to stay at a downtown hotel.
d. She's going to Chicago.
e. He's going to see the aquarium.
f. No, she isn't.
g. She's going to visit museums, the zoo, and have an interview.

F. Complete each question. (Answers may vary. Suggested responses below.)

1. Where ___is___ Yuri ___going/traveling/staying___ for his vacation?
2. Who ___is___ Yuri ___eating/going to/having___ dinner with?
3. Why ___is___ Lisa ___visiting___ Chicago?
4. Where ___is___ Lisa ___having___ a job interview?
5. How ___are___ the Greccos ___traveling___ ?
6. How long ___are___ they ___staying___ ?

| go |
| travel |
| eat |
| visit |
| have |
| stay |

Going on Vacation   225

D. *Who* questions.
Ask students to complete the activity on their own. Then, replay the audio and have them check their answers.

Suggestion
For additional oral practice, ask students to use the information on the chart to make statements about the different travelers. For example: *Yuri is going to travel by train.*

E. Match each question with the correct answer.
Have students complete the activity individually. Check the answers by calling on different students to read the matching questions and answers.

F. Complete each question.
Point out the six verbs in the box. Ask students to complete the questions in their books using *did* plus one of these verbs. Review the correct answers with the whole class.

Audio Script

(Continued from page 224.)

The Greccos:
The Greccos love the snow, and they take a long vacation every winter. This winter, they're going to drive to Denver, Colorado. They're going to spend two weeks away from home. It's a long drive from Louisiana to Colorado, so they're going to spend two days on the road. In Colorado, they're going to stay at a comfortable hotel in the mountains. They're going to go skiing every day. They're going to take a lot of pictures. And, they're going to eat at a different restaurant every night. The Greccos are going to have a great vacation.

Teacher's Guide, Unit 15   **225**

Reading:
An Alaskan Vacation

A. Before You Read.

• Say the word or phrase below each picture and ask students to repeat. Then, invite students to say something about each picture. You might ask questions such as:

Who has gone river rafting?
Where did you do it?
Where is the closest glacier?
What is the difference between a house and a lodge.

• Point out the map of Alaska. Remind students to refer to it as they read the story. It will help them understand the reading.

• Ask students to read the story on their own. When they finish, invite them to ask about anything they don't understand, but try not to get involved in figuring out what a sentence means in a word-by-word fashion. Encourage students to add their comments about the reading.

Suggestion

If students can't understand a certain passage, try paraphrasing it in simple English.

Reading: An Alaskan Vacation

A. Before You Read. Read the vocabulary and look at the pictures.

river rafting   wild animals   glaciers   lodge   whales

bears   moose   caribou   salmon

It is impossible to see all of Alaska in one visit. Alaska is a very large state, and it has many natural wonders. There are many things to see and to do in Alaska, so most people only choose three or four places to visit.

Fly to Anchorage, the state's largest city. From there, rent a car and drive to the Kenai Peninsula.① The Kenai River offers the best salmon fishing in the world. You can catch a thirty- to forty-pound salmon. The largest salmon ever caught in this river was 98 pounds. If you like water, and if you like something fast and exciting, you can go river rafting on the Kenai River.

Drive back to Anchorage and buy a ticket for your trip on the Alaska Railroad to Denali National Park.② This eight-hour ride passes beautiful mountains, rivers, and valleys. The only way to see Denali is in a park bus. Make a reservation for the bus. From the bus, you can see the interesting, wild land of Alaska. Look carefully for bears, moose, and caribou. If it is a clear day, you will see Mt. McKinley, the highest mountain in the United States. You can camp in the park or stay a few nights in one of the few lodges inside the park. Then, take a bus back to Anchorage.

Finally, fly to Juneau,③ the state capital. The city is beautiful, and it is popular to take a day trip on Mendenhall Glacier. You will want to spend most of your time on the water. Many small companies offer trips in the waters near Juneau. You can stay from one day to one week. You can watch for whales, view the wildlife, or look at the giant

glaciers. If you choose a smaller boat, you can go to a beach for a picnic lunch, fish from the boat, or walk up to a glacier.

A visit to Alaska takes a lot of planning. Visitors need to make reservations for flights, hotels, and cruises before they arrive. Remember to bring your camera and extra film. You will want to record your many memories of this wild, beautiful state.

B. After You Read.

1. This article describes three areas to visit in Alaska. <u>Underline</u> these three areas. Find these three areas on the map. What can you do at each location?
2. What's the best way to travel in Alaska? **flying, going by train, taking a cruise**
3. Complete the chart below. Check (✓) a good place for each activity.

	Kenai	Denali	Juneau
1. I can view wild animals.		✓	
2. I can fish.	✓		✓
3. I can watch for whales.			✓
4. I can take great pictures.	✓	✓	✓
5. I can see the largest mountain in the U.S.		✓	
6. I can see glaciers.			✓
7. I can take a river rafting trip.	✓		

Writing Our Stories: My Next Vacation

A. Read these topics. Choose one. Write in your notebook.

1. **My next vacation.** Where are you going to go on your next vacation? How are you going to get there? How long are you going to stay? What are you going to do there? What can a tourist do and see in each place?

2. **A visit to my country.** A tourist is going to visit your country. Describe three places to visit.

> **Writing Note**
> Before you hand in your composition, check your verb forms.

B. After You Read.

- Discuss questions 1 and 2 with the whole class. Have students read quotations from the story to back up their answers.
- Ask students to complete the chart on their own. Encourage them to go back and reread sections of the story to be sure they have found the correct answers. Put a blank chart on the board and invite different students to fill in one line each. As you go over the chart, ask students to read aloud passages from the story that prove their points.

Writing Our Stories: My Next Vacation

A. Read these topics.

- Read aloud and discuss the two topics students have to choose from. Suggest that as soon as they choose a topic, they make a list of all the ideas that they may want to include in their stories. Tell them not to worry about writing complete sentences or putting their ideas in the correct order. Emphasize that the purpose of this part of the exercise is just to get a lot of ideas down on paper.
- Tell students that if they choose *A visit to my country,* they can pattern their stories after the one on pages 226 and 227.
- To get started, ask several students to write one or two sentences they might use in their stories. Have different students read these sentences aloud and check them for meaning and grammar.

☀Practicing on Your Own

A. Complete with the question word.

Students complete this activity on their own. Check the answers with the whole class.

B. Put the words in the questions in the correct order.

Have students write the questions in their books. Ask different students to write one question each on the board. Make any necessary corrections and have the rest of the class check their own sentences.

Suggestion

If you have time and students seem interested, have them form groups and write their own scrambled *going to* questions on a sheet of paper. Groups exchange papers and work together to write out the correct questions.

☀ Practicing on Your Own

A. Complete with the question word.

| How | What | Who | Why | When | Where | How many | How long |

1. __What__ is she going to do there?   She's going to ski.
2. __How long__ is he going to stay?   One week.
3. __How long__ is it going to take?   Three hours.
4. __When__ are you going to return?   Next Sunday.
5. __Who__ is going to meet you there?   My sister is.
6. __Why__ are they going to go there?   Because the weather is good there.
7. __How__ is he going to get there?   He's going to drive.
8. __How many__ cities are you going to visit?   Four.
9. __Where__ is she going to stay?   At her friend's house.

B. Put the words in the questions in the correct order. Then, answer the questions. (Answers to questions will vary.)

1. what / you / do / tonight / are / going to
   What are you going to do tonight _____?

2. when / you / study / going to / are
   When are you going to study _____?

3. going to / what time / the students / go / home / are
   What time are the students going to go home _____?

4. your country / going to / you / when / are / visit
   When are you going to visit your country _____?

5. going to / the teacher / give / a test / tomorrow / is
   Is the teacher going to give a test tomorrow _____?

A. Where are Americans going to go on summer vacations? Read the list of the top ten places.

1. Go to a beach or a lake
2. Visit friends and relatives
3. Visit a city
4. Attend a cultural event
5. Visit a historic place
6. Go fishing
7. Go camping, hiking, or climbing
8. Visit a theme park such as Disneyland
9. Travel in an RV (Recreational Vehicle)
10. Stay in a resort

(Source: Travel Industry Association of America)

(Answers will vary.)

1. Are you going to take a vacation next summer?
2. Which of the ten activities are you going to do? Are you going to do something that is not on the list?
3. Survey your classmates. Make a top ten list. Ask, "What are you going to do next summer?"

Grammar Summary

1. Yes/No questions			
Am I going to visit a friend?	Yes, you are.	No, you're not.	No, you aren't.
Are you going to see your relatives?	Yes, I am.	No, I'm not.	
Is he going to take the train?	Yes, he is.	No, he's not.	No, he isn't.
Is she going to rent a car?	Yes, she is.	No, she's not.	No, she isn't.
Are we going to stay at a hotel?	Yes, we are.	No, we're not.	No, we aren't.
Are they going to drive?	Yes, they are.	No, they're not.	No, they aren't.

2. Wh- questions	
When am I going to visit?	Next week.
What are you going to do there?	I'm going to go hiking and swimming.
How long is she going to stay?	She's going to stay for 10 days.
How long is it going to take?	It's going to take three hours.
How are we going to get there?	By train.
Why are they going to go there?	Because it's not expensive.
Who is going to pay for the tickets?	My parents are.

☀ Looking at a Top Ten List: Summer Vacations

A. Where are Americans going to go on summer vacations?

- Discuss the top ten list and the answers to questions 1 and 2 with the class. Then, have students move around the room interviewing each other about what they are going to do next summer.
- Collate the results of the interview in list form on the board. Ask a student to write the name of one activity on the board. Have the rest of the class raise their hands if they are going to do that activity. The student writes the total on the board. Repeat for several activities.
- When you have ten items on the board, go back and rank the activities from most popular (1) to least popular (10).

Grammar Summary

- Review the summary with the class. Invite students to make up alternate sentences for each example in the chart. For example, in place of *Are we going to stay at a hotel?* a student might say *Are we going to fly?*
- See the Grammar Summary Expansion on page 242 for a more complete explanation of these grammar points.

Grammar Summary Expansion

Unit 1

1. Statements: *Be*

Affirmative Statements		
Subject	*be*	
I	**am**	a student.
We	**are**	from Russia.
You	**are**	at home.
They	**are**	married.
He	**is**	a child.
She	**is**	single.
It	**is**	a table.

Negative Statements		
Subject	*be* + not	
I	**am not**	a teacher.
We	**are not**	from Mexico.
You	**are not**	at school.
They	**are not**	divorced.
He	**is not**	a man.
She	**is not**	married.
It	**is not**	a desk.

Notes

- *You are* is used in two ways. We use *you are* when talking directly to one person. *You are a student.* We also use it when talking directly to several people. *You are my students.*
- Some uses of the verb *be* are:
  - to identify people and things: *I am a student. It is a table.*
  - to describe a person's origin: *We are from Russia. We are not from Mexico.*
  - to describe people in other ways: *She is not married. They are married.*

2. Contractions

Full forms	Contractions
I am	I**'m**
You are	You**'re**
He is	He**'s**
She is	She**'s**
It is	It**'s**

Full forms	Contractions
We are	We**'re**
You are	You**'re**
They are	They**'re**

Notes

- We often use contractions when we speak, but we usually use full forms in writing.
- We sometimes use contractions in writing.

3. *Yes/No* questions

Questions			Short Answers		
Be	Subject		Affirmative	Negative	
Am	I	in room 9?	Yes, you are.	No, you **aren't**.	No, you**'re not**.
Are	you	from Cuba?	Yes, I am.		No, I**'m not**.
Is	he	married?	Yes, he is.	No, he **isn't**.	No, he**'s not**.
Is	she	at work?	Yes, she is.	No, she **isn't**.	No, she**'s not**.
Is	it	3:00?	Yes, it is.	No, it **isn't**.	No, it**'s not**.
Are	we	safe?	Yes, we are.	No, we **aren't**.	No, we**'re not**.
Are	you	hardworking?	Yes, we are.	No, we **aren't**.	No, we**'re not**.
Are	they	brothers?	Yes, they are.	No, they **aren't**.	No, they**'re not**.

Notes

- The answer to a *Yes/No* question is usually a short answer.
- Short answers always use a pronoun, not a noun: *Yes, he is.* NOT *Yes, ~~John~~ is.*
- We never use a contraction with a *yes* answer: *Yes, we are.* NOT ~~*Yes, we're.*~~
- There are two ways of making negative contractions for all personal pronouns, except for *I*. You can't say, ~~*No, I amn't.*~~

1. Adjectives

Subject	be	Adjective
Brazil	is	**beautiful.**
My house	is	**quiet.**
My parents	are	**hardworking.**

Notes

- Adjectives describe people, places, or things.
- In sentences with *be,* we put the adjective after the verb.
- Adjectives are never plural in English. *My sisters are thin,* NOT ~~My sisters are thins~~.
- Adjectives have many different endings: *mes<u>sy</u>, beauti<u>ful</u>, talka<u>tive</u>, intelli<u>gent</u>, hardwork<u>ing</u>, ti<u>red</u>, dange<u>rous</u>.*

2. *Who* questions

Questions			Answers	
Who	*be*	Adjective	Subject	*be*
Who	is	tired?	I	am.
Who	is	talkative?	You	are.
Who	is	intelligent?	Juan (He)	is.
Who	is	relaxed?	Raisa (She)	is.
Who	is	sad?	We	are.
Who	is	thin?	You	are.
Who	is	busy?	They	are.

Notes

- The word *Who* asks questions about people.
- Never use *are* to ask a *who* question with an adjective. ~~Who are hungry?~~ The correct question, even when asking about several people, is: *Who is hungry?*
- *Who is* is often abbreviated (*Who's*), especially in speech. *Who's thirsty?*

3. *Or* questions

Questions					Short Answers	
Be	Subject	Adjective	*or*	Adjective		
Is	Arnold	talkative	**or**	quiet?	He's	quiet.
Are	the students	hardworking	**or**	lazy?	They're	hardworking.

Notes

- An *or* question gives the listener two choices.
- The two choices are often opposites.
- The short answer to an *or* question contains one of the choices given.

1. Singular nouns

Articles *a/an*	Examples		
a before consonant sounds	**a** computer		**a d**esk
an before vowel sounds	**an e**levator		**an u**mbrella
a/an before sounds of "u"	**a u**niversity (/y/ sound)	BUT	**an u**mbrella (/uh/ sound)
a/an before sounds of "h"	**a h**ouse (/h/ sound)	BUT	**an h**our (no /h/ sound)

Notes

- The article *a* comes before words (both nouns and adjectives) that begin with consonant sounds, whereas the article *an* comes before words that begin with vowel sounds.
- In the words *university, used car, unit,* and *useful,* the letter *u* at the beginning is pronounced as a consonant. With words like these, we use the article *a.*
- In the words *umbrella, uncle,* and *unusual,* the *u* at the beginning is pronounced as a vowel. With words like these, we use the article *an.*
- In the words *hotel, hill,* and *house,* the *h* at the beginning is pronounced as a consonant. In words like these, we use the article *a.*
- In the words *hour* and *honor,* the *h* at the beginning is not pronounced. In words like this, we use the article *an.*

2. Plural nouns

Rules	Examples
Add **s** to make a plural noun.	erasers/pens/students
Add **es** to words that end in **-s, -ch, -sh.**	buses/watches/dishes
Change **y** to **i** and add **es.**	dictionaries
Do <u>not</u> add **s** to adjectives.	young students

Note

One-syllable words that end in *y* do not use the *ies* ending. For example: *city → cities,* but *day → days,* NOT ~~daies~~.

3. *There is/There are/There is no/There are no*

There	be	(no)	
There	**is**		a notebook in my backpack.
There	**are**		three pens on the desk.
There	**is**	**no**	window in this room.
There	**are**	**no**	computers in this room.

Notes

- We use *there is* with singular items and *there are* with plural items.
- We use *there* instead of *it* or *they* to say that something exists.
  There is a window in the room. NOT ~~It is a window in the room.~~
  There are three men in the class. NOT ~~They are three men in the class.~~
- We use *there* only the first time we mention something.
  There *is a window in the room.*
  It *is near the door.*
  There are *no computers in the classroom.*
  They *are in the computer center.*

1. Possessive nouns

Maria is Robert**'s** mother. Robert is Maria**'s** son.
The waitress**'** (waitress**'s**) sister is the cook.
The waiters**'** families are from India and China.
The children**'s** father lives in Colombia.
My son-in-law**'s** eyes are blue.

Notes

- Add *'s* to most singular nouns, whether they end in a vowel or a consonant.
- Add *'* (or *'s*) to singular nouns that end in *s*.
- Add *'* to most plural nouns.
- Add *'s* to irregular plural nouns.
- Add *'s* to the last word in a hyphenated noun.

2. Possessive adjectives

Possessive adjective	Noun	
My	sister	is an engineer.
Your	eyes	are brown.
His	father	is in New York.
Her	doctor	is from Russia.
Our	backpacks	are heavy.
Your	house	is large.
Their	books	are in the bookcase.

Notes

- A possessive adjective comes before a noun.
- A possessive adjective shows who owns something.
- The possessive adjective remains the same whether the noun is singular or plural. *Our parents are hardworking.* NOT ~~Ours~~ *parents are hardworking.*

1. Prepositions

The answering machine is **in** the living room.
It's **on** an end table.
The end table is **next to** the couch.
The couch is **between** two windows.
There's a telephone book **under** the couch.
The TV is **across from** the couch.
The cat likes to sleep **in back of** the couch.
It's sleeping **behind** the couch right now.
There's a coffee table **in front of** the couch.

Notes

- Some prepositions of place consist of more than one word: *next to, across from, in back of, in front of.*
- *In back of* and *behind* mean the same thing.
- *On* is used to describe an object resting on a surface. *The book is on the table.*
  On is also used to locate objects in a city or on a map: *on Center Street, on the corner of River Road and Center Street.*

2. *Can* statements

Subject	*can*	Base form	
We	**can**	**walk**	to the park.
You	**can**	**get**	the bus here.

Notes

- The word order is subject + *can* + the base form of the verb.
- In these sentences *can* means *be able to.*
- *Can* never has an *s* ending. *He can park on Main Street* NOT ~~He cans park on main Street.~~

1., 2. Simple present tense: Statements

Subject	Verb	
I	eat	breakfast at 7:00.
We	get up	at 6:00.
You	watch	TV after dinner.
They	eat	pizza every night.
He	goe**s**	home after school.
She	walk**s**	to school every day.

Notes

- The simple present tense describes regular activity and repeated actions: *I work on Saturday. I leave work at 7:00.*
- This tense also shows that something is true all the time: *I love my sister.*
- Simple present verbs following *I, you, we,* and *they* don't have an *s* at the end.
- Simple present verbs following *he, she,* and *it* have an *s* at the end.
- The third person singular forms of the verbs *do* and *go* have an *es* at the end. The verb *have* is irregular.
  Go: I *go,* he/she *goes*
  Do: I *do,* he/she *does*
  Have: I *have,* he/she *has*

3. Negatives

Subject	do/does + not		Base form	
I	**do not**	**(don't)**	watch	TV in the morning.
We	**do not**	**(don't)**	brush	the dog's teeth.
You	**do not**	**(don't)**	work	on Sundays.
They	**do not**	**(don't)**	shave	every day.
He	**does not**	**(doesn't)**	take	the bus to work.
She	**does not**	**(doesn't)**	take	a shower at night.
It (the bus)	**does not**	**(doesn't)**	leave	in the morning.

Notes

- We use *do not* (*don't*) + base form to make negative statements with *I, we, you,* and *they.*
- We use *does not* (*doesn't*) + base form to make negative statements with *he, she,* and *it.*

4. Time expressions and *How often ...?*

How often questions	Time expressions	
How often do you go to the gym?	I go to the gym	**every day.**
How often does she see a doctor?	She sees the doctor	**once a year.**
How often do we have class?	We have class	**twice a week.**

Notes

- *How often ...* questions ask about the number of times something happens in a given period of time.
- The answer to a *How often* question always contains a time expression that tells the number of times something happens in a given period of time.
- These time expressions usually come at the end of the sentence. (They sometimes come at the beginning.)

5. Adverbs of frequency

With verbs other than *be*				
Subject	Adverb of frequency	Verb		
I	**always**	study	on Monday night.
He	**usually**	drives	to work.

Notes

- Adverbs of frequency tell how often something happens.
- Adverbs of frequency come before all verbs except the verb *to be.*

With the verb *be*			
Subject	*be*	Adverb of frequency	
We	are	**sometimes**	late to class.
She	is	**never**	on time.

Note

- Adverbs of frequency come after the verb *to be.*

1. Yes/No questions

Questions			Short Answers	
Do/Does	Subject	Base form	Affirmative	Negative
Do	I	**work?**	Yes, you **do.**	No, you **don't.**
Do	you	**cook?**	Yes, I **do.**	No, I **don't.**
Do	we	**read?**	Yes, we **do.**	No, we **don't.**
Do	they	**walk?**	Yes, they **do.**	No, they **don't.**
Does	he	**help?**	Yes, he **does.**	No, he **doesn't.**
Does	she	**study?**	Yes, she **does.**	No, she **doesn't.**
Does	it	**move?**	Yes, it **does.**	No, it **doesn't.**

Notes

- Simple present tense *Yes/No* questions use the base form.
- Simple present tense short answers use *do* or *does*.

2. Wh- questions

Wh- word	*do/does*	Subject	Base form
Where	do	I	sit?
When	do	you	leave?
What days	do	we	go to school?
Why	do	they	work at night?
Where	does	he	live?
What hours	does	she	work?
Where	does	it	go?

Note

Simple present tense *Wh-* questions use *do* or *does* + the subject + the base form.

3. Who questions (*Who* as subject)

Who	Present tense verb		Subject	*do/does*
Who	sells	tickets?	She	**does.**
Who	earns	$10 an hour?	They	**do.**

Notes

- Short answers with *he, she,* and *it* as the subject use the verb *does.*
- Short answers with *I, we, you,* and *they* as the subject use the verb *do.*

Unit 8

1. *There is/There are:* Statements

There	*be*	Quantity expressions	Noun	
There	**is**	a	bus stop	on the corner.
There	**are**	a few	benches	on the campus.
There	**are**	several	students	in the library.
There	**are**	some	garbage cans	behind the student center.
There	**are**	a lot of	lights	in the parking lot.

Notes
- *A/an* is used with a single item; *a few, several,* and *some* are used with small numbers of items; *a lot of* is used with large numbers of items.
- *There is* is used with single items; *There are* is used with groups of items.

2. Affirmative and Negative

There	*be*	*a/an/no/any*		
There	**is**	an	administration building	on campus.
There	**is**	no	day care center.	
There	**isn't**	a	day care center.	
There	**are**		desks	in the classroom.
There	**are**	no	benches.	
There	**aren't**	any	benches.	

Note

Any is used in negative statements following a plural verb.

3. *How many* questions

Questions				Answers	
How many	Noun			*There is/are*	Number
How many	books	are there	in the bookstore?	**There are**	15.
How many	dogs	are there	in your dorm?	**There is**	one.
How many	lights	are there	in this room?	**There aren't**	any.

Note

Questions with *How many* . . . use the words . . . *are there.*

1., 2., 3. Present continuous tense: Time expressions; Statements

Subject	*be*	*-ing* form	Time expression
I	am / am not	working	right now.
He	is / is not / isn't	reading	at the moment.
She	is / is not / isn't	studying	at the present moment.
It	is / is not / isn't	working	now.
We	are / are not / aren't	writing	at the moment.
You	are / are not / aren't	talking	right now.
They	are / are not / aren't	sleeping	at the present moment.

Notes

- The present continuous tense is used to talk about an action that is happening right now.
- Some verbs that show states of mind are not usually used in the present continuous. We don't say: ~~I am knowing~~ *how to fix refrigerators.* We use the simple present: *I know how to fix refrigerators.*
- We usually use contractions when we speak and full forms in writing.
- We sometimes use contractions in writing.

4. Spelling

Most verbs	
pack	packing
wear	wearing

Add *-ing* to most verbs.

Verbs that end with *e*	
live	living
drive	driving

When a verb ends in *e*, drop the *e* and add *-ing*.

One-syllable verbs that end with a consonant, vowel, consonant	
run	running
get	getting

When a one-syllable verb ends in consonant, vowel, consonant, double the final consonant and add *-ing*.

Verbs that end with *x, y,* or *z.*	
play	playing
fix	fixing

When a verb ends in *x, y,* or *z,* do not double the final consonant.

1., 2. Present continuous: *Yes/No* questions

Questions				Short Answers	
Be	Subject	*-ing* form		Affirmative	Negative
Am	I	eating	a hamburger?	Yes, you **are.**	No, you **aren't.**
					No, you**'re not.**
Are	you	cooking	dinner?	Yes, I **am.**	No, I**'m not.**
Is	he	looking at	the menu?	Yes, he **is.**	No, he **isn't.**
					No, he**'s not.**
Is	she	drinking	decaf?	Yes, she **is.**	No, she **isn't.**
					No, she**'s not.**
Is	it	working?		Yes, it **is.**	No, it **isn't.**
					No, it**'s not.**
Are	we	going	home?	Yes, we **are.**	No, we **aren't.**
					No, we**'re not.**
Are	they	serving	lunch?	Yes, they **are.**	No, they **aren't.**
					No, they**'re not.**

Notes

- The answer to a *Yes/No* question is usually a short answer.
- Two different contracted forms can be used for all negative short answers, except for short answers using the pronoun *I.* The contraction ~~*I amn't*~~ is never used.

3. *Wh-* questions

Questions				Answers
Wh- word	*be*	Subject	*-ing* form	
Where	am	I	sleeping?	In the living room.
When	are	you	leaving?	I'm leaving now.
What	is	he	doing.	He's resting.
Why	is	she	eating?	Because she's hungry.

4. *Who* questions

Questions			Answers	
Who	Present continuous		Subject	*be*
Who	is cooking	dinner?	Leroy	is.
Who	is talking?		Alice and Carlos	are.

Notes

- The word *Who* asks questions about people.
- Never use *are* to ask a present continuous *who* question. ~~*Who are having coffee?*~~ The correct question, even when asking about several people, is: *Who is having coffee?*
- *Who is* is often abbreviated to *Who's,* especially in speech: *Who's working today?*

1. Count and non-count nouns

	Count	Non-count
Food	a bean—beans an egg—eggs	flour, butter, soda, tea
School	a desk—desks a school—schools	education, fun, work

Notes

- Count nouns are things we can count. Count nouns can be singular or plural.
- Non-count nouns are things we can't count. We do not use plural s with non-count nouns.
- We can put count and non-count food in containers and count the containers.
  a box of donuts, two boxes of donuts, a bag of rice, two bottles of oil

2. Count nouns

- The quantifier *some* is used with affirmative statements containing count nouns:
  There are <u>some</u> potatoes in the bag.
- It is not necessary to use *some* with count nouns in affirmative statements:
  There are potatoes in the bag.
- The quantifier *any* is used with negative statements containing count nouns:
  There aren't <u>any</u> tomatoes in the bag.
- The quantifier *any* is used with questions containing count nouns:
  Are there <u>any</u> tomatoes in the bag?

3. Non-count nouns

- The quantifier *some* is used with affirmative statements containing non-count nouns:
  There is <u>some</u> milk in the refrigerator.
- It is not necessary to use *some* with non-count nouns in affirmative statements.
  There is milk in the refrigerator.
- The quantifier *any* is used with negative statements containing non-count nouns:
  There isn't <u>any</u> milk in the refrigerator.
- The quantifier *any* is used with questions containing non-count nouns:
  Is there <u>any</u> milk in the refrigerator?

1. Past tense

Regular verbs		Irregular verbs	
Present	Past	Present	Past
open	opened	be (am, is , are)	was, were
mail	mailed	come	came
like	liked	do	did
use	used	eat	ate
study	studied	have	had
cry	cried	read	read
stop	stopped	sit	sat

Note

- See Student Book page 172 for a more complete list of spelling changes in regular past tense verbs.
- See Student Book page 173 for a more complete list of irregular past tense verbs.

2. Past tense Statements

Subject	Verb	
I	**called**	my sister.
We	**washed**	the dog.
You	**listened**	to the news.
They	**visited**	their friends.
He	**broke***	a cup.
She	**found***	her purse.
It	**made***	noise.

*Irregular past tenses

Notes

- Simple past tense statements describe actions in the past.
- Regular past tense verbs end in *ed*.
- Irregular past tense verbs have many different forms.

3. Negatives

Subject	*Did not/Didn't*	Base form	
I	**did not**	**call**	my sister.
We	**didn't**	**wash**	the dog.
You	**did not**	**listen**	to the news.
They	**didn't**	**visit**	their friends.
He	**did not**	**break**	a cup.
She	**didn't**	**find**	her purse.
It	**did not**	**make**	noise.

Notes

- Negative past tense statements use the words *did + not* (or the contraction *didn't*) before the simple form of the main verb.
- The contraction *didn't* is more common than the full form *did not*.
- The full form *did not* is usually used for emphasis: *I did <u>not</u> take your book!*

1. *Yes/No questions*

Questions				Short Answers	
Did	Subject	Base form			
Did	I	win	the game?	Yes, you **did.**	No, you **didn't.**
Did	you	go	to college?	Yes, I **did.**	No, I **didn't.**
Did	he	retire?		Yes, he **did.**	No, he **didn't.**
Did	she	die	last year?	Yes, she **did.**	No, she **didn't.**
Did	it	work	well?	Yes, it **did.**	No, it **didn't.**
Did	we	get	the correct answer?	Yes, we **did.**	No, we **didn't.**
Did	they	move	to a new house?	Yes, they **did.**	No, they **didn't.**

2. *Who questions*

Questions			Short Answers	
Who	Base form			
Who	wrote	this letter?	I	**did.**
Who	came	here first?	You	**did.**
Who	found	a job?	He	**did.**
Who	grew up	in Cuba?	She	**did.**
Who	got	a new car?	We	**did.**
Who	cooked	dinner?	They	**did.**

Note

The word *Who* asks questions about people.

3. *Wh- questions*

Wh- word	*did*	Subject	Base form
What	did	we	need?
Where	did	she	go?
How	did	you	meet?
When	did	they	arrive?
Why	did	he	leave?

Note

Past tense *Wh-* questions use *did* + the subject + the base form.

1. Future tense statements

Subject	be	going to	Base form		Time expression
I	am / am not	going to	stay	home	Saturday night.
He	is / is not	going to	study		this weekend.
She	is / is not	going to	watch	TV	this evening.
We	are / are not	going to	have	a party	tonight.
You	are / are not	going to	go	to college	next year.
They	are / are not	going to	visit	New York	next month.

Notes

- The *going to* future uses *going to* + the simple form of the main verb.
- *Going to* is usually pronounced as *gonna,* but it is always written as *going to.*

2. Future time expressions

Notes

- Future time expressions can go at the beginning or end of the sentence.
- When the future time expressions is at the beginning of the sentence, it is followed by a comma.
  I'm going to take my driving test <u>the day after tomorrow.</u> <u>The day after tomorrow</u>, I'm going to take my driving test.

3. Pronunciation

Notes

- In natural, conversational style speech, *going to* is pronounced *gonna.*
- To emphasize urgency or importance, pronounce each word separately.
  I am going to go now.
  You are going to have a test on Monday.

1. *Yes/No* questions

		Questions				Short Answers	
Be	Subject	*going to*	Base form				
Am	I	going to	visit	Paris?		Yes, you **are.**	No, you **aren't.** No, you**'re not.**
Are	you	going to	take	a train?		Yes, I **am.**	No, I'm **not.**
Is	he	going to	go	hiking?		Yes, he **is.**	No, he **isn't.** No, he**'s not.**
Is	she	going to	visit	friends?		Yes, she **is.**	No, she **isn't.** No, she**'s not.**
Are	we	going to	stay	at a resort?		Yes, we **are.**	No, we **aren't.** No, we**'re not.**
Are	they	going to	go	to a beach?		Yes, they **are.**	No, they **aren't.** No, they**'re not.**

2. *Wh-* questions

Wh- word	*be*	Subject	*going to*	Base form	Answers
Where	are	we	going to	swim?	In the lake.
What	is	she	going to	do?	Go hiking.
How long	are	you	going to	stay?	Two weeks.
How	is	he	going to	travel?	By train.
Why	are	they	going to	drive?	They have a new car.
Who	am	I	going to	meet?	My brother.

Skills Index

Speaking

Ask and answer, 6, 13, 21–22, 24, 38, 52, 62, 67, 68, 82, 84, 96, 99–100, 125, 133, 140, 142, 143–144, 158, 169, 191, 193, 195, 203, 218, 219, 220, 221–222

Conversations, 13, 23, 53, 70, 130, 175–176, 188

Descriptions, 192, 208

Discussions, 86, 131, 132, 145, 146, 207, 216

Interviews, 63, 131

Introductions, 1, 3, 11

Pair practice, 9–11, 21–22, 24, 35, 38, 52, 67, 69, 82, 84, 99–100, 110, 125, 133, 142, 143–144, 171, 186, 204

Pronunciation
  Contractions, 5
  does he/does she, 101
  -ed words, 171
  Final *-s*, 35, 83
  going to/gonna, 204, 213, 221
  I'm, 130
  Money amounts, 143
  of, 157
  or questions, 21
  Prepositions, 67
  there/they, 112
  what's, 52

Repeating, 2–3, 7, 18, 21, 32, 36, 37, 46, 54, 60, 61, 64, 76, 77, 108, 123, 138, 152–153, 168, 184, 185, 200–201, 204, 214–215

Restaurant orders, 144

Technology

Internet, 45, 159

Test-Taking Skills

Circle answers, 6, 9, 10, 24, 26, 28, 35, 36, 38, 41, 42, 63, 70, 88, 94, 95, 96, 104, 112, 118, 132, 134, 148, 150, 154, 160, 187, 194, 208, 224

Matching, 8, 23, 41, 55, 92, 94, 115, 123, 124, 141, 157, 179, 225

Multiple-choice, 26, 36, 84

Sentence completion, 8, 14, 20, 36, 41, 47, 51, 52, 55, 61, 63, 64, 66, 72, 74, 81, 87, 92, 95, 96, 97, 124, 128, 129, 131, 133, 136, 138–139, 141, 147, 155, 156, 163, 164–165, 166, 167, 169, 171, 175, 189, 195, 197, 202, 204, 205, 207, 209, 216, 218, 225, 228

True/false, 28, 38, 42, 70, 88, 94, 95, 103, 104, 112, 114, 118, 130, 169

Topics

College campuses, 108–121

Complaints, 175–176

Countries and cities, 22–23, 23, 25, 28–29

Daily activities, 76–77, 85, 88, 89, 168–174, 177

Downtown, 66–71, 74, 75

Families, 46–57

Food, 152–167

Growing up, 184–189, 192–198

Home, 60–63, 72, 75

Introductions, 1, 3, 11

Neighborhoods, 64–65, 73

Occupations, 50–51, 92–107

Parties, 190–192

Planning weekends, 200–213

Population figures, 31

Registration forms, 7–8, 12

Restaurants, 138–151

Schedules, 78–84, 86–90

School, 37–43, 62

State fairs, 180–181

Teachers, 14

Time, 36

Vacation, 214–229

Writing

Abbreviations, A.M. and P.M., 105

Capitalization, 15, 29, 73, 81, 105

Conversations, 23, 27, 53, 62, 144, 156, 222

Descriptive writing, 19, 24, 26, 29, 43, 149

Interviews, 103

Lists, 11, 40, 148, 154, 155, 156, 157

Proposals, 210

Punctuation
  Commas, 119, 190, 211

Questions, 13, 140, 150, 189, 192

Recipes, 165

Registration forms, 7–8, 12, 121

Sentences, 10, 24, 27, 39, 69, 73, 85, 103, 109, 110, 113, 131, 136, 161, 177, 211

Spelling, 137, 172

Stories, 15, 43, 57, 89, 105, 135, 147, 149, 181, 197, 227

Times, 36

Titles, 135

Vocabulary words, 33, 40

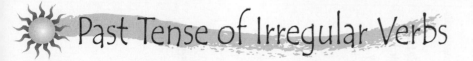

Past Tense of Irregular Verbs

be	was / were	leave	left
become	became	lose	lost
begin	began	make	made
bite	bit	meet	met
break	broke	pay	paid
bring	brought	put	put
buy	bought	read	read
catch	caught	ring	rang
choose	chose	run	ran
come	came	say	said
cost	cost	see	saw
do	did	sell	sold
drink	drank	send	sent
drive	drove	sit	sat
eat	ate	sleep	slept
fall	fell	speak	spoke
feel	felt	spend	spent
fight	fought	stand	stood
find	found	steal	stole
fly	flew	swim	swam
forget	forgot	take	took
get	got	teach	taught
give	gave	tell	told
go	went	think	thought
have	had	understand	understood
hear	heard	wake	woke
hold	held	wear	wore
hurt	hurt	write	wrote
know	knew		

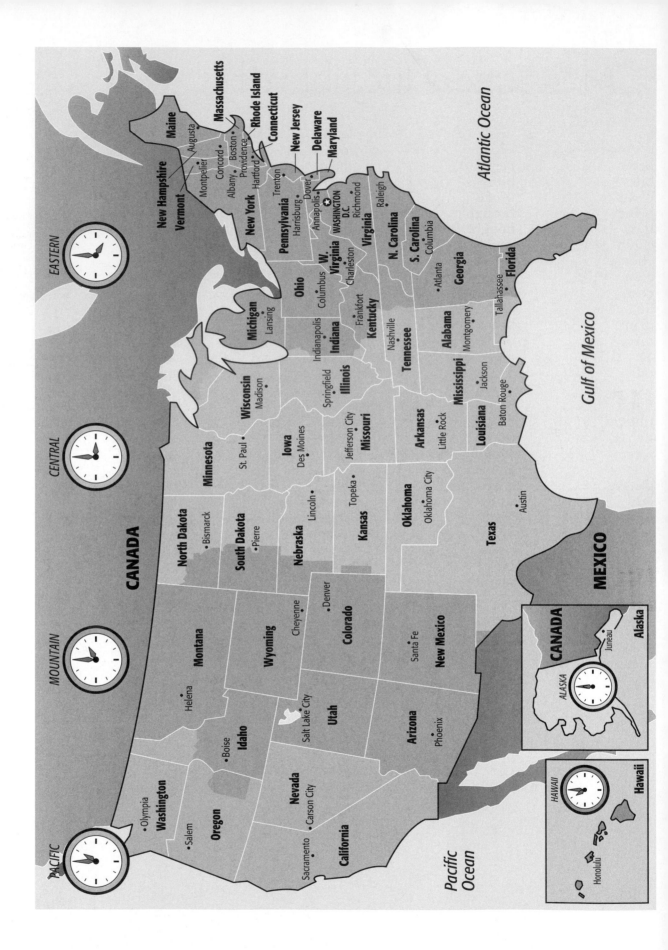

Atlantic Ocean

EASTERN

CENTRAL

MOUNTAIN

PACIFIC

CANADA

Maine
Augusta
New Hampshire
Vermont
Montpelier
Concord • Boston • Massachusetts
Albany • Providence • Rhode Island
New York • Hartford • Connecticut
Trenton • New Jersey
Pennsylvania • Dover • Delaware
Harrisburg • Annapolis • Maryland
WASHINGTON
D.C.
Richmond
W. • Virginia
Virginia • Raleigh
Charleston • N. Carolina
Ohio • Columbia
Columbus • S. Carolina
Frankfort
Kentucky • Atlanta • Georgia
Nashville
Indianapolis • Tennessee • Alabama
Indiana • Montgomery • Tallahassee • Florida
Michigan
Lansing
Illinois • Mississippi
Springfield • Jackson
Wisconsin • Jefferson City • Arkansas • Baton Rouge
Madison • Missouri • Little Rock • Louisiana
Minnesota
St. Paul • Iowa
Des Moines
Topeka • Oklahoma City
North Dakota • Lincoln • Kansas • Oklahoma
Bismarck • Nebraska • Austin
South Dakota
Pierre • Denver
Montana • Cheyenne • Colorado • Santa Fe
Helena • Wyoming • New Mexico
Texas
Salt Lake City
Idaho • Utah
Boise • Arizona
Phoenix
Washington • Nevada
Olympia • Carson City
Salem • Sacramento
Oregon • California

Gulf of Mexico

Pacific
Ocean

MEXICO

CANADA
ALASKA • Juneau • Alaska

HAWAII • Hawaii
Honolulu